The Prospect of Immortality

by Kelly Richard Nicholson

Dr. Nicholson is available for motivational speaking engagements, business conferences, courses, lectures, and seminars. Contact the publishing company listed below or send e-mail to Kr7arjuna@aol.com.

First Edition 1999

Library of Congress Catalog Card Number: 99-90129

ISBN 0-9668911-1-2

The Prospect of Immortality

Homeward Bound Publishing, Inc.
P. O. Box 1468 • 499 East Parowan Way • Draper, UT 84020
Toll Free 1-888-433-1130 • Fax (801) 816-1170
e-mail: homewardpb@aol.com

www.need2read.com

Printed in the United States of America

Cover design Ranée Stam

For Mama,

whose own radiance has been my guiding light

What lies across the sea he cannot tell; his special expectations may all be mistaken; but his insight into the clear meanings of present facts may persuade him beyond doubt that the sea has another shore.

Harry Emerson Fosdick, *The Assurance of Immortality*

Table of Contents

Introduction

The man Kant, writes Unamuno,

> was a man much preoccupied with the problem - I mean with the only real vital problem, the problem that strikes at the very root of our being, the problem of our individual and personal destiny, of the immortality of the soul.[1]

Such is the problem. It is *the* problem, insists Unamuno - not another puzzle for academic wonderment, but the single life-issue from which others derive. It is the vital problem that strikes at the root of our being. And it is the man Kant who addresses this problem - a concrete man of flesh and bone, one possessed of passion and pain and sensibility. A man, insists the Spaniard, and not a mere theoretician.

This book, as its title indicates, concerns the prospect of a future life - a new and greater life beyond the present for ourselves and for those with whom we now share the journey. It is inspired, in part, by this sharing, by moments spent along the way with these companions who have trod the same path. It is inspired by the hope that they might one day receive the joy and the justice all too often denied them in this world.

---

[1] Miguel de Unamuno, *The Tragic Sense of Life*. Trans. J. E. Crawford Flitch (New York: Dover, 1954), p. 4.

This book is eclectic in its choice of materials, citing sources in and out of the scholastic mainstream and from more than one religious tradition. It is concerned, be it said now, with survival in a full-blooded sense of the word - with our active and conscious continuation of life beyond its present bounds. It thus disavows itself of mere figurative versions of the thesis - those involving, say, our continuing effect on future generations by our present actions, or our participation, in some way, in eternal truths within the duration of this life alone.[2]

In this book I maintain that the thesis of survival is reasonable - that it is consistent, on the whole, with rational principle and with our present corpus of scientific information. I argue likewise that there exist grounds for accepting it. Belief in survival, I maintain, is integral to our conception of ourselves as free and responsible agents and to a broadly religious conception of life.

Such a belief, I notice, is not especially widespread among current philosophers, nor has the thesis any particular fashion in the academic community. "If we have done all that we can to live," writes George Graham, "death marks the

---

[2] Thus D. Z. Phillips, for example, calls it foolish to speak of eternal life "as some kind of appendage to human existence, something that happens *after* human life on earth is over." For eternity, he insists, is merely "the reality of goodness, that in terms of which human life is to be assessed." D. Z. Phillips, *Death and Immortality* (London: Macmillan, 1970), p. 48. The reader who seeks a definition of 'immortality' in Aldous Huxley's discussion will find it explained therein as "participation in the eternal now of the divine Ground." See *The Perennial Philosophy* (New York: Harper and Row, 1970). While Huxley does not deny the reality of conscious survival (it is, he notes, the fate of those "partially delivered" into some heaven or purgatory), he has little to say about it in concrete terms. For the relevant part of his discussion see pp. 211-16.

point when we should feel we have lived *enough*."[3] Few current philosophers, it seems, wish to entertain another possibility. Thus words like 'soul' and 'survival', for example, do not figure in the Blackwell *Companion to the Philosophy of Mind*, presumably being discounted as remnants of another era.[4] The going trend instead is reductionism - the analysis of human beings, and of reality as a whole, solely in terms of events in the natural world. Such an analysis allows little prospect of personal survival.

In recent years, in fact, much of religion itself has become earth-bound, as members of this community have shifted their focus of concern from the next world to this one. Our final good and evil, believes Jesus biographer John Crossan, are with us here and now. What matters is not what may await beyond, but "how we live our lives here below."[5] Indeed the implausibility of certain traditional afterlife pictures has effected a widespread silence on the topic even among those theologians who still profess a belief in it. Our modern inability "to conjure up some convincing and appealing notion of Heaven," writes Paul Johnson, "ends by casting doubt on its very existence."[6] The paradise, he

---

[3] George Graham, *Philosophy of Mind* (Oxford: Blackwell Publishers, Ltd, 1993), p. 34.

[4] Samuel Guttenplan, ed., *A Companion to the Philosophy of Mind* (Oxford: Blackwell Publishers, Ltd, 1996).

[5] John Dominic Crossan, *Who Is Jesus?* (New York: HarperCollins Publishers, 1996), p. 166.

[6] Paul Johnson, *The Quest for God: A Personal Pilgrimage* (New York: HarperPerennial, 1996), p. 174.

imagines, may be real, but we are a long way from those ancients and medievals who could envision it as an Olympus or a Valhalla. For many American scholars and clerics, proclaims one timely newsstand article, "Heaven can wait."[7]

Philosophers of this past century, swept hard upon its analytic current, have produced accounts foreign to the common ear, accounts far removed from what ordinary folk envision as a "just reward." In some cases these accounts have been so abstract as to be virtually meaningless.[8] It is likewise argued, in some quarters, that our relationship to the divine has nothing to do with personal survival at all.[9] Thus there has arisen in this century an effort to understand the Christian gospel, for example, as a social doctrine, the end of which is a more balanced earthly order. This new focus, observe Colleen McDannell and Bernhard Lang, asks for

---

[7] David Van Biema, "Does Heaven Exist?", *Time* (New York: Time Inc., March 24, 1997). Vol. 149, no. 12, pp. 70-78.

[8] Consider, for one, the commentary of Alfred North Whitehead: "An enduring personality in the temporal world is a route of occasions in which the successors with some peculiar completeness sum up their predecessors. The correlate fact in God's nature is an even more complete unity of life in a chain of elements for which succession does not mean loss of immediate unison. This element in God's nature inherits from the temporal counterpart according to the same principle as that by which in the temporal world the future inherits from the past. Thus in the sense in which the present occasion is the person *now*, and yet with his own past, so the counterpart in God is that person in God." Alfred North Whitehead, *Process and Reality* (New York: Macmillan. 1929), pp. 531-32. This passage is reprinted with commentary in John Cobb, Jr., and David Ray Griffin, *Process Theology* (Philadelphia: Westminster Press, 1976). See pp. 118-24.

[9] See, for example, discussion of the philosophy of Charles Hartshorne in chapters 1 and 2 of this volume.

nothing less than the rejection of a privatized, individualized afterlife in exchange for a regenerated social order on earth. The other-worldly orientation of previous generations of Christians had to be eliminated not because it contradicted reason or science, but because it ignored the fundamentally social concerns of the New Testament.[10]

And yet if concern with a future life is gone from some arenas, it is not gone from all. For there remain persons in this day, as in all days past, persons from all walks and every corner, who believe that this life cannot be all, that it cannot be meaningful unless it is part of something more. Sooner or later, writes Richard Purtill,[11] whether at life's end or in our youth, we face certain questions about the meaning of the life in which we are engaged. Some persons, it is true, find sufficient meaning within this life alone. But we ought to bear in mind, says Purtill, that if the materialist conception of things is right, death will one day claim the human race as surely as it claims the individual. When this day comes, all human hopes and aspirations will be as if they had never been. Thus it will be correct to say, at such time, that the whole story is (in Shakespeare's famous phrase) "a tale told by an idiot ... signifying nothing."[12]

The real life blood of religion, thinks Purtill, is the conviction that there exist satisfying answers to questions about the nature of life and its direction. He maintains that some conception of a life to come is essential to making sense of

---

[10] Colleen McDannell and Bernhard Lang, *Heaven - A History* (New Haven, Connecticut: Yale University Press, 1988), page 334.

[11] Richard Purtill, *Thinking About Religion* (Englewood Cliffs, New Jersey: Prentice-Hall, 1978).

[12] *Macbeth*, act V, scene 5.

the life that we now have. The crucial difference between a secular view of life and a genuinely religious one, he explains, is the value that a religious view places upon the life of the individual. Take, for instance,

> a young Indian mother who is starving to death, along with her child, after a life of hunger, hardship, and degradation. What is it to her that a classless society, or a psychologically adjusted society, or any perfect society you like, may someday exist? She would trade all such grandiose hopes for a little food or for some immediate hope for her child. The secularist can hope and work for a society in which no one is starved or degraded, and this is a noble objective. But it offers no personal hope to those starving or degraded now or in the past.[13]

If indeed we survive, where might we be headed? There exist, notes Purtill, certain glib answers to this question. One is that we are simply born again into this world to reap the *karma* (roughly, the moral payback) that we earn by our present actions. Purtill's reaction to this idea is poignantly expressed in his brief dialogue between middle-aged father Ed Kelly and his son Tom, who has left his own religious tradition and has developed an infatuation with the wisdom of the East. Ed's wife has recently died a painful death from cancer. *Karma*, explains Tom, makes sense of this event. For the suffering we have in this life, he imagines, is merely the effect of our own past actions.

Did she, asks Ed, deserve the illness that took her life? Not in this round, thinks his son, but in some other. Yet her noble response to this difficulty has moved her "up the scale" and closer to *nirvana* (some, says Tom, "call it Nothingness") and the end of all desiring. Ed can make no sense of this. For if indeed his wife is now reborn as his son imagines, then she cannot now know or

---

[13] *Ibid.*, p. 139.

remember them, and soon they will not know or remember her, either. And, he adds, "if the end of the whole business is to lose all personal identity, what's the use of all the suffering and trying anyway?"

This little piece of drama, of course, is not meant to represent in any detail the real content of "Eastern" thought. It is intended rather to illustrate our need to examine the issue of our own destiny. What do we believe about ourselves and our direction? What is the real end of this present life?

In chapter 1 of this book I cite and discuss several expressions of the belief that survival is either unlikely or unimportant. One such example is that of Bertrand Russell, who supposes that belief in survival requires not only gullibility, but also a false conception of what is involved in the development over time of a human personality. Noted also are the views of Corliss Lamont, Charles Hartshorne, Antony Flew, and Walter Kaufmann, each of whom supposes that the importance of personal survival is commonly exaggerated.

In the second chapter I offer replies to some of these claims. I address the argument, for example, that consciousness is dependent upon brain activity and so cannot exist apart from it. I discuss also the issue of personal identity. Afterward I respond to the claim that belief in survival is unimportant - that it is antagonistic, as some say, to a serious life-philosophy, and owes somehow to confusion or personal selfishness. Citing the discussions of Burnett Hillman Streeter, C. S. Lewis, and others, I argue to the contrary that belief in survival is naturally aligned with a respect for justice and for the innate worth of individual human beings.

The third chapter is devoted to further examination of our moral experience. In this chapter I argue that our moral conduct involves us implicitly in certain beliefs about ourselves and about reality as a whole. I argue it involves us likewise in an embrace of our own spirituality. Here I cite the example of Kant, who began this tradition, and then discuss versions of the argument presented (whether sympathetically or not) by philosophers since. Following Kant's example, I maintain that our practical respect for moral demand warrants certain assumptions, in turn, about ourselves and the universe in which we live. I argue that this respect carries with it the implicit assumption that we are destined for another life.

In succeeding chapters I discuss the insights and contributions of several philosophers whose works have centered in notable ways around the survival issue. In chapter 4, I discuss Frederick Myers, a vibrant and adventurous figure of the nineteenth century who helped to found the Society for Psychical Research. I begin with a brief historical summary of the aim and development of this organization, and discuss afterward some of the principal theses and case-materials of Myers' classic *Human Personality*. Following this I note some related events in the field in years afterward.

Chapter 5 is devoted to the extraordinary Spanish philosopher Miguel de Unamuno, whose work *The Tragic Sense of Life* is one of the masterpieces of existentialist literature in the past century. I discuss what might be termed Unamuno's healthy obsession with the prospect of human survival, and his contention that survival is indeed the preeminent question in all of philosophy.

Chapter 6 examines the work of John Hick, who has made, in my estimate, the most valuable contribution to this issue of any philosopher in recent decades. I address first Hick's theory of knowledge, as it bears upon his account of religious belief, and second his conception of "soul-making" in relation to our present life challenge. I then recount his exploration of Eastern and Western eschatological outlooks in his great work *Death and Eternal Life*.

The seventh chapter continues an exploration of human destiny. In this chapter I cite the data of psychical research and near-death experiences, as well as the efforts of a number of thinkers, both traditionalists and innovators, to offer a plausible account of what the next world holds in store. I trace out a few of the common denominators in various accounts, seeking to determine what conception thus emerges and what connection it has with my own discussion. Last I cite possible intimations of eternity within our present daily experience.

Before opening the first chapter I might comment briefly upon some common reactions to an enterprise of this kind. It is a source of puzzlement to some. For how, they wonder, can there ever be research or investigation of such a thing? Where does one find evidence of it, or any real sense of its content?

The issue, I concede, is a species unto itself. There is little prospect, I think, for proof in this arena; one cannot demonstrate survival as one can demonstrate more "solid" things - say, the reality of an ancient American culture, or the chemistry of photosynthesis. For this issue runs deeper, it is more basic, than these others; it is not just an investigation, in the usual sense, but an inquiry into the meaning of our very existence.

Some, it is true, find proof at hand. One hears all the time, they will say, of those who have had some vision of this other world, or have briefly "crossed over" to it and come back, or have seen its gates open in their last earthly moments. Such claims are interesting and they sometimes merit, I believe, serious attention.[14] But the notion that these experiences constitute *proof* is open to at least two objections; first, it takes for granted the sincerity of those who report them, and second, it assumes that experiences of this kind (when reported in good faith) cannot be explained in terms of natural events.

I believe nonetheless that the subject of our destiny may be approached and that it admits of investigation. There are things to be said on behalf of survival, I think, even if it cannot be confirmed in the manner of a scientific hypothesis. Our reflection upon the nature of conscious experience, for example, may tell us that a future life is not ruled out by materialistic arguments commonly alleged against it. Our examination of values, by the same token, may lead us to acknowledge a source of reality that transcends the natural world. And our investigation of purported encounters with the other world as found, for example, in the data of mediumship and alleged otherworld contact, may persuade us, on balance, that there is more to life than meets the eye.

Exploration of this kind expands the conceptual horizon. It enables us to reexamine our own assumptions as to what is *real* in the first place. In so doing

---

[14] Thus in several places, and particularly in chapters 4 and 7, I give attention to the experiences of those who claim to have seen or conversed with the other side. On examination it is far from obvious, I think, that all such data can be easily assimilated within a materialistic account of reality.

it may bestow an awakening. Exposure to new ideas and testimony may confirm our basic instincts about what is true and valuable. It may occasion a vitally new perspective on our daily life-encounter. It may occasion self-discovery.

This, again, is not proof. Nor, I think, is anyone likely to establish, on theoretical grounds, a spiritualist account of reality over a materialist one. For this difference of outlook lies deep; it owes, in some measure, to core differences in human beings themselves. Some, as Evelyn Underhill reminds us in her esteemed classic, find truth in the test tube, others in the poet's fancy; "some before the altar, others in the slime."[15] We begin, it seems, with strong dispositions in this regard. It may thus happen that one man or woman will find in reality nothing but the motions of particles; another sees in it an event of the spirit, a miracle of sound and light invested with a greater meaning. Such differences have been present in the race from its beginning. I see little prospect of their end.

Yet the investigation, I believe, is no less necessary. The rule of philosophy is that of reason. Thus the demand of philosophy is universal and unyielding. Yet one individual's philosophy cannot be every other. For always it is grounded, as Unamuno tells us, in that unique and private well-spring of an individual's own experience. The according task of philosophy, I think, is to provide not so much solution as *resolution*; to this end we must each take stock of our experience, must forge out of it, when all is said and done, the view of life that best accords with our own deepest instincts.

---

[15] Evelyn Underhill, *Mysticism* (New York: New American Library, 1974), p. 4. This book first appeared in 1911.

I am one of those, I confess, who feels the pull, one who senses, at odd moments, that life is not accident, but homeward venture. In this book I hope to convey something of this feeling to the reader, and to explain its place, as I see it, in the development of a personal philosophy. In so doing I will offer a more daring world-view than one usually finds in the mainstream; I will advocate a willingness to entertain such a view and a trust in those intimations that betoken it. For this tendency toward reductionism in the past century is not progress, I suspect, but historical mood-swing. The spiritual dimension of life is real, and it is not going anywhere. Logic by itself does not confirm its reality, nor does logic dissolve it. The method of philosophy is that of reason, but its substance, I am convinced, is more. Real philosophy owes to the life-blood of each philosopher. It is a product of instinct, intuition, indeed the very substance of the thinker himself - his strength, his character, his spiritual condition. Out of this source, I maintain, will come his philosophy. So will come each response to it.

Chapter I

Voices of Denial

> To struggle, to protest against the metaphysical limit of human existence is not only foolish, it is essentially impossible.
>
> Herbert Marcuse, "The Ideology of Death"

Materialism and the Dissolution of Personal Identity

Philosophy in the past century has been none too friendly to the possibility of a future life. Various reasons are offered to account for this fact. It represents, say some, a genuine advance - the forsaking of an old and sentimental idea for a harder, more realistic view of our place in the cosmos. The notion of persons surviving their own natural demise, it is said, is fantastic.

Whatever the merit of this skepticism, it has some connection to the rise of the sciences; to our realization, first, that we are not truly at the center of things, that we are furthermore blood kin to the animals, that consciousness itself is connected, in some intimate way, with events in the natural world. Such discoveries have encouraged many to think that we are but a part of nature, material in constitution, accidental and fleeting in our appearance.

Philosophy itself, over the past hundred years, has acquired a scientific tone. It prides itself also on *reduction*, on containing reality within the world that science investigates. But if this outlook is in fashion, it is nothing new; it is present even in the philosophy of the fifth-century B. C. Greek atomists. Reality, say these early materialists, is but a sea of particles (*a-tomoi*, or un-cuttables), tiny and indivisible, adrift in space.[1] Consciousness likewise, they imagine, is but a collection of particles, soon dispersing and gone.

We know nothing after death, maintains Epicurus, an atomist of a few centuries later. This, he reasons, may not be such a bad thing. For if death is the end of sensation, so also is it the end of pain. In which case, it seems, death can bring no evil. Epicurus is the hero of the Roman philosopher Lucretius, who later credits him with liberating human beings from baseless and oppressive fears (principally, the fears of death and divine retribution) that have long plagued them.

Our consciousness, Lucretius argues, is material. For we see it moving the limbs, changing the expression of the face, and "guiding and steering the whole man" - all functions requiring physical properties. Here he offers the favorite evidence of skeptics ancient and modern, namely, the close and conspicuous agreement of mind and body. We see that these two things "are born together, grow up together and together grow old." With a delicate frame goes an infirmity of judgment; with robust vigor "a steadier resolve and a maturer strength of mind." As the body fails with age, so does the mind. When the body

---

[1] For a succinct explanation of this philosophy, see Merrill Ring, *Beginning with the Pre-Socratics* (Mt. View, California: Mayfield Publishing Company, 1987), pp. 149-57.

"suffers the horrors of disease and the pangs of pain, so we see the mind stabbed with anguish, grief and fear."[2] What, then, is death, but our annihilation?

This line of thought finds revival in modern times with insight into the natural order. Everything, says La Mettrie,[3] writing a century before Darwin, "depends on the way our machine is running." One need only look to see, for example, the influence of age on reason. Just as obvious is the effect of nutrition. Raw meat conduces to fierceness in animals, and it would do the same to ourselves, were we in the habit.[4] Hunger, when severe enough, can bring us to a fury wherein we may devour one another.

Even the will, adds La Mettrie, seems to depend upon the body's mechanism. One man thus may cry like a child at the approach of death, while another will jest. What is needed, he asks,

> to change the bravery of Caius Julius, Seneca, or Petronius into cowardice or faintheartedness? Merely an obstruction in the spleen, in the liver, an impediment in the portal vein? Why? Because the imagination is obstructed along with the viscera, and this gives rise to all the singular phenomena of hysteria and hypochondria.[5]

---

[2] Lucretius, *On the Nature of the Universe*. Trans. R. E. Latham (London: Penguin Books, 1994), p. 78.

[3] Julien Offray de La Mettrie, *Man a Machine*. Trans. Gertrude Bussey, et al. (La Salle, Illinois: Open Court Press, 1993), p. 95.

[4] Empirical support, he avers, is found in the example of the English, "who eat meat red and bloody," and who seem to share "more or less in the savagery due to this kind of food, and to other causes which can be rendered ineffective by education only." (p. 94).

[5] *Man a Machine*, p. 91.

With cognition it is the same. For "when feeling is stifled, thought also is checked," as in cases of apoplexy, lethargy, and catalepsis. Observation will show, too, that man bears a structural resemblance to other animals. Examine the human embryo of six, eight, or fifteen days with a microscope. Hereafter, plain observation will suffice. One sees the gradual development of a mature organism from something plain and primitive. Such observation reveals a uniformity in nature, and an analogy, not only between man and animal, but between entire plant and animal kingdoms.

While La Mettrie does not reject altogether the possibility of a continued existence,[6] such facts as he cites are often marshaled to this end. The development of causal explanation, says Bertrand Russell,[7] leaves little room for traditional ideas of free will and the soul's immateriality. During the seventeenth century, Russell notes, it became apparent that the laws confirmed by experiment and observation might well determine the behavior of all matter. No reason, it seemed, existed for making an exception in favor of living bodies.

Compromises were attempted, but were quickly shown to be implausible. The French philosopher Rene Descartes, for example, maintained that animals were automata, while human beings were possessed of consciousness and moral freedom. But the progress of physics soon discouraged any such solution. It was

---

[6] "Let us not say that every machine or every animal perishes altogether or assumes another form after death, for we know absolutely nothing about the subject." (p. 147).

[7] Russell, "Soul and Body", contained in Russell's *Religion and Science* (London: Oxford University Press, 1961).

suggested by some that there might exist separate worlds of mind and matter, each with its own event-series and rules of sequence. A parallel timing of these worlds would allow mental and physical events to coincide just as they would if they were causally connected. Yet the two worlds, it was said, might still be independent of each other.

This latter theory, as Russell observes, was not only hard to believe, but had the further disadvantage that it could not salvage the notion of free will in any case. For the parallel timing of these two worlds implied "a strict correspondence" between states of body and states of mind, such that when one state was known, the other could in principle be inferred. An individual who knew this and who understood the laws of physics could predict a forthcoming series of mental occurrences just as well as physical ones. If so, it was hard to see where any freedom might remain.

The later emergence of a "vital force" theory among anti-materialists, Russell continues, offered little more prospect of liberating human nature from the material world. This theory holds, in some fashion, that science cannot understand the human body, or that it can do so only by invoking principles other than those of conventional physics and chemistry. But the work that has been done in such areas as embryology, bio-chemistry, and the artificial production of organic compounds makes it more and more likely that the characteristics of living matter "are wholly explicable" in material terms.

A related skepticism arises in the modern age concerning the nature of personal identity. We commonly suppose that human beings are distinct and enduring entities, that they remain somehow, and despite their changes, the same individuals over the course of a lifetime. In 1739 this belief was challenged in a bold new volume written by a young Scottish philosopher. It was called *A Treatise of Human Nature*[8] and its author was David Hume.

The book was deemed an oddity, if not an outrage, by those who gave it attention. Its questions were radical and its conclusions were outrageous: Why, asked Hume, do we suppose that the world will behave *today* like it did *yesterday*? Where, in our observation, do we find objective elements of *good* or *evil*? What does it mean for one thing to *cause* another?[9] In short, are we ever justified in believing the things that we take for granted in the course of daily experience? Hume's answer, in the main, was that these common-sense beliefs have no real support, but owe instead to our own peculiar nature.

Radical questions, to be sure, were nothing new. Descartes had raised a few of his own in the previous century. But he had managed, when all was said and done, to align his views with both common sense and church doctrine. Our whole view of reality, he maintained, has a foundation in reason. "I think, therefore I am" - the self, he argued, is something immediate, an immaterial substance self-evident and persisting. It is directly knowable, a logical starting

---

[8] David Hume, *A Treatise of Human Nature* (Oxford: Clarendon Press, 1951). Edited by L. A. Selby-Bigge. See especially section I. 4. 6.

[9] For a splendid account of Hume's general philosophy, see Barry Stroud, *Hume* (London: Routledge and Kegan Paul, 1977).

point for inquiry of any kind.[10]

But what is this self, Hume asks, of which we are so confident? Our thinking about identity in general, he observes, is careless. Our belief in the lasting sameness of material objects, for example, fails to pass examination. For these objects are really successions of related yet different things.

Consider, he says, some piece of matter before us. We might ascribe an identity to this mass if all of its parts "continue uninterruptedly and invariably the same." But when mass has a slight addition, or subtraction, it is not precisely the same thing as before. Yet the passage of our thought from one entity to the other is "so smooth and easy" that we scarcely notice.

Or again, when we observe a change in some object, the greatness of this change is measured, in our thinking, not by its size *per se*, but by its proportion to the whole. Thus the gain or loss of a mountain, it seems, "would not be sufficient to produce a diversity in a planet," while "the change of a very few inches" is crucial elsewhere. A thorough change, when it is produced gradually and insensibly, may not disrupt identity at all. The reason, writes Hume, is that

> the mind, in following the successive changes of the body, feels an easy passage from the surveying [of] its condition in one moment to the viewing of it in another, and at no particular time perceives any interruption in its actions. From which continu'd perception, it ascribes a continu'd existence and identity to the object.[11]

---

[10] See Part IV of Descartes' *Discourse on Method*. Trans. Donald A. Cress (Indianapolis, Indiana: 1980). For discussion, see also chapters 1 and 2 of Margaret Wilson's *Descartes* (London: Routledge and Kegan Paul, 1993).

[11] *Treatise*, p. 256.

We tolerate also a great deal of change in an object when there is "a reference of the parts to each other, and a combination to some common end." So, for example, a ship that has undergone continued reparation may be counted the same regardless of its alteration. Similarly with plants and animals - we find here parts working in a coordination, and so we attribute identity to these organisms despite their thorough change over time. (Thus the oak that has grown from a small plant is the same, we imagine, throughout this whole process.) Or again, we say that a church that has fallen has itself been "rebuilt" of new materials.

Our common sense attitudes, thinks Hume, bear closer watch. Such is the case, he maintains, with our notion of personal identity. We think of selfhood as being a single thing, something that lasts through time, even across great changes. Yet is there, Hume asks, really such a thing as a self or soul, a "me" that is present throughout this history?

"For my part," he writes famously, "when I enter most intimately into what I call myself, I always stumble on some particular perception or other, of heat or cold, light or shade, love or hatred, pain or pleasure."[12] One does not find oneself at any time without a perception,[13] nor anything present in consciousness but the perception itself. When all such episodes are removed, as in sound sleep, what remains?

---

[12] *Ibid.*, p. 252.

[13] Without, that is, some given momentary conscious state, involving particular episodes of thought, mood, volition, sensation, and so on.

Our belief in the self, thinks Hume, is thus ungrounded. We find no enduring subject in this succession, and have no idea what it would even look like. To all appearances, we are "nothing but a bundle of different perceptions, which succeed each other with an inconceivable rapidity, and are in a perpetual flux and movement."

This account flies in the face of both common sense and tradition. If Hume is right, then there is no one - no you or me - that lasts through this conscious succession. Nor can there exist any prospect of another life, or at least, not of the kind that we imagine. For "we," as it turns out, do not endure even in this one.

Hume's discussion has had powerful influence in the time since. "The apparent permanency of the ego," writes Ernst Mach, "consists chiefly in the single fact of its continuity, in the slowness of its changes." The thoughts and plans of yesterday are carried over and give rise to the feeling of an enduring selfhood. But it is a feeling, says Mach, without basis in fact. With time and development comes thorough change in personal nature. There can hardly be greater differences between two persons than exist within one across a lifetime. "When I recall to-day my early youth," he writes,

> I should take the boy that I then was, with the exception of a few individual features, for a different person, were it not for the existence of the chain of memories. Many an article that I myself penned twenty years ago impresses me now as something quite foreign to myself.[14]

---

[14] Ernst Mach, *The Analysis of Sensations* (London: Open Court Publishing Company, 1914), pp. 3-4.

The ego, then, has in it as little "absolute permanency" as the body. That very thing, adds Mach, that we dread so much in death, namely our annihilation, actually occurs within life in the course of this personal evolution.

Criticism of traditional ideas about the soul and personal identity appears in a much-reprinted essay by Bertrand Russell entitled "Do We Survive Death?". Before we can meaningfully discuss the possibility of life hereafter, says Russell, we must be clear about "the sense in which a man is the same person that he was yesterday." Our common-sense notion of selfhood, he maintains, is the product of confusion.[15]

There was a time, Russell notes, when philosophers imagined that there existed definite *substances* of soul and body both. The soul, it was believed, remained in existence from the time of its creation to eternity, and the body, though dissolved at death, was reconstituted for all time in resurrection. Surely, says Russell, this notion of an enduring body is no longer tenable. For we know today what happens to an organism through its growth and development. Indeed we know that the very atoms themselves are not the discrete and lasting things that science once supposed. The continuity of the human body, seen in this light, is one "of appearance and behavior, not of substance."[16]

The same, thinks Russell, is true of the mind. Over time, there is the activity of thought, feeling, and action; but there is not, he contends, some further

---

[15] Bertrand Russell, "Do We Survive Death?", contained in Russell's *Why I Am Not a Christian* (New York: Simon and Schuster, 1957).

[16] *Ibid.*, p. 89.

thing, identifiable as mind or soul, beneath these events that "does or suffers" them. Our alleged sameness is no more than "a continuity of habit and memory": All that constitutes a person is "a series of experiences connected by memory and by certain similarities of the kind we call habit." The whole notion of a future life, thinks Russell, counts upon a misconception of what we are in the first place.

Our mental activity, he continues, is conspicuously related to our nervous system. Personal characteristics, whether natural or acquired, are bound up with the condition of certain bodily structures. Our thoughts and emotions, our reactions to language, our so-called moral or immoral habits of behavior, are related of necessity to events within these structures.

It is not rational argument, then, that causes belief in a future life, but emotion. One such emotion is fear of death. Another is our admiration of human "excellence." Thus it is said of man that

> His mind is a far finer instrument than anything that had appeared earlier - he knows right and wrong. He can build Westminster Abbey. He can make an airplane. He can calculate the distance of the sun ... Shall, then, man at death perish utterly?[17]

We must be wary, says Russell, of values. For their intrusion has always been a hindrance, and not an asset, where investigation is concerned. It was once believed, for example, that the planets must move in circles, on the grounds that the circle is "the most perfect curve"; that species must be immutable because "God would only create what was perfect"; that it was useless to combat

---

[17] *Ibid.*, p. 91. The quotation is taken from Bishop Barnes, whose article appeared in the book *Mysteries of Life and Death*, in which Russell's own piece was included.

epidemics because they had been sent as punishment for sin, and so on. But nature, it seems, is indifferent to our values. Thus if we are to understand her ways, we had better leave such notions behind.

Our values, writes Russell, are natural facts; they develop out of material forces in our struggle for existence. Nothing about them is divine or supernatural. In one of Aesop's fables, he notes, a lion is shown pictures of huntsmen catching lions. The lion remarks that were he the artist, the tables would be turned.

What is good, what is impressive, thus depends on the observer. We may find it thrilling that human beings are able, say, to design aircraft. But what of the common housefly that can walk on the ceiling? None of us has ever managed it. On this basis, writes Russell, "a very telling argument could be constructed by a theologically-minded fly, which no doubt the other flies would find most convincing"!

Hume's thought surfaces in recent discussion, as well. One is that of Derek Parfit in his book *Reasons and Persons*. We operate, thinks Parfit, with a great misconception of what is involved in the sameness of a person over a period of time. For we suppose, once again, that persons are singular entities - core substances, of a certain kind, beneath their experience and outward disposition. We are thus inclined to think that the question of their identity - whether this one is the same as that earlier - must be answered *yes* or *no*. Such sameness, we assume, is all or nothing.

Yet there are imaginable cases,[18] says Parfit, where the question has no clear answer. For example, what if only a very small part of my brain were replaced with material just like it? It would be odd to think that I have now ceased to exist. What, then, of a 10% replacement? Or 30%, or more? It is hard to see where one draws the line. But we err, thinks Parfit, in thinking that there is any such line to be drawn.

Suppose, again, that the brain of a single individual could be divided and each half made to function afterward in a separate body. Each resulting individual might think himself to be identical with the first. Which would be correct? If personal identity is (as we assume) a definite fact, then either one, or both, or neither should be right.[19] But it does not appear that there exist grounds for any one of these verdicts.

Cases of this kind lead Parfit to adopt what he calls a reductionist view of personal identity. On this view, the development of a human being over time can be understood without reference to sameness. Personal identity is a non-issue, and questions involving sameness or difference can be reduced to (or put in terms of) particular events within this development.

---

[18] Derek Parfit, *Reasons and Persons* (New York: Oxford University Press, 1984). See pp. 234-36.

[19] Note, in this regard, pp. 253-61. See also Parfit's "Personal Identity", *Philosophical Review*, 80 (1971), pp. 3-27. This essay is reprinted in John Perry, ed. *Personal Identity* (Berkeley: University of California Press, 1975) and is discussed by Godfrey Vesey in his *Personal Identity: A Philosophical Analysis* (Ithaca: Cornell University Press, 1977). See also a related discussion in chapter 6 of Hywel Lewis' *The Elusive Self* (Philadelphia: Westminster Press, 1982).

What links two stages of an individual, thinks Parfit, is psychological *connectedness*,[20] the holding, in other words, of particular psychological characteristics (such things as belief, desire, intention, and memory) that exist over a period of time. A human being is thus not a solid and singular thing that endures through this process; his or her existence lies not in any core identity, but in the holding of certain connections, certain *common features of personality*, across the stages. What makes the later individual more or less the same as the one earlier is some appreciable amount of this connection. This sameness, then, is not something crucial and decisive. It is instead a matter of degree - the holding of enough of these chain-elements to make this individual close in makeup to one later.

Perhaps rough comparison can be made with a river. There is an outward and phenomenal sense in which this entity remains one thing over time. But if we look more closely, we see that it is not so much a thing as a series of things - it is more or less the same from one moment to the next, but this sameness diminishes with time. With enough time comes a whole turnover.

Strong connectedness, Parfit observes, is not identity as we commonly understand the term. For one thing, it is not transitive. Identity, after all, passes along, so that if A = B and B = C, then A and C are likewise identical. Applying this to persons over time, we might say that if person X at *time 0* is identical with later person X\` at *time 1*, and that individual with still later person X\`\` at *time 2*, then X at *time 0* must be identical with X\`\` at *time 2*, as well.

---

[20] *Reasons and Persons*, p. 206.

By contrast, while X may be strongly connected to X\` and X\` to X\`\`, it does not follow that X is strongly connected to X\`\`. (To find some point of comparison, again, we might think of certain other non-transitive relations, such as *resembles*, or *is blood kin to*. While person A may have the relation to B, and B to C, it does not follow that A and C are so related.)

If the point seems complex, perhaps another illustration will help. Take some individual Jan Jones at different ages - one, let us suppose, who was pursuing her first degree in biology at 25, was raising a family while working on her Master's thesis in embryology and studying cinema at 40, and who now helps her children run an art-film theater thirty years later. Perhaps we could add (at the risk of loading her life rather heavily) that Jan at 25 enjoys checkers and chess, at 40 chess and backgammon, and at 70 backgammon and bridge.

How might we now describe what has occurred over these many years? There are, it seems, relations of similarity that hold between the first and second of these - between Jan at 25 and Jan at 40. Likewise, between the second and third. The one of 25 has a good deal in common (in terms of habits, actions, predominant interests, and so on) with the one of 40. The one of 40 may likewise resemble the one of 70. But this relationship does not carry over. While Jan at 25 is noticeably similar to Jan at 40, and that Jan, in turn, to the one at 70, the first and third of these Jans (or, if one likes, these Jan-slices) have little in common with each other.

In which case, thinks Parfit, it makes little sense to speak of a self-same individual over the whole process. There is no *one,* he maintains, who lasts through it. The relation of a person X at a given time with one later, he believes, should thus be understood not in terms of identity, but in terms of causal sequence and development. Each is a stage in the process. Their tie is not one of strict personal sameness, but of participation in these overlapping chain-relations of resemblance.

Persons, on this view, are not substances that retain their identity as some "deep further fact" beneath the changes. They are really more akin to such things as clubs, nations,[21] or political parties. Think of what happens when one of these entities changes its constituency, a little at a time, down to the last member. Is it still the same? To see the arbitrariness of the answer, one might envision other changes of other kinds: Imagine that a given organization of persons one day ceases to hold its meetings, and at some later date reconvenes. Are the organizations at these respective times identical, or is the latter one "new"? Or suppose, again, that the party divides. What then? We might adopt the language of sameness to describe some of these relations. But need we?

The point of these cases, says Parfit, is that we can know *all that is to be known* about them[22] without even raising the issue of identity. We may, if we like, adopt the rule that the club is the same when it reconvenes. We may say, as well, that the nation "endures" through its generations. Or again, in each case,

---

[21] Cf. Hume: "I cannot compare the soul more properly to any thing than to a republic or commonwealth, in which the several members are united by the reciprocal ties of government and subordination, and give rise to other persons, who propagate the same republic in the incessant changes of its parts." *Treatise*, p. 261).

[22] *Reasons and Persons*, p. 260.

we may say otherwise. But this sameness, or lack of it, is not some mysterious and further fact beneath those present. Our verdict in each case is a matter of choice.[23]

Similarly, then, with human beings. The individual, so-called, who has undergone sizeable changes, over time, in habits, interests, and qualities of character is hardly the same as the one who bore her name several decades ago. Although a process of development historically links them, the two may be no more the same, in any meaningful sense, than are two distinct persons with whole different life-histories.

The strangeness of this account, its departure from common sense, is shown by Parfit's example of "teletransportation."[24] Let us imagine, he says, that technology one day offers us the chance to visit another planet by being replicated - that is, by having our cell-states copied there while our bodies are destroyed here on earth. Some, we may suppose, would balk at this chance, imagining that this alleged travel is tantamount to extinction. Others would accept it, figuring that they will be effectively reproduced in a new environment.

Which reaction is correct? In fact, thinks Parfit, each counts upon a false assumption, namely again that the question has a definite answer. For we do not survive, even under ordinary circumstances, he thinks, in the way that we

---

[23] One might also consider, for illustration, several time-slices of one baseball team - say, the New York Yankees of 1982, 1988, 1994, and 1999. While there exist some similarities (i. e., some players common to rosters) from one team to the next, the teams differ in constitution, and the first and last are thoroughly distinct.

[24] See initially chapter 10, "What We Believe Ourselves to Be".

imagine. Life is not the journey, as it were, of a self-same traveler along for its duration. Over time this "one" undergoes thorough change, whether acknowledged or not. Those refusing teletransportation would do so because they think that something (i. e., their "real" self) is lost in the transition. But what they think would be missing, says Parfit, "is always missing."[25] Thus there would be little lost, he thinks, in this process of being destroyed and copied elsewhere, for teletransportation is about as good as ordinary survival. (And conversely, he adds, because ordinary survival is about as bad as teletransportation!)

Parfit's account has interesting consequences. One is that our usual concerns about remaining in existence are largely ungrounded. For they presuppose something (namely, our absolute and continuing sameness) that does not exist. We commonly think of our existence as being a solid "further" fact present through all of life and then abruptly ending. With this view comes a good deal of anxiety:

> When I believed that my existence was such a further fact, I seemed imprisoned within myself. My life seemed like a glass tunnel, through which I was moving faster every year, and at the end of which there was darkness.[26]

But on the view being developed, there is no such crucial fact. Rather there are, at bottom, only experiences and their various connective relations, all in flux over a natural lifetime. One might then redescribe the event of his own death in appropriately less decisive terms as follows:

---

[25] *Ibid.*, p. 280.

[26] *Ibid.*, p. 281.

> Though there will later be many experiences, none of these experiences will be connected to my present experiences by chains of such direct connections as those involved in experience-memory, or in the carrying out of an earlier intention. Some of these future experiences may be related to my present experiences in less direct ways. There will later be some memories about my life. And there may later be thoughts that are influenced by mine, or things done as the result of my advice. My death will break the more direct relations between my present experiences and future experiences, but it will not break various other relations. This is all there is to the fact that there will be no one living who will be me.[27]

With the acquisition of this view, says Parfit, comes relief. The walls of the tunnel disappear so that one may "live in the open air" with a diminished sense of the difference between self and others. One becomes less concerned about one's own life, and more concerned about that of others. Death, seen in this new perspective, seems "less bad" than before.

To offer, then, a word of summary: There exist serious questions as to whether we can speak of consciousness as existing independently of the material processes with which it is associated. There exist questions, too, about the sameness of individuals in any meaningful sense over an extended period of time. The claim that human beings are spiritual entities, that they are persisting souls, is regarded likewise as being implausible.

By some accounts, the notion of a soul apart from a body is incoherent. For, it is said, if souls are (as traditionally imagined) immaterial, then presumably they lack such things as mass, shape, or location. In that case, how can one soul be distinguished in theory from another? And what is its relationship to this world

---

[27] *Ibid.*

once it departs? It is hard, thinks Antony Flew, to make sense of the notion of an individual *witnessing his own funeral*.[28] And if souls lack materiality, ask some, how can we know that other people (whom we know, presumably, only by appearance) are the same from one time to the next? I will address these issues and others in the following chapter.

Some have thought the prospect of survival to be unworthy of serious attention whatever its theoretical status. In the remainder of this chapter I will trace developments of this position in the twentieth century. One of these is the Humanist philosophy of Corliss Lamont, and another is the view of Charles Hartshorne. Each of these men denies the likelihood of personal survival. Each maintains furthermore that concern with a future life is inessential and perhaps even antagonistic to the cultivation of a meaningful life-outlook.

Humanism: Survival Discounted as Being Neither Likely Nor Essential

There is a positive connection, many imagine, between ethics and belief in personal survival. Religious folk, it seems, are likely to have a strong sense of values. This much stands to reason, since we often receive, in our formative years, moral and religious instruction from a common source. Moral views are likewise apt to inhere in a religious outlook.

---

[28] Antony Flew, "Can a Man Witness His Own Funeral?", reprinted in Flew's *God, Freedom and Immortality* (Buffalo: Prometheus, 1984).

One might suppose, then, that belief in a life hereafter is naturally associated with a high moral development. Yet some philosophers deny that there is any such connection. Some maintain that the relationship is actually inverse - that belief in another life expresses an inferior personal ethic.

Perhaps we would be better persons if we were denied this hope. A frank acceptance of our shared "inevitable doom," writes Clarence Darrow,[29] might make us more considerate toward one another in the time that we are here. It is argued likewise by some that a non-survivalist view makes possible the truest form of unselfishness. For, it is said, persons who anticipate survival tend to see their virtue here as contributing, in the long run, to their own reward. Those who lack this expectation must choose the good for its own sake.

Perhaps the staunchest critic of belief in personal survival in the twentieth century is Corliss Lamont, who denies that a future life is either likely or important. Survival, says Lamont, is unlikely in view of the obvious congruence of mind and body. But rejection of belief in another world, he adds, does not preclude a meaningful philosophy of life. Rather it is Humanism[30] that offers the prospect of real living and the improvement of the human condition.

---

[29] Clarence Darrow, "The Myth of the Soul", reprinted as "The Myth of Immortality" in Paul Edwards and Arthur Pap, eds., *A Modern Introduction to Philosophy* (New York: Macmillan, 1973).

[30] Corliss Lamont, *The Philosophy of Humanism* (New York: Philosophical Library, 1957). The term 'humanist', notes Lamont, came into currency in the early sixteenth century and was used to refer to the writers and scholars of the European Renaissance. The contemporary version of humanism, he explains, incorporates the most enduring values of that era, while in some respects going beyond it in scope and significance.

Humanism is a philosophy "of joyous service for the greater good of all humanity in this natural world and according to the methods of reason and democracy." It is not an outlook merely for scholars, but is "a way of thinking and doing for average men and women seeking to lead happy and useful lives." It does not appeal to the intellectuals by pretending some great originality of thought, nor to the multitude by promising easy fulfillment, either here or in "some supernatural dream-world" to come.

Among the tenets of this philosophy, Lamont explains, are a naturalistic attitude toward reality and the dismissal of all purported elements of the supernatural as myth; the view that man is "an evolutionary product of this great Nature of which he is part"; a faith in human beings to solve the problems that afflict them, principally by means of reason and scientific method; a rejection of fatalism in favor of the view that we are "masters of their own destiny"; and an ethic that grounds all values in "this-earthly experiences and relationships." It has as its goal the establishment of an earthly happiness for all of the human race.

Further, Humanism believes in "the widest possible development of art and the awareness of beauty, including the appreciation of Nature's splendor" and in making aesthetic experience a pervasive reality in human life. It seeks to establish, throughout the world, peace and democracy, as well as a high standard of living. Humanism intends to implement reason and scientific method in the social structure. It advocates the unending questioning of basic assumptions, whether those of tradition or even its own.[31]

---

[31] *Ibid.* See especially chapter I, "The Meaning of Humanism".

For Humanism, writes Lamont, as for most other philosophies, the first question with respect to the nature and destiny of man is that of mind and body. Is their relationship so close as to constitute an indissoluble unity, or is it so loose and inessential that human personality might exist on its own? Is man, in short, a "one-ness" or a "two-ness"?

This issue, thinks Lamont, is crucial. For if human beings think that their careers are limited to this world, they are more than half-way to becoming Humanists whatever they may think about reality otherwise. According to Humanism, writes Lamont, body and personality live, grow, and perish together. The facts of science, he maintains, offer overwhelming evidence in support of such a thesis.

In the first place, biology has shown beyond rational doubt that all forms of life, including our own, are the result not of divine creation, but of a naturally explicable process stretching over some two billion years. In this gradual development from one-celled life to more complex organisms, body is "prior and basic." Mind appears "at the present apex of the evolutionary process and not at the beginning." The human body is "an organism of the most prodigious intricacy, its multitudinous parts adjusted to one another" in harmony with natural law.[32]

It is the relative complexity of the brain, and especially of the cortex, explains Lamont, that bestows on human beings the power of thought. It is this feature that raises them immeasurably above all other creatures on earth. Just as in the species, where mind and personality appear at a certain stage, so it is in the

---

[32] *Ibid.*, p. 69.

individual. Neither the embryo nor the newborn possesses this capacity, which exists as yet only in potential. The laws of heredity, moreover,

> show in the first instance the intimate correlation between the physical organism and the self. The laws of sex, with their ever-powerful influence on behavior, character and aptitude, tell the same story. It is obvious that certain profound differences between the male and female personalities depend primarily upon different bodily organization. Always the general rule is that the kind of personality one has is conditioned by the kind of body one has and by the more fundamental changes that take place in that body.[33]

It is the misuse of abstraction, Lamont argues, that gives rise to our confusions about the mind-body problem. Terms like 'mind' and 'personality' are ones that we use, like 'digestion' and 'respiration', to denote certain activities of human beings. Our habits of language make it easy to separate mental processes from the natural functions that bring them about, and to think of them, at times, as if they were self-subsisting. It is obvious, of course, that digestion and respiration are bodily based; the body's generation of the mind, by contrast, is less so. For this reason it is easier to think of mental activity apart from its physical basis.

Examination of the purported accounts of the hereafter casts further doubt upon the notion. The activities of persons on the other side, it seems, require need not only a bodily mechanism, but also "a substantial and complex environment," if they are to have meaningful content. In the modern age, writes Lamont, some afterlife proponents make their accounts of the next world less

---

[33] *Ibid.* For related discussion, see section III, "The Verdict of Science", contained in *The Illusion of Immortality* (New York: Frederick Ungar Publishing Co., 1965).

specific in order to salvage their dignity. Alternatively, some re-create a whole scenario of objects and pastimes, "from cheap cigarettes to expensive limousines,"[34] fleshing out that world with a duplication of this one.

If there is survival, who qualifies? Logic seems to demand immortality for all living things if it demands them for any. The survival of other life-forms is needed not only "to round out" the next-world environment, but also to avoid logical favoritism. It is most difficult "to draw a reasonable line barring from a like destiny the creatures of the animal world from which man is descended and to which he is kin." The heavenly pageant, then, must include "in addition to all the millions and billions of men and submen who ever lived, the entire past, the entire past and present population of the animal kingdom." Those who enjoy the affection of a household pet should agree that if an infant of ten days or ten months goes on to the greater life, surely "good old Rover," a family member for ten years, is worthy of a similar fate.

Once we are apprised of the facts, thinks Lamont, we will find it hard to believe that human beings are destined for any life but this. The dualistic hypothesis, he contends, runs afoul of the law of parsimony, which holds that explanation should employ "the fewest possible assumptions necessary for it to

---

[34] Cited on pages 80-81 is a passage from a famous book detailing the communication about the next world to Sir Oliver Lodge from his departed son Raymond, wherein "Everything that is necessary to man, everything that man in a sense makes his own, has an etheric duplicate ... It may be that the chair you see at home, your material chair, and the chair we see, which is your chair on our side, the etheric chair, are one and the same thing really ... You can mold an etheric body for a thing - a piano, a clock, a desk - by loving and liking to have it with you." No wonder, says Lamont, that contemporary spiritualists tend to shy away from offering close descriptions of the next world.

account adequately for all the facts involved."[35] This law was first enunciated by the fourteenth century English philosopher William of Occam, who said famously that "Entities are need not to be multiplied beyond need."[36]

Such a law, put in negative terms, holds that no hypothesis is worthy of our acceptance until it meets " the requirements of affirmative empirical proof." This does need not deny that nature herself may operate in an exceedingly complex manner, or that we should ignore such complexity where it is observed. It only means that we ought need not to bring in hypotheses when they are unnecessary.

The development of astronomy furnishes an example. When Copernicus had no new facts to confirm his heliocentric hypothesis,[37] his initial advantage over the old Ptolemaic theory lay in mathematical simplicity.[38] Fewer assumptions about planetary motion were required to explain the observed facts on Copernicus' view, and this was a reason, in principle, to take his view (all things equal), over

---

[35] See again *The Illusion of Immortality* and particularly the discussion in chapter 3, "The Verdict of Science".

[36] For an extensive discussion of Ockham's philosophy, see Ernest A. Moody, "William of Ockham", contained in volume 8 of *The Encyclopedia of Philosophy* (New York: Macmillan, 1967). Paul Edwards, general editor.

[37] The view, in other words, that the sun, and not the earth, was the center around which the planets (and the heavens) revolved.

[38] For a detailed account of his transition, see Edwin Burtt's classic *The Metaphysical Foundations of Modern Physical Science* (New York: Doubleday, 1932). A chapter on the new astronomy is contained also in Herbert Butterfield's *The Origins of Modern Science* New York: The Free Press, 1957).

the other. In time, Newton was able to go yet further in this direction when he was able to account for the movements of the earth and the heavenly bodies by a single law of gravitation.

Parsimony, thinks Lamont, is aligned in principle with rationality and with scientific progress. He cites further the example of Galileo, who discovered mountains on the moon, and who was "refuted" by one conservative who (to maintain traditional belief in the pristineness of this heavenly sphere) answered that the apparent valleys on the moon were filled with an invisible crystalline substance. Galileo replied that if this were so, perhaps the moon had on it mountains, made of this same substance, ten times as high as those he had observed![39]

Dualistic theories, by the same token, are a holdover. In pre-scientific days, supernatural forces were routinely assigned to forces of nature to explain their activity; trees could need not grow on their own account, nor streams flow, nor thunderstorms thunder. Souls, or gods of some sort, were read into these phenomena as "moving principles" behind their manifestations. Diseases such as insanity[40] and hysteria were the result of evil spirits entering the body. But this time is past, and we seem to be the better for it.

---

[39] An entertaining account of scientific progress set against prevailing religious spirit is found in Bertrand Russell's aforenoted *Religion and Science*. See especially chapter 2, "The Copernican Revolution".

[40] See, for example, Russell's "Demonology and Medicine", contained in the same volume.

How is it, then, that belief in a future life is so widespread? The sad yet common frustration of ideals and ambitions here, writes Lamont, provides an insight. Most of mankind has had little access to the better things in life. Countless individuals have gone to the grave without realization of their natural promise, and so it continues today. The tendency to fashion another world, then, may be understandable in this light. But a wish is no index of reality.[41]

Death, says Lamont, is integral to life, neither evil nor mysterious. The very existence of our fuel, food, clothing, shelter, furnishings, and reading materials all depend, in large part, upon its operation. Life and death are thus "essential and correlative parts" of the same process. An understanding of death's "indispensable place in Nature" may well be an antidote to our fear.

Humanism, then, disavows itself of any belief in a higher world. It argues furthermore that survival is inessential to the meaning of life. Human beings need not seek their purpose in any world but this one. For they can find

> plenty of scope and meaning in their lives through freely enjoying the rich and varied potentialities of this luxuriant earth; through preserving, extending and adding to the values of civilization; through contributing to the progress and happiness of mankind during billions and billions of years; or through helping to evolve a new species surpassing man.[42]

This philosophy thus constitutes "a profound and passionate affirmation of the joys and beauties, the braveries and idealisms of existence upon this earth."

---

[41] If human beings, notes Lamont, desired to be "as big as all space instead of as eternal as all time," this desire would hardly presage its fulfillment. (*The Illusion of Immortality*, p. 178)

[42] *The Philosophy of Humanism*, pp. 89-90.

It embraces healthy and life-enhancing pleasures, whether those of a vigorous youth or a mellowed age, whether of food and drink or of fine art and literature. It extols the beauty of love and the magnificence of nature. It views the individual as being a living unity of body and personality.

Humanism, in sum, adheres to the highest moral ideals and fosters "the so-called goods of the spirit," such as culture and art and responsible citizenship. Its ethic is "positive," one wherein conscience plays not just the role of a vetoing censor, but is creative, bringing to the fore "new and higher values." It advocates the greater enjoyment of earthly goods on the part of all; it repudiates ascetic other-worldliness in favor of "a buoyant this-worldliness"; it opposes defeatist ideals of worldly renunciation and acquiescence in the social injustice that plagues us here.

This ethic, Lamont contends, is better and saner than one that postpones our happiness to a world hereafter. It is opposed to the notion, quite prevalent in Christian tradition, that there exists an "inherent wickedness" in human beings, and that the sexual impulse, in particular, is essentially bad or base. Thus it finds nothing admirable in the idea, for example, that Jesus was born of a virgin and in violation of ordinary law. While Humanism recognizes the necessity of "high standards" in sexual relations, it does not regard sexual emotion itself as being evil. It holds likewise that excessive concern with sexuality as a keystone of value has resulted in an unhealthy narrowing of our moral attention. Tradition, says Lamont, has long slighted the value of love between man and woman. In a sound philosophy, its worth would be higher.

Moral judgments are a species of value judgment. For this reason, Lamont observes, it is hard to gain a consensus on them. Yet a true science of ethics, he maintains, is possible and will yet be established. We must realize, however, that no action is good or bad of itself, but can only be judged so in terms of its social consequences. Our knowledge of the good can thus be "worked out" if we can learn to think less in terms of divine pronouncement and more in terms of human welfare.

Embedded in our own religious tradition, writes Lamont, is a tendency toward anti-intellectualism. Supernaturalist religions, he notes, have generally had a low estimate of the worth of human reason. In this regard they fail to see the relationship between reason and ethics. A moral law, a moral system, is always "relative to the particular historical period and to the particular culture" of which it is a part. What was good for Hebrews of 4,000 years ago, or for Greeks of Athens, or for Europeans of the past century, is not necessarily good for Americans of the present day. This does not mean that we need think of moral systems as being merely subjective, or must suppose that the past is irrelevant to our situation.

Humanism teaches "the formation of sound moral habits as well as of guiding moral principles," but asks that neither habits nor principles become rigid. It may be, for example, that a lie is objectionable in one context, yet not in another. Certain minor acts of deception may be justified by their value in extricating us from difficult situations or in sparing the feelings of other persons. (A doctor, then, might well be pardoned for deceiving his patient to avoid aggravating his condition.) And while non-violence may seem, on the whole, to be a good ideal, it also seems that one is justified in shooting a mad dog in order to save the life of a child.

Those philosophies that maintain a future life, Lamont observes, tend to rest their ethics ultimately upon self-interest. So Plato, he explains, advocates in his dialogues nothing more, in the end, than a long-range personal advantage.[43] Christianity has preached likewise an ethic of "building up credits" of worth in the next life. Humanism, on the other hand, allows the real devotion. It advocates a system wherein the social and sympathetic tendencies of human beings are encouraged over egoistic ones. It recognizes that a society aimed at the collective well-being will make more progress than one in which self-interest is predominant.

Happiness, writes Lamont, is not definable in terms of "the glorified heavenly rest-home" or "the passive contemplation" that is the mark of supernaturalist tradition. Nor is it found in the withdrawal of oneself to an ivory tower, of one kind or another, away from the mainstream. Human beings are inherently active creatures. For this reason, the most pathetic sight on earth is not the tired businessman, but the re-tired one. A human being cannot remain satisfied with past success. The psyche, it seems, is no exception to the law, present from the level of the atom to that of the star, that nature is ever active.

---

[43] Lamont may have in mind, for one, the defense of justice in Plato's *Republic*, where, it seems, the argument turns upon the fact that virtue and happiness are (by Socrates' reckoning) congruent, justice always benefitting the soul and injustice always harming it both here and hereafter.

Nor is happiness found in the acquisition of one object of desire after another. We are familiar with the empty feeling that often follows the realization of a goal we have long pursued. The thrill of achievement gives way soon to the emptiness of boredom. For this reason Humanism seeks human success in the condition of "equilibrium in activity" - in a dynamic harmony achieved under the guidance of wisdom.

The goal of Humanism, in brief, is that of "happiness, freedom, and progress for all humanity." It advocates a synthesis of values, the result of which is "a greater and greater sharing of the good things of life on the part of more and more persons in every country"; its logical end, at the level of world civilization, is thus the goal of the greatest good for the greatest number, of "democracy in its most meaningful and far-reaching sense." It allows and indeed advocates the free examination of all ideas, including its own, hence fostering improvements in all areas of human interaction, such as those of economics, cultural development, and race relations.[44]

A number of writers in recent years have agreed with Lamont in thinking that a future existence has little bearing on the meaning of life. Some have denied that the prospect of a future life is even especially attractive. Thus Russell, for example, feels more at home in a universe empty of spiritual significance; cosmic

---

[44] See chapter 6, "The Affirmation of Life", and especially section 3, "A Humanist Civilization".

accident, he writes, offers a "less painful" account.[45] Charles Hartshorne,[46] whose view I will discuss shortly, regards it as neither sad nor unjust that our existence should be restricted to its earthly limit.

Walter Kaufmann argues likewise that the presence and acknowledgment of this limit is integral to the conduct of a truly good life. "The life I want," he says, "is a life I could not endure in eternity. It is a life of love and intensity, suffering and creation, that makes life worthwhile and death welcome. There is no other life I should prefer. Neither should I like not to die."[47] And again,

> As one deserves a good night's sleep, one also deserves to die. Why should I hope to wake again? To do what I have not done in the time I've had? All of us have so much more time than we use well. How many hours in a life are spent in a way of which one might be proud, looking back?[48]

For most of us, Kaufmann maintains, death does not come soon enough. Lives are "made rotten" by the sense that it is distant. For this reason, we are better off if we face life instead with a mortal urgency. Kaufmann quotes the poet Holderlin:

---

[45] Russell, "Do We Survive Death?", reprinted once again in Russell's *Why I Am Not a Christian and Other Essays on Religion and Related Subjects*. "I believe," he writes elsewhere, "that when I die I shall rot, and nothing of my ego will survive. I am not young, and I love life. But I should scorn to shiver with terror at the thought of annihilation." See his essay "What I Believe" in this same volume.

[46] Charles Hartshorne, "Time, Death and Everlasting Life", reprinted in Hartshorne's *The Logic of Perfection* (La Salle, Illinois: Open Court, 1962).

[47] Walter Kaufmann, *The Faith of a Heretic* (Garden City, New York: Doubleday and Company, Inc., 1961).

[48] *Ibid.*, p. 386.

A single summer grant me, great powers and
A single autumn for fully ripened song
That, sated with the sweetness of my
Playing, my heart may more willingly die.

The soul that, living, did not attain its divine
Right cannot repose in the netherworld.
But once what I am bent on, what is
Holy, my poetry, is accomplished,

Be welcome then, stillness of the shadows' world!
I shall be satisfied though my lire will not
Accompany me down there. Once I
Lived like the gods, and more is not needed.[49]

Further on he cites a familiar line from Shakespeare's *Tempest*, wherein

We are such stuff
As dreams are made on, and our little life
Is rounded with a sleep.[50]

It is possible, says Kaufmann, that this is mistaken. There may be surprises in store. But why hope for it? Instead, he says, let those who have nothing worthwhile in this life wish for something beyond. But they, it seems, are the ones who would gain the least from it. If one lives and loves with intensity, claims Kaufmann, the time comes when death seems bliss. Those who have loved with all their hearts, and who have cared for others amidst life's travails, he contends, will understand this message.

A religion, thinks Kaufmann, that holds out the promise of another life to its adherents is open to moral question. Accordingly he champions a this-worldly Old Testament ethic over that of Christianity. In the former, our happiness is

---

[49] "A Single Summer" (quoted by Kaufmann on p. 381).

[50] *Tempest*, act IV, scene 1 (quoted by Kaufmann on p. 385).

"scarcely considered" next to the real issue of God's will; in the New Testament, on the other hand, each man's "overruling concern" is his own eternal reward. The Old Testament tells us to treat others justly for their sake, and not ours. To the Jesus of the Gospels, on the other hand, "social justice as such is of no concern." The Sermon on the Mount, says Kaufmann, "is centered not in the neighbor but in salvation," whereas the demands of Moses and the prophets are "categorical." The Jesus of popular worship appeals at bottom "to each man's self-interest."[51]

I think that Kaufmann is right in saying that death gives to life a unity and a moral scheme that it might lack otherwise. Death as a backdrop can provide life with a sense of urgency. It can spur us to action. It offers us a sense of completion as we move through life's stages, and gives us an opportunity for moral choices that we would not have otherwise. I think, too, that absent-mindedness about one's own demise can make it easier to fritter away time on trivial entertainments.[52]

As to whether belief in survival is furthermore inessential to a meaningful philosophy of life, I will say more in the following chapters. In the remainder of this chapter I will take note of one other denial of survival (as survival, at least, is ordinarily understood) as contained in the philosophy of Charles Hartshorne.

---

[51] See *The Faith of a Heretic*, chapter 8.

[52] Worth citing, in this regard, is Tolstoy's classic on the subject (discussed with admiration by Kaufmann in the chapter quoted above), which examines a man's sudden confrontation with his own mortality. See Leo Tolstoy, *The Death of Ivan Ilych*. Trans. Aylmer Maude (New York: Signet Books, 1960).

A Religious Denial of the Importance of Personal Survival

Many persons imagine that they will be paid back in another life for good deeds unrewarded in this one. Yet genuine love of God, contends Hartshorne, bids us to abandon this idea. The time and place to look for virtue's rewards, "is here and now. Not only will there be 'no marrying and giving in marriage' in the heavenly mansions, there will, I imagine, be no personal actions of yours and mine other than those we enact before we die."[53] Nor should we think that God will "insult" those who value love for its own sake with post mortem compensations such that "a reasonable man could think of nothing else if he really took them seriously."[54]

It is, thinks Hartshorne, precisely in our limitations that our identity consists. In these limitations, too, is our immortality - our eternal place in reality, which is the only immortality that we have. Granted, we are finite creatures, limited in space and time, but this does not make us nothing. For death, we must understand, is not sheer destruction. Once an individual "is there to refer to," says Hartshorne, "he continues to be there even after death, as object of reference, as a life which really has been lived."[55]

---

[53] *The Logic of Perfection*, p. 254.

[54] To know more of Hartshorne's conception of the divine nature and his reasons for believing that God exists, see discussion in this same volume.

[55] *Ibid.*, p. 247.

What, then, is death? It is "the last page of the last chapter of one's life, as birth is the first page of the first chapter." Given the existence of a first page, the book is opened. It remains to be seen, of course, how rich and how complete this book will be. But there is no question of its reality, at this point, for it is real now. True, the book may be truncated - may be ended without apt content or conclusion. An individual may perish before his basic purposes have been carried out, but even this, contends Hartshorne, cannot mean annihilation. For in that case there would be nothing, rather than something that is broken off before its time. In this way death actually "presupposes indestructibility" of the life that it ends. (Thus, to cite one case, "Washington having died is at least Washington.") This individual, once having had his place, is forever "a unique unity of experience and decision and thought" that has made up this particular biography.

But there is a distinction, Hartshorne continues, between reality in the form of retained actuality, and reality in the form of continuing actualization. The actuality of an individual lies in his or her thoughts, feelings, and activities - all of these "evermore as real as when they occurred." But this does not imply that new events of this kind are occurring in heaven as part of the same conscious stream. Such a continuation would mean new reality, not the indestructibility of the old. Our eternity needs to be understood instead in terms of our permanent place in the story. Various traditional claims about our survival might thus be read as "mythical ways of trying to grasp the truth that death is not ultimate destruction but simply termination, finitude."[56]

---

[56] *Ibid.*, p. 251.

Comparison of life and literature goes further: To say that life is a book, says Hartshorne, suggests that there exists some potential reader of its contents. Something that cannot be known by any possible mind is scarcely a book, and "is doubtfully distinguishable from nonentity." Who, then, are these potential readers? The first answer that comes to mind is posterity. Thus we might have a "social immortality," consisting in our children, in the readers of books that we have written, in the spectators who will behold the words and monuments we have left behind.

Does this eventuality make for eternal life? It has, thinks Hartshorne, severe limitations. For no human being will ever truly "read" even a single page in the life-book we have written. Even while we live, none sees its exact content. Those who view our outward signs, such as our facial expressions, cannot know what bits of experience (a slight discomfort, an impulse of sympathy) lie behind them. And if such things elude our closest contemporaries, they are missed all the more by posterity.

Thus the only real reader, the only genuine audience, must be someone who is not subject to such limitations. For this reason, it seems, our adequate immortality

> can only be God's omniscience of us. He to whom all hearts are open remains evermore open to any heart that ever has been apparent to Him. What we once were to Him, less than that we never can be, for otherwise He Himself as knowing us would lose something of His own reality ...[57]

---

[57] *Ibid.*, pp. 252-53.

The meaning of omniscience is a knowledge coextensive with reality. As such it is a measure of reality. If we can never be less, in God's eyes, than we have been, we are never diminished. "Omniscience and the indestructibility of every reality are correlative aspects of one truth." What God understands can never be removed from existence. Death, then, is not the destruction, or even the fading, of the book of one's life; it means instead "only the fixing of its concluding page." Death may write *The End*, but nothing further is added or subtracted. Life's content is fixed for eternity.

The impossibility of subtraction, notes Hartshorne, is more certain than the impossibility of addition. For personal conscious survival does not seem to be "an absolute absurdity," provided that we keep in mind the difference between continuing chapters, on the one hand, and an infinite number of pages, on the other. For this notion of absolute unlimitedness, he believes, runs afoul of the boundaries of human nature.

But even this somewhat more modest notion of new chapters - the supplying of fresh canvas, as it were, on which "the artist will paint new pictures in some finer medium" - strikes Hartshorne as being dubious. The time to paint, he explains,

> seems to be here and now, and there will not, I suspect, be another - for us. Our chance to do right and not wrong, to love God and in God all creatures, is here and now. Not only will there be "no marrying and giving in marriage" in the heavenly mansions, there will, I imagine, be no personal actions of yours and mine other than those we enact before we die.[58]

---

[58] *Ibid.*, p. 254.

Neither, then, will there be any such thing as our feeling sorrow as punishment for our past ill deeds, or bliss as reward for our good ones. The time to look for virtue's reward is here. If one cannot now find good in doing good and ill in doing ill, then one is unlikely to find such things in heaven. If love is the motive in virtuous conduct, then "scheming for reward or avoidance of punishment" at some future date cannot be a part of it.

The latter part of Hartshorne's essay is devoted to an explanation of why this denial of conscious survival is consistent with an affirmation of divine benevolence. The old idea of heaven and hell, he writes, is a colossal error, and "one of the most dangerous that ever occurred to the human mind." Yet it is associated, he adds, with certain truths. Death, understood rightly, is not the destruction of an individual's reality, but only the fixing of its "quantum." It thus says, in effect, "More than you already have been you will not be. For instance, the virtues you have failed to acquire, you will now never acquire. It is too late. You have had your chance."

This, he observes, accords well with the idea of a Last Judgment. When our time is done, our lives will be estimated and our accounts will be closed. Nothing will be added or taken away. This limit applies to rewards and punishments, as well. If an individual has no present objection to being an ugly soul, or to living without the deeper harmonies of love and understanding, then no further punishment will be meted out. Sadistic or vengeful men may wish that such a person be further punished, but God by His nature cannot share such impulse.

To each of us, then, is given a choice: We may fall down into self-hatred over our failures; or again, we may persist in a state of mind so dense that we do not fully understand what we are consequently missing; or last, we may demand of ourselves a life of kindness and insight into ourselves and those around us. Between these respective fates, here and now, we may choose, and we shall not escape judgment. But God, reasons Hartshorne, does not trample again upon the bodies or souls of those who choose for ill; nor will He give more to those who have found virtue to be a sufficient reward.

This absence of *post mortem* rewards and punishments does not imply that there are no good or bad results to be anticipated from our lives once they are over. It may well be that another will live more richly for what I have done. In this, I may find a reward for courage or generosity. But my own enjoyment of this reward is here and now. It does not lie elsewhere.

Such a reward, Hartshorne admits, may seem modest in comparison with the one traditionally promised. But it is not to be despised. Indeed the nobler the spirit, he imagines, the more it will suffice. Thus Moses, for example, did not need to enter the promised land so long as he knew that it would be entered by those who survived him. It was enough that he had led them there.

Consider, says Hartshorne, an analogy. There are many persons who cannot bear the thought that they are no longer eligible for the joys of young love. This is common among middle-aged men who leave their wives for women of the next generation. In this way, such men think that they avoid the fate of growing old.

Yet herein they are the victims of a kind of "metaphysical confusion": Seeing that young love is a beautiful thing, they draw the conclusion that it is good that they themselves have it. Such a good is missed, they suppose, if it passes them by. What they must see instead is that this particular good, like all others, has its place. It should be had, not necessarily by anyone, but by those best fitted to it.

Much of the art of life, Hartshorne continues, lies in being able to distinguish between truth-claims like, "this possible beauty of life ought to be actualized" and "it ought to be actualized by and for me." For this qualification "by and for me," he explains, is irrelevant. "There is a good in the life of person A" and "There is a good in the life of person B" each imply the existence of a certain good. Since they are given to different individuals, they are different goods. But one is not inherently better. From God's point of view, their value is the same. Granted, if I am person A, I may find the first prospect more attractive. But this does not mean that it has higher objective worth.

To love God unreservedly is to understand the truth of this proposition: *That is good which is good in the eyes of God.* Thus an old man or a young man, for example, may occupy the central place in a young woman's life, but as a general rule, one must think, it should be the latter. The older man who believes himself to be the better candidate must either have "very unusual reasons"[59] for so thinking, or else must imagine that the only real good is his own.

---

59 There must be circumstances present in the situation, I take it, that make the older man a happier choice.

In this latter case the man falls prey to both selfishness and intellectual confusion. He needs to understand that the closing of his life is not the closing of life itself. The ending of his youth is not the ending of youth altogether. The secret of living consists in the service of good as an end in itself, and not merely when it is mine: "The devoted imagination can win such reward as it needs from joys that only others are to possess directly."

For the nontheist, Hartshorne observes, the ultimate future good is that of posterity. But how can I know what will benefit posterity? Perhaps I shall misjudge the effects of my actions, or will have bad luck in carrying these actions out. And much of what I do - say, when I listen to Mozart for an hour - will mean nothing to posterity in any case. But there is one to whom my experiences may mean something. While God is familiar with Mozart, He is not yet familiar with the experience that I myself may have of him, an experience that will differ from others according to my own alertness, sensitivity, and imagination. For this reason all of my life can be a kind of sacrifice to deity, one whose quality depends upon its devotion to all good things, not specifically as mine, but as belonging to all of God's creatures and so to God Himself. A life that is thin and discordant, owing to its lack of openness, is thus "a poor gift to the divine valuer of all things."

Heaven, writes Hartshorne, is thus the divine apprehension. It is the awareness of all that has ever happened and has ever been experienced. Such a "book" is never read by any mortal creature, of course, except in fragments, but it is read by God in its entirety. Hell, by the same token, is just that ugliness contained therein, as a result of our own perversity. In which case, there is no sinner in hell, except insofar as some may feel themselves to be there on earth. And afterward, only God will know that one has made a poor excuse of oneself to the immortal memory. But here this one will have felt the consequences, or else will have stupefied himself to the point of missing this and many other things worth knowing.

In this regard we have an active role in deciding what God will see in us; we "mold the picture which forever will hang in the divine mansion." God will make as much out of the picture as can be made, but how much will depend upon the sort of picture it is. The true immortality, thinks Hartshorne, is everlasting fame before God.

Some will doubtless be disappointed. It may be felt, he writes,

> that the consolations of the old faith are lost in this doctrine. What, no chance to make amends for errors in this life! No chance to grow deeper in insight and devotion beyond the grave! No compensation for bad luck in one's earthly career![60]

Yet these objections involve the confusion noted above, namely, that between good, or life, in general, and the more limited element of my own good, or life, in particular. How selfish, how stunted, is this outlook, thinks Hartshorne, when seen from the outside. Granted I myself cannot have, cannot know, all things. But others, again, "will make amends, will develop deeper insight and devotion, will be lucky where I was not." All good cannot be mine; only God Himself is heir to all the good that exists.

---

[60] *The Logic of Perfection*, p. 259.

True, it would be a good thing if there were more of life than exists in this world. But if our developing view of the cosmos is correct, there may be countless hospitable planets out in the vastness. Who can say what life they will support or what good they will contain? To suppose that you or I must have this good, writes Hartshorne, is like supposing that you or I must be the one who marries this young girl. Our grasp of this truth requires an act of renunciation, an admission that the good of others is no less valuable than our own.

Perhaps it will be said that while we ought not to demand personal survival for ourselves, it is all right to demand it for others. This is but another instance of conflating the general with the particular. (If I need not require, once again, that it is I who marry the young girl, neither must I require that some other middle-aged man does.) Perhaps it will be said that if God loves us, He will not allow us to be destroyed. But death, once more, is not destruction. It is "the setting of a definite limit, not the obliteration of what is limited." Does God love us as we are here on earth merely for the sake of what we will be in some future life, or does He love us for the sake of ourselves "as we really are"? God, imagines Hartshorne, loves us in our present reality for its own sake.

Each of us, he concludes, is a theme with variations. No theme other than that of the divine nature "can admit an infinity of variations all significant enough to be worth making a place for in reality." Life is self-exhaustive. Those who live appreciably beyond the prime of life are a woeful illustration. Perhaps some marvelous resurrection, restoring everyone to full vitality, could change this, but there are other means by which an equal good can be accomplished.

Seeing this resurrection instead as "the synthesis of one's life in God," writes Hartshorne, we may believe in it without the old confusion. We are individuated by our place in time and space; God is individuated by containing all reality in Himself. Our function is to be novel, and not to enjoy novelty ourselves without limit. We, as individual themes, are parts of an eternal synthesis that undergoes variation through all of time. But this eternal process is not something that we ourselves shall experience, save in our own limited contemplation. To live without end can scarcely be our privilege, but we can earn an everlasting place within the one life that will be lived evermore and in endlessly new ways.

Chapter II

Voices of Affirmation

> Nature is mortal; we shall outlive her. When all the suns and nebulae have passed away, each one of you will still be alive. Nature is only the image, the symbol ...
>
> C. S. Lewis, "The Weight of Glory"

The Soul as an Immaterial Agent

Some philosophers, as we have seen, think it unlikely that we survive death. Some believe, as well, that the importance of survival is commonly exaggerated. We would do better, they say, to look elsewhere for the prospect of meaning in our lives. Are such claims warranted? In this chapter I will discuss them further.

Much is made by skeptics, as we have seen, of the close relationship between body and mind. This connection, it is said, provides us with strong evidence that death brings with it the end of conscious experience. For if mind and brain vary together, it seems, they must perish together, as well. Thus an indication of their unity, writes Lamont, "is the way in which the physical exterior of a man may reflect his essential being."[1] Consider, he says, how the faintest trace of alteration of the eyes, the mouth, the hands, the voice, can inform us of an individual's frame of mind. He cites the words of the poet John Donne, who says of a high-spirited young girl,

> Her pure and eloquent blood
> Spoke in her cheeks, and so distinctly wrought
> That one might almost say her body thought.[2]

Certainly mind and body have an intimate connection. But does this fact rule out our chance of survival? This inference is discussed by William James in his classic essay "Human Immortality".

Observation, says James, reveals the connection of the brain with conscious experience. Thus everyone knows "that arrests of brain development occasion imbecility, that blows on the head abolish memory or consciousness, and that brain-stimulants and poisons change the quality of our ideas."[3] The laboratory is daily establishing this connection in ever more detail: Certain kinds of brain activity are associated with certain kinds of experience. Those who see this, says James, tend to summarize it by saying that thought is a *function* of the brain. They imagine that the brain thus produces consciousness in much the way, for example, that a kettle produces steam.

---

[1] *The Illusion of Immortality*, p. 87.

[2] *Ibid.*, p. 88. Lamont quotes from Part II of Donne's *An Anatomy of the World*.

[3] William James, "Human Immortality", contained in James' *The Will to Believe and other essays in popular philosophy* and *Human Immortality* (New York: Dover Publications, 1956), p. 8.

They imagine likewise that consciousness is dependent for its existence upon the brain's activity. Thus they effectively deny that consciousness survives apart from this relationship. But the facts in evidence, says James, fail to support this conclusion. Those who accept it think that the relationship is analogous, again, to that of steam and kettle, or of electric light and the circuit on which it depends. They think, in other words, of *production*. But what we see, James insists, is consistent with another and crucially different interpretation. For there exist other kinds of functional relationship.

One, in particular, is *transmission*. Take, for example, a colored glass through which light may pass. In this case the light is "sifted" by the glass and is limited in its color. The light cast is thus a function of the instrument through which it passes. It varies, in other words, with that instrument's condition. But the light is not produced by the glass. Were the glass removed, the light would still exist, albeit without its present qualification. Similarly, thinks James, with respect to consciousness and the "prism" (that is, the brain mechanism) through which it presently operates.

So it may be that the whole universe is but "a mere surface veil of phenomena, hiding and keeping back the world of genuine realities." Our brains, says James, may be parts of that veil where consciousness is shaped into its various modes of expression. Hence, he observes, Shelley's verse,

> Life, like a dome of many colored glass,
> Stains the white radiance of eternity.[4]

---

[4] *Ibid.*, p. 16. James cites from Shelley's *Adonais: An Elegy on the Death of John Keats.*

We may thus entertain entertain a very different picture with respect to this observed connection of brain and consciousness. For this co-variance may arise from the fact that the brain is *the means through which consciousness presently operates*.

The brain, on this view, is the filter or medium through which conscious activity finds its expression. Its condition may thus decide, in some measure, our present talents, aptitudes, and inclinations. It may provide the cognitive and temperamental medium through which life is lived. But the brain, in this case, does not produce consciousness. Nor does it determine our choices. For it is not the source of our actions, but their means. If the brain is the mechanism through which consciousness operates, relevant changes in its state will alter our experience. But this does not mean that consciousness is grounded in brain activity, or that it can have no existence apart from this present connection.

This picture, says James, is not irrational or anti-scientific, for it accords, just as well as does the production theory, with the observed facts. It likewise enables us to see that this intimate connection of self and body is consistent with their basic difference. It is true that the body provides, at times, a reliable and even exquisite expression of conscious states. But what else should one expect, if indeed the it is the vehicle through which consciousness now acts?

James' conception of the mind as an agency working through the medium of the brain has found a number of adherents in the past century, among them Minot Savage. This close relationship between brain and consciousness, claims Savage, need not discourage us from thinking that consciousness has a viable existence of its own. To take a rough illustration, he says, one may consider the attachment of a dynamo (i. e., a generator) to some machine. When the machine is removed, one has not destroyed this source of energy. It may be attached to another machine, and may operate again with "all the old-time power." The "I", he writes,

> that is back of the brain, or above it, may use it as the organ of thought and the communication of my thoughts to others in my present condition. But that does not prove at all that the "I" ceases to exist, and that there is no thinking done, when this brain gets tired and goes back to dust.[5]

The view has more recent adherents, as well. Among them is Huston Smith, world-renowned scholar of comparative religion. Mechanists, says Smith, imagine that the mind is a part of the body, but this is a mistake. "The brain," he contends, "breathes mind like the lungs breathe air."[6] He cites, in this regard, the testimony of several of the world's most respected physiologists, among them Charles Sherrington and Wilder Penfield. Sherrington, notes Smith, maintains that a dualistic account of human nature (one, in other words, that sees human beings as being essentially different from their bodies) offers no less inherent probability

---

[5] Minot Savage, *Life Beyond Death* (New York: The Knickerbocker Press, 1899), p. 289. See related discussion in chapters 4 and 7 of this volume. In fairness, it should be added that James' view has not met with the same agreement in other quarters. For an antagonistic review, see chapter 3 of Lamont's *The Illusion of Immortality*. Lamont bases most of his objection on the problem of how an immaterial mind can *act upon* the brain. For related discussion see chapter 2 of my *Body and Soul: The Transcendence of Materialism* (Boulder, Colorado: HarperCollins Publishers, 1997).

[6] Huston Smith, *Forgotten Truth* (San Francisco: HarperCollins, 1992), p. 63.

than a monistic one.[7] So far as observation is concerned, it seems just as reasonable. In his book *The Mystery of the Mind*, Penfield relates some of his laboratory experiences as they bear upon questions concerning mind and brain. Such experiences, he maintains, do not advance the case for materialism. Perhaps they even tell against it.

An electrode, explains Penfield, can trigger in a patient certain crude sensations. It can cause him to turn the head and the eyes, to move the limbs, to vocalize, and to swallow. But there is nowhere in the cortex, Penfield insists, where such stimulation will cause him to *believe* or to *decide* anything. There is thus a sense in which an individual "remains aloof" from those alterations produced by electrode stimulation - a sense in which he stands apart and "passes judgment on it all."[8]

The view thus encouraged, says Penfield, is not one of dependence of mind upon brain. It is rather a relation of mind to brain in much the way of an operator to an instrument. Thus after years of seeking to explain the mind on the basis of brain-action alone, he concludes that "it is simpler ... if one adopts the hypothesis that our being does consist of two fundamental elements." It is

---

[7] *Ibid.*, p. 64. See related discussion in Wilder Penfield, *The Mystery of the Mind - A Critical Study of Consciousness and the Human Brain* (Princeton, New Jersey: Princeton University Press, 1975). Penfield cites (p. 4) this same remark, which concludes Sherrington's foreword to an updated edition of his own 1906 work *The Integrative Action of the Nervous System* (Cambridge: Cambridge University Press, 1947).

[8] *The Mystery of the Mind*, p. 77. For kindred discussion, see Karl R. Popper and John C. Eccles, *The Self and Its Brain* (New York: Springer International, 1977). Note, for example, chapter 1 (P3), "Materialism Criticized".

simpler, in other words, if one allows that mind is something active - something more than a material by-product. This, as he notes, leaves open the possibility that consciousness survives the brain's destruction.

This notion of the mind's agency is actually presupposed, I think, by our necessary faith in our own *rationality*. In order to do philosophy at all, we must first think that we are able to perceive the rational merit, or lack of it, in a given proposition, and to accept or reject it on these grounds. Yet if materialism is true, our consciousness is dependent ultimately upon material events that themselves have no such allegiance - no conformity, in other words, to principles of truth or validity. Our thoughts, in that case, conform not to ideal, but to accident.[9]

Thus if we have any faith in our own reasoning, we must assume, it seems to me, that we are in some way independent of these events. We must suppose that consciousness is active - that it is free, that it is viable, that it can apprehend rational principle and act upon it. We must think likewise that it transcends the events of neurochemistry.

Of course, as mentioned in chapter 1, there exist a variety of objections to this separation of consciousness from the material events with which it is associated. Surely, it is said, we cannot be something other than our bodies. The

---

[9] Indeed if this is the case, then arguments for materialism itself are produced in the same way. Thus a materialist must admit that he has no rational basis for trusting his own mental operation. For this reason, says John Hick, acceptance of materialism amounts to "logical suicide." See section #'s 1 - 3 in chapter 6 of his *Death and Eternal Life* (Louisville: Westminster / John Knox Press, 1994). For related discussion, see again chapter 2 of *Body and Soul*. See also the book by Popper and Eccles just noted, which discusses several versions of the materialist theory. An extensive discussion is contained in chapter P3, "Materialism Criticized".

notion of an immaterial self - a *soul* - makes no sense, since two (or more) such entities cannot be individuated as physical objects can. A rock and a tree, for example, can be distinguished from each other by their respective physical properties - their mass, shape, chemistry, and so on. Even if two objects are similar, to all appearance, they can still be distinguished by their locations in space. Yet no such criteria seem to be available to point out different souls, which have no size and are not made of anything. The very notion of a soul, it is said, is thus invalidated, since there is no distinction, in principle, between one such entity and another.

I think, however, that this objection begs the question. For it assumes that the only meaningful criteria for distinguishing entities from one another *are* material. And this is just what immaterialists deny. Granted, a soul may not have such properties of weight, position, or shape. But it may have other qualities appropriate to its nature; consider, for example, things like *freedom*, *intelligence*, and *moral development*, as well as a whole content of experiential history. Properties like these, I think, might suffice to make two souls distinguishable. Are such properties meaningless? Perhaps it will be said that they are suspect, since they have no explicit material nature.[10] But to disqualify them for this reason is to assume the very thing, it seems to me, that is at issue. It assumes that material properties are the only ones that are legitimate.

---

[10] And again, it is not obvious that all things normally counted as real must have a material nature. Consider, for example, such things as space, time, numbers, ideas, and even properties themselves, none of which seem to be explicitly material in their type.

Does the dualistic conception of reality involve us in skepticism about other minds? It is said, once again, that if persons are immaterial entities, they cannot be judged to be the same from one time to the next merely by outward bodily appearance. (There might, for all we know, be a different person, from time to time, animating the same body.) For the real person, on this account, is an elusive thing. It has no tangible features. Thus if we accept dualism, goes the argument, we are committed to a very strange position regarding other persons.

Is such an argument conclusive? Bruce Reichenbach, I think, offers a very sensible reply.

> What is embodied here in our language, the dualist suggests, is the fact that personal identity is not to be found in my physical body. My posture, movement, and appearance express myself, but they are not the real person. They are the mode by which that person is manifested to others. By watching the bodily movements or gestures of another and by listening to what he has to say, I can make inferences to the nature of his real self. There are acts of revelation by which the true self is made known, but are not constitutive of the true self.[11]

Thus we may, thinks Reichenbach, distinguish between persons and bodies and still believe with good reason that persons (normally, at least) "remain" with the same bodies over time. This basis is found in the continuity of their outward behavioral appearance, which provides the appropriate evidence.

It is possible, on this outlook, that different souls do successively "invade" a single body undetected by observation. For that matter, there are any number of common sense assumptions (say, the existence of the external world) that may

---

[11] Bruce Reichenbach, *Is Man the Phoenix?* (Grand Rapids, Michigan: Eerdmans, 1978), pp. 42-43.

be called into question, whatever our view of mind and body. But this does not mean that we must be troubled by such things without particular cause.

As for the problem of changing souls, it might be added, there may actually arise circumstances on rare occasion that raise serious questions as to who or what it is that now animates a given body. One example is that of abrupt personality change[12] and another is that of alleged demonic possession.[13] But in each case we have some behavioral warrant for our doubt.

The Viability of Personal Identity

Noted also in chapter 1 was another problem concerning personal identity. We operate, say some philosophers, with a basic misconception of what is involved in the history of a human being. For we normally suppose, once again, that this entity has duration - that he or she lasts, in other words, as a single being throughout the process of a given personal lifetime. But we are not, say these revisionists, the persisting and substantial things that common sense would make of us.

---

[12] For an entertaining (and surely controversial) account of an individual actually "switching" bodies, see T. Lobsang Rampa's allegedly autobiographical *The Rampa Story* (New York: Bantam Books, 1960).

[13] See, for example, Malachi Martin's *Hostage to the Devil: The Possession and Exorcism of Five Living Americans* (New York: Harper and Row, 1987). Regarding alleged problems with spirits and their individuation, he remarks, "our denying that spirits exist because they literally will not 'stand up and be counted' does not seem to impress them"!

A so-called individual, they say, is really a series of things, better understood as a process than as a substance, and has no identity of the kind that common sense imagines. Derek Parfit, once again, denies that there is any single person who endures throughout the course of a lifetime. The individual I am today is of course different, in appearance and in mental character, from the one who bore my name twenty years ago. No one will deny this. But further, claims Parfit, there is no decisive sense in which he and I are really the same person at all. There is not, as we often imagine, some inner or underlying *me* who makes the journey through these stages. The process of growth, of maturation and personal change, makes this present individual a different entity from the one earlier. The two are related, of course, in their historical development, but they are not in any crucial sense identical. The earlier individual does not last through this process, but merely constitutes one of its stages.

While this account is intriguing, it has consequences that are counterintuitive in the extreme. Consider again Parfit's case of "teletransportation," in which we are replicated, in all our present details, at some remote locale, as an alternative to ordinary travel. This arrangement, thinks Parfit, would be "about as good" as our usual mode of life-continuation, for it offers more or less the same prospect.[14] For in such cases a continuity of conscious states is preserved as well as it might have been otherwise.

---

[14] One might imagine another case, says Parfit, in which the first individual is not destroyed at once by the machinery, but is only mortally injured by it. Even in such a case, when the lives of original and replica overlap, he imagines, nothing appreciable is lost by the first in the process. (See *Reasons and Persons*, pp. 199-200.)

Nor would it matter that the cause of this relation (replication, that is, instead of ordinary brain continuity) is unusual. Copying will do just as well. For consider, says Parfit, our attitudes toward artificial eyes that would restore sight to those who have lost it. If they gave to their owners sensations like those had by sighted persons, we would not reject them on the grounds that they *caused* the sensations in a different manner. (Here, in other words, the replica is just as good as the original.) Thus it seems that bodily replication, by analogy, might serve as a suitable cause of personal continuity.

How well does Parfit's view square with our ordinary thinking about personal identity, and with the facts of experience? Is it true that my replacement by a replica is about as good as ordinary survival? (Or that ordinary survival is about this bad?) It is true that an artificial eye would be about as good as a natural eye, in terms of its usefulness *to the one who uses it*. But what bearing does this have on the relationship between a given human being and a materially similar replica?

The replica, it is true, would be "about as good" as the original in appearance. For it would look like the other and would have have memories and mental characteristics continuous with those of the one earlier. He or she would have likewise a congruent role in connection with other persons, who would respond to this individual as they would respond to the other. Thus if identity means simply *playing a similar role* within an environment, there is no appreciable difference between the two. The content of experience, and the outward appearance, remain the same.

Yet personal identity, we normally think, means more than this. The fact that some entity could thus effectively take my place in the world does not convince me that either of us might as well do so. It may be that a replica is functionally just as good as an original, but this, I think, does not itself mean that the replacement is inconsequential *to the first individual himself*.

Parfit, again, thinks that my concern is misplaced, since I do not survive even under ordinary conditions in the way that I imagine. He also believes that his view accords well, in certain ways, with our moral attitudes. He notes, for example, that we tend to be increasingly *lenient* toward wrong-doers with the passing of time.[15] This, he thinks, suggests that we regard human beings as becoming gradually *different* individuals in much the way that his thesis maintains. With diminishing connectedness, it seems, comes diminishing moral desert. Thus an individual might, over some period of time, cease to deserve punishment altogether. This diminution, claims Parfit, is hard to accommodate on a non-reductionist view.

It is true, I think, that our desire for retribution toward a given individual tends to lessen with time. Perhaps indeed this feeling is veridical; perhaps this individual becomes less deserving of punishment as time passes. It may be true, as well, that this deservedness lessens with diminishing degrees of psychological connection. (Thus we may, for example, count the middle-aged benefactor as being a virtually different person from the 15-year old delinquent he was decades ago.) But this, I think, need not commit us to a reductionist account of personal

---

[15] *Reasons and Persons*, pp. 323-26.

identity. It is consistent, I believe, with our recognition of the profound sameness of human beings over time. I think it possible, in other words, that the individual of today is less deserving of punishment than was the offender - and yet that he and this younger individual are substantially identical. I think that we may view this change as being part of a developmental process within a single individual.

There are perhaps a number of ways in which this diminution of desert might come about. One is that the offender has, by subsequent effort, repaid the debt to the offended party. This, in some cases, would make punishment unnecessary, or make a less severe punishment appropriate. Another is that he has met with great misfortune in the time since he committed the offense; in some cases, I believe, this fact might temper our retributive impulse, particularly if he himself has changed for the better in the process. We might show lenience, in this case, simply because we feel that a natural justice has in some measure been accomplished. But such thinking need not conflict with the view that this later individual is identical with the one earlier.

Of particular importance in cases involving desert, it seems, is the issue of changed character. If this individual has developed in some positive direction, if he is, years after the fact, a better and more compassionate individual, we might prefer that he not be punished at all. But we need not think, it seems to me, that this change has made him an essentially *different* person. We may continue to regard him as being the same one who committed the offense. Indeed the very attitudes that we tend to adopt in such cases - the recognition, for example, of how *this individual* has changed, our related admiration of his or her moral *progress*, and perhaps most of all *forgiveness*[16] - tend, if anything, to express our recognition of the profound sameness of this individual across time, of qualitative changes within one person.[17]

A similar recognition, I suspect, may lie at the heart of the claim, expressed in certain moral and religious contexts, that we ought to see value in other persons, even if their present condition is less than admirable. This claim is perhaps inspired by our realization that these individuals have the potential to be more than they are now. But again, if we believe that *they themselves* are one day to fulfill this promise, we must suppose that they will endure to this (perhaps remote) future date. In order to do this, it seems to me, we must think of them in spiritual terms, as substantial, selfsame entities who are involved in the journey to its end. We cannot think that they are merely stages in a developmental sequence.

I have suggested that a reductionist account of personal identity is at odds with certain instincts that we have regarding ourselves and others. What, it may be asked, do we find when we attend to our own consciousness firsthand? Some philosophers have thought that memory provides a direct inner testimony to our basic (or "deep further") sameness across periods of time. Thus in reflecting upon some past episode, it seems, I remember what *I myself* was experiencing on that occasion.

---

[16] See related discussion in chapters 6 and 7 of this volume.

[17] Similarly, I believe, is *restitution* appropriate no matter what the degree of change that has taken place in the offender.

Parfit, on the other hand, thinks that it gives evidence of nothing more than "mere psychological continuity."[18] Thus while it is possible, he says, that we are more than this, memory gives no evidence of it. We have no guarantee from memory that we have lasted through the time in question.

But as Richard Swinburne observes, it is often hard to distinguish our self-awareness from a given act of perception itself. For, as he notes,

> The division between what we perceive and what we remember having perceived is a fairly arbitrary one. Do I remember what I first came to know through perception two seconds ago, or is it part of what I am still perceiving? The boundaries of the 'specious present' are unclear. My memory of what I perceived merges into my present perception. So my memory of who I was merges into my awareness of myself as a common subject of different perceptions at very close moments of time ...[19]

For that matter, even the briefest moments of consciousness are hard to understand if we try to subtract the concept of selfhood from their occurrence. Just what is the experience, say, of a red color, a sharp jab or a shrill noise without some*one* to have it? As Paul Badham writes,

> the notion that doing, suffering and thinking can be isolated from agents, sufferers and thinkers seems to me to be as impossible as the notion of a Cheshire cat vanishing and leaving only its grin behind. When Wittgenstein allegedly declared that in the expression "I have a toothache ... the 'I' does not denote a 'possessor'", I can only comment that I wish he were right![20]

---

[18] *Reasons and Persons*, pp. 223-26.

[19] Richard Swinburne, *The Evolution of the Soul* (New York: Oxford University Press, 1986), p. 168.

[20] Paul Badham, *Christian Beliefs About Life After Death* (London: Macmillan, 1976), p. 99.

Swinburne makes a related point concerning introspection. While Hume, he notes, may not catch himself at any time without a perception (i. e., without a particular episode of experience), the "bare datum" of his discovery "is not just 'perceptions', but successions of overlapping 'perceptions' experienced by a conscious subject." Hume insists, once again, that he does not find in this sequence an enduring subject. But what sort of thing, asks Swinburne, is he looking *for*? Is it merely another perception within the inventory? (Might it be, for example, a constant background noise? Or some shape that never leaves his visual field?) The thing sought, after all, "is supposed to be the subject, not the object of perception." Finding it, then, consists in being aware of multiple conscious events within oneself.

And this, it seems, is just what Hume has done. Indeed, his claim to have found a *succession* of perceptions is hard to interpret otherwise.[21] The fact that these perceptions are part of a common series suggests that there is some shared arena (which is to say, a single conscious stream) wherein they occur. Thus over short periods of time, at least, personal identity "is itself experienceable by the subject, as directly as anything can be experienced."[22]

---

[21] "Change itself," writes Willam Ernest Hocking, "to be known as change, must register itself upon an unchanging subject." Thus our consciousness, he explains, may need these particular contents, but "we are not they; they are ours." See Hocking's *The Meaning of Immortality in Human Experience* (New York: Harper and Brothers, 1957), p. 198. This book is an expanded version of Hocking's self-copyrighted 1937 work *Thoughts on Death and Life*.

[22] It is perhaps worth noting, in this regard, Hume's own dissatisfaction with the account of personal identity noted earlier. See the *Treatise* Appendix, pp. 633 and following.

Parfit argues that such identity is not discoverable even in this apparent succession.[23] For consider again the case of the teletransporter. Suppose that I have two thoughts, one of which follows naturally from the other. Suppose also that my replica on a distant planet is now activated to begin its conscious life with the second of these. It will seem to him that this thought is part of a sequence through which he has persisted, when in fact the situation is quite different. Yet no immediate fact in the experience of the replica, observes Parfit, inform him of this. Thus, he argues, we cannot take our own alleged experience of succession to indicate anything like a persisting and deeper selfhood. Our seeming existence through time might thus be likened to a relay progression in which mental characteristics are passed, like batons, from one stage of experience to another in the absence of a single carrier.

I think that Parfit is right in pointing out the logical possibility of this "baton" model. For that matter, it is possible, too, that the whole world has come into being only a short time ago, thus putting all of us in the epistemological situation of that replica. But it is a separate question, I think, whether we should choose such a hypothesis over one that seems more natural. Perhaps instead we ought to have more faith in what experience tells us. There is, explains Swinburne, an element of trust at the heart of all rational activity. For this reason he holds that "apparent" memories - those, in other words, that seem to be genuine - ought to be taken at face value in the absence of contrary evidence.

---

[23] See *Reasons and Persons*, pp. 223-26.

This is a particular instance of what he calls *the Principle of Credulity*,[24] according to which we ought, barring the emergence of counter-evidence, to take our experience as furnishing us with some indication of how things really are.

Of course, this acceptance must be tentative, and open to the possibility of evidence that may change our minds. But as Swinburne explains, any new information will count upon this same trust if it has weight. Faith in our own perception is the basis for belief, and for doubt, as well.[25]

What does this have to do with personal identity? As Swinburne points out, our common-sense thinking about the sameness of a person across time is founded upon memory. We *recall*, for example, that our identity is tied in some fashion to brain continuity. (It is unlikely, for example, that we would consent to a change of brain as we might a transplant of the liver!) In a different world, Swinburne observes, we might have a different opinion.[26] There is no logical reason why personal identity should be associated with our brains, or even with our bodies, at all. But we hold this view on the basis of what we remember.

What, then, does memory tell us about ourselves? Says Swinburne, it tells us not only what was done (i. e., by those former selves connected with our own), but that it was *we ourselves* who did it. Parfit, he writes,

---

[24] *The Evolution of the Soul*, pp. 11-13.

[25] Thus doubt, in Ludwig Wittgenstein's peculiarly succinct phrase, "comes *after* belief." This remark from his work *On Certainty* (# 166) is cited by Norman Malcolm in his article "The Groundlessness of Belief", contained in Stuart C. Brown, ed., *Reason and Religion* (Ithaca, New York: Cornell University Press, 1977), p. 143.

[26] *The Evolution of the Soul*, chapter 9.

> claims that the only datum provided by memory is an awareness of psychological continuity, an awareness, that is, of an overlapping series of quasi-memories (memories 'from the inside' that so-and-so was done and experienced, which do not have as part of their content that the doer was the same as the rememberer). But that is just false. It is as much part of what seems to the subject to be the case that he did or experienced so-and-so as that so-and-so was done or experienced.[27]

For this reason, says Swinburne, we need a separate argument to show why this face-value evidence ought not to be accepted. In the absence of such an argument, the principle of credulity warrants its acceptance.[28]

This, again, does not mean that memory is infallible. Some persons' memories are distorted, and some are selective. Perhaps each is in some degree flawed. But memory cannot be ignored. Indeed our very recognition of its problems depends upon what we remember about human faculties and their limits. If memory suggests to us that we are persisting individuals, then we have some reason to suppose that this is the case.

This does not mean that the reductionist theory must be wrong. It only means that memory does offer us some *prima facie* reason to favor an alternative. Memory tells us something about what *we* have done and experienced. Herein we have some reason to think of ourselves as having persisted through the duration - as having lasted, in other words, from the time of the event being remembered to the present. We have reason to think that selfhood is something deeper and more fundamental than a mere continuity of successive conscious episodes.

---

[27] *Ibid.*, pp. 170-71.

[28] *Ibid.*, pp. 170-71.

This effort to dissolve personal identity, to reduce it to a series of discrete conscious moments, is not peculiar to philosophers in the west. Some adherents of Buddhism - those, in particular, who take a traditional stance toward the Buddha's *anatta* or "no soul" doctrine - maintain that our common-sense notion of personal identity is an illusion.[29] It is, they imagine, part of a general and errant human tendency to take transient states of affairs for reality. A recent expression of this view is found in the account of V. F. Gunaratna. The mind, he writes, is not an enduring entity; it is actually

> a stream of successive thoughts which are continually arising and passing away from moment to moment. Each thought is succeeded by another with such a rapidity as to give the mind a semblance of something stable and permanent. A stick burning at one end and turned rapidly round and round in the dark creates the illusion of a ring or circle of fire to onlookers at a distance who do not know what is actually happening ... So it is with the mind where thoughts succeed each other with a much greater rapidity.[30]

But does this suffice to explain our sense of self? The explanation, as John Hick[31] observes, seems to presuppose the very thing it denies, namely, an enduring consciousness in which the succession is contained. If it is a *series*, after all, that gives rise to the illusion, then *in what consciousness* is it contained? The event in question cannot occur at a single "point-instant" of consciousness,

---

[29] For a summary of conservative Buddhist thought, see Wapola Rahula, *What the Buddha Taught* (New York: Grove Weidenfeld, 1974).

[30] V. F. Gunaratna, *Rebirth Explained* (Kandy: Buddhist Publication Society, 1971), pp. 16-7.

[31] Gunaratna's statement is reprinted with discussion in Hick's *Death and Eternal Life*, p. 336. See section # 1 of chapter 18, "The Buddhist Conception of Rebirth".

since this contains only the awareness of the moment. An illusion of the kind that Gunaratna describes, it must be the result of a perceptual sequence, of something occurring within a selfsame consciousness over a period of time. But this itself presupposes the existence of a persisting conscious subject.

A good deal of philosophy would find itself adrift without this idea of a real and enduring personality. Consider, for one, the literature of existential philosophy. This literature has, as a central theme, the meeting of consciousness with an outside world and its active shaping, by this challenge, of a life-course. Thus William Barrett, for example, writes of our need to take stock of ourselves as concrete agents within this process. There is no agency, thinks Barrett, apart from an agent, nor responsibility either. While this enduring self may not be another datum along with particular thoughts, moods, feelings, and sensations, it is needed, as a part of our conceptual scheme, to make practical sense of our situation.

It is especially hard, thinks Barrett, to make sense of *moral* activity without this assumption. Noting with concern the abandonment of substance as a personal concept, he writes, "If we try to construct consciousness out of mental atoms - sense impressions or whatever - we shall find that these atoms always imply the more inclusive structure of mind in which they are found."[32]

It is neither logically nor morally sound, thinks Barrett, to try to dissolve this reality (*a la* Hume) into separate fleeting episodes. There is, once again, no

---

[32] William Barrett, *Death of the Soul - From Descartes to the Computer* (New York: Anchor, 1987), p. 109.

series of experiences without a persisting subject. Nor, it seems, can there exist moral choicemaking apart from the enduring character from which it issues. This cannot mean a fixed character, frozen in its capacities, if such choices are to be free. But there must be some relatively stable background (some basic *kind* of person, in other words, that one is) to provide leverage for change if this change is to have direction (say, toward personal improvement). This need for stability, again, invites the notion of an enduring personality.

Such a notion, as we have seen, raises difficult questions. Yet no more of them, it seems, than arise from its abandonment. The idea of a soul, says James, is so much integral with our overall world view that its rejection leaves us at a loss. The idea of a soul, insists psychical researcher William McDougall, is needed to make sense of the most basic and immediate facts of experience. He concludes,

> if any hypothesis is so logically necessary that its rejection must involve the rejection of our belief in the most fundamental logical principles, it is, *ipso facto*, justified, and bears the highest possible credentials. Has any scientific hypothesis any better justification, or can any better one be conceived? Why do we believe that the earth is round? Surely only because to deny it would involve the mistrust of logical reason! No one has directly perceived the earth as a round object.[33]

Why, he asks, do we believe any of the things that science tells us, even when we do not find their immediate verification? Why do we believe in energy, magnetic force, electricity, atoms, electrons?"

---

[33] From McDougall's "Animism", first published in his *Body and Mind* and reprinted in *William McDougall: Explorer of the Mind* (New York: Garrett, 1967), Raymond Van Over and Laura Oteri, editors. See pp. 294 ff.

We believe in these things, he writes, "for the same good pragmatic reason, namely, that our intellect finds the conceptions of these things necessary for the building up of the conceptual scheme of things by means of which we seek to render intelligible the facts of immediate experience." In similar fashion, we are entitled to accept that datum of experience that is given to us directly, namely our own profound and irrecducible *sameness* over time. There are some, perhaps, who will refuse the option. Better, they will say, to "lie on the ragged edge" and "gnaw the file forever." Instead, says McDougall, let us choose "a less desperate alternative" and "retain a modest confidence in human reason, and accept the hypothesis of the soul!"

Criticism of soul-theories, as noted in the previous chapter, sometimes concerns the soul's function apart from the body. What manner of existence, it is asked, can a soul have on its own? How, asks Antony Flew, might an individual witness events taking place in the world after he himself has left it?[34] It is easy enough to imagine what one's own funeral will look like to those who will attend it. But what would it mean for *oneself* to be present, without a body, as one of the observers?

Certainly it would make no observable difference to those alive and (materially) in attendance. If we envision first a funeral attended only by living persons, and then one attended also by the (immaterial) guest of honor, we cannot actually *see* the difference. What, then distinguishes the events?

---

[34] See again Flew's earlier cited essay "Can a Man Witness his Own Funeral?".

Immateriality itself is a negative property. It forbids us to ascribe to a soul properties such as size or mass, which seem to be implicit in the idea of a thing's being present in some place. Thus an immatreial thing, it seems, cannot have location in a given vicinity, such as that of a funeral. But it does not follow from this, I think, that the concept of a *soul* is meaningless, or that a *post mortem* spiritual life must be empty of experiences. Rather the problem lies in knowing how to make sense of such experiences apart from their present medium.

One proposed answer is that the soul, while it is distinct from the body, actually has (as one of its vehicles) a material property that is not available to ordinary perception. On this view, soul and body are separate things, yet death does not divorce the soul altogether from material reality. This idea, as will be noted later, belongs to a long tradition of belief in a finer realm that interpenetrates the one in which we live. We share, on this account, in this subtle or "astral" world[35] even as we reside in this one. While such a world, of course, is an issue unto itself, an account along these lines may help to make sense of certain unusual elements of human experience.[36]

---

[35] The term 'astral' is related to that of the Latin *'astrum'*, or star. For an overview of this theory and its language and development, and its going revival in some circles, see Benjamin Walker, *Beyond the Body* (Routledge and Kegan Paul, Ltd., 1974).

[36] One of these is the so-called "out-of-body" experience, discussed by Walker in *Beyond the Body*. This notion of another and subtler body within the outward physical frame, as Walker observes, is a persistent one across many cultures, and seems to exist within native societies of both Africa and Australia, as well as those of Egypt, China, and Tibet. For discussion of laboratory attempts to verify such experiences, see Alfred Douglas, *Extra-Sensory Powers - A Century of Psychical Research* (Woodstock, New York: Overlook Press, 1977).

This theory of a finer material world will be noted again in subsequent chapters. But it is not the only way in which philosophers have tried to deal with the problems that arise in connection with alleged disembodied experience. Another proposed solution is to maintain that while the soul is immaterial, it lives (at one stage, at least, of its *post mortem* development) in an experiential world of its own making. On this view the soul has no size or location, yet it has perceptions of the kind normally associated with this life. Such a suggestion is made by philosopher and psychical researcher H. H. Price in his article "Survival and the Idea of 'Another World'".[37]

What would it mean, asks Price, for a disembodied soul to have experiences? In our present condition, of course, we depend on our nervous system for experience of any kind. But what if the next world were an immaterial world made up of conscious experience itself? Perhaps it is an "image" world of sights, sounds, and various other sensations, one best likened to the world that we inhabit in our dreams. It has no spatial relation to ours, and no reality independent of the mind(s) creating it. Still, it might have a vividness and a relative permanence that make it experientially as real to the subject as this one. In such a world, says Price, a subject might operate as a sort of mental artist, fashioning new scenes out of the stock of raw materials gained in this world.

Perhaps, too, there could be some telepathic "sharing" of worlds between persons sufficiently compatible. The laws of such a world might be mainly those

---

[37] This essay is reprinted in John Hick's *Classical and Contemporary Readings in the Philosophy of Religion* (Englewood Cliffs, New Jersey: Prentice-Hall, 1964).

of wish-fulfillment. Freed from its material limitations, thinks Price, the mind might work with an efficiency that it did not have here. (This last feature does not insure that the next world is an unconditionally pleasant one. For it may be, as he notes, that certain debased types of mind, operating in this new and less restricted circumstance, might produce something more akin to hell than heaven.)

Perhaps, then, there exist ways of making sense out of disembodied souls and their experiences. Each line of strategy noted here, I think, is an interesting one.[38] Each, too, has the advantage, for what it is worth, of making sense also of a good deal of the literature of spiritualism and psychical research.[39] It remains to be asked whether the prospect of survival has any significance.

---

[38] It may be, however, that this latter account is in need of some modification. For as John Hick observes, the principles of wish fulfillment and telepathic sharing of the next world are in some tension with each other. For as long as the desires and ambitions of the inhabitants of this image-fashioned world are at all varied, they will have to be compromised at times if they are to be fulfilled at all. Such a world could not be satisfying to all if it were too plastic to the desires of one. Furthermore, says Hick, the next world cannot offer us much in opportunities for growth and moral development if it is fashioned wholly by our desires. Unless this growth is to wane hereafter, there must be some degree of objectivity in the world to come. See discussion, for example, in section # 1, chapter 14, "The Survival of the Disembodied Mind", in *Death and Eternal Life*.

[39] Price notes the literature of mediumship and automatic writing, much of which stresses the principle of wish fulfillment and a quality of life that corresponds to an individual's level of development.

The Importance of Survival to the Meaning of Life

A number of writers, as noted in the last chapter, have maintained that belief in survival is irrelevant or even injurious to a sound philosophy of life. It arises, some say, not out of insight or devotion, but out of a basic egocentricity. Is the belief, as these types claim, at odds with a genuine ethic or a mature religious outlook?

Those who disparage belief in another life sometimes have, I think, legitimate reason. Belief in survival, as Kaufmann suggests, may reflect at times an absent-mindedness or a want of personal direction. Some instances of this belief have reflected, in fact, meanness and inanity, perhaps even outright cruelty.[40] Thus denial of the survival hypothesis may be aligned in some cases with moral insight. Perhaps, too, as Darrow suggests, an earth-bound sense of shared and impending doom would (in some nobler types, at least) inspire a greater humaneness in the race. But this does not mean, I think, that belief in a life hereafter, or the desire for such a life, is aligned of any necessity with moral defect. C. S. Lewis reflects upon this issue in his memorable essay "The Weight of Glory".

We have at times, says Lewis, the intimation of a reality beyond present experience. We are likewise conscious at moments of a desire "which no natural

---

[40] See, for example, related discussion in the first section of chapter 6 concerning belief in hell as it has appeared in the Christian mainstream.

happiness will satisfy."[41] It is an uncertain desire, one that has no conspicuous object. Some forms of sensory experience - a vibrant piece of music, a haunting landscape - may give us an inkling. Yet it is not *in* these things, contends Lewis, but *through* them that the object reveals itself.

Contained in present experience, he maintains, is the apprehension that we are meant for more than the present life. In the flights of great poets we gain some hint of it; in the promises of scripture, he contends, it is explicit. For herein we are promised that we will (if we walk rightly) be with God, that we will have glory, that we will in some way be rulers.

Is such a desire legitimate? Some philosophers, as we have seen, maintain that belief in another life tends to compromise the worth of our actions - that it makes us do the right thing for the wrong reasons. There is indeed such a thing, Lewis observes, as mercenary action. It occurs when one pursues an end from an irrelevant motive, as, for example, when one marries for money and not love, or wages a battle merely for the sake of personal advancement. On the other hand, there is also such a thing as a rightful reward for one's actions, as when one marries for love, or fights for principle. There is nothing wrong, thinks Lewis, with the desire for heaven if it is the end for which we were created.

Belief in survival, in fact, provides an occasion for our awareness of the worth of other persons. In reflecting upon this prospect we are reminded of our

---

[41] C. S. Lewis, "The Weight of Glory", contained in Lewis' *The Weight of Glory and Other Addresses* (New York: Collier Books, 1980), p. 8. For related discussion of this element and its relation to Lewis' own philosophical growth, see his autobiographical *Surprised by Joy - the Shape of My Early Life* (San Diego: Harcourt Brace and Company), 1955.

possibilities. What exists of the personality here, bearing in mind this greater and extended picture, is but a small part of what exists of it in potential. If life continues beyond its earthly duration, even the least comely here and now may one day be more than we can presently fathom. Reflecting upon this thought, Lewis remarks,

> There are no ordinary people. You have never talked to a mere mortal. Nations, cultures, arts, civilizations - these are mortal, and their life is to ours as the life of a gnat. But it is immortals whom we joke with, work with, marry, snub, and exploit.[42]

The idea, thinks Lewis, is staggering. If we continue in our development beyond this life, who knows what we may yet become? "It is a serious thing," he writes, "to live in a society of possible gods and goddesses" - to think that the dullest and least interesting person you meet today may one day be one whom you would, in your present condition, be tempted to worship.

This does not mean that we should suspend our present judgment. A spiritual outlook need not preclude anger or condemnation here and now when it is appropriate. Along the way we may take offense at our fellows, may forsake and even go to war with them,[43] if the situation requires. But if they are more than the flesh, then whatever we think of them here and now, we cannot dismiss

---

[42] *Ibid.*, p. 19.

[43] For related discussion, see "Why I am Not a Pacifist", contained in the same volume.

even the least of these individuals as being essentially bad or worthless.[44] For within them is promise. Nor does this prospect of greater development contradict the claim that God loves us, as Hartshorne has maintained,[45] even as we are. The reality of this present love in no way rules out a greater destiny in store.

Reflection on the progress that is possible, in an individual, over a relatively short period of time, may give us perspective. Human beings are capable of fundamental changes, sometimes within a short period of time. When one considers the prospect extended indefinitely, the thought is astonishing. In this idea we find an insight into human potential. What we lack today may be reality tomorrow. Our assessment must be tempered by this recognition.

Our present difficulties with other people are thus cast in a different light when we take stock of this fact. If personal development continues beyond the confines of this world, then we are indeed far more than we may presently imagine. Such an attitude, were it taken seriously, might well improve the quality of personal relationships everywhere. Belief in survival makes possible just this attitude, in which case, it seems, it has something in its moral favor.

---

[44] Or if we think that they are somehow inherently bad, then we cannot continue to regard them in the same way that we do at present. For to the extent that we hold such persons accountable for their failure, we must acknowledge the possibility of their eventual success. Suppose, for example, that we count a man guilty of cowardice. If so, we must think that he has willfully chosen this act. But this belief presupposes that he is capable of choice *in either direction*. In which case, we cannot be sure of his choice on the next occasion. A freedom toward evil is presumably a freedom toward good, as well. A coward, if he is truly a coward, is thus capable of heroism. And if life continues hereafter, there is no foreseeable limit to what this freedom may realize.

[45] See again relevant discussion in the concluding portion of the last chapter.

To explore further the relationship between ethics and belief in survival, let us return for a moment to the earlier-cited "transmission" theory offered by William James. While it is not, perhaps, the only way of construing the survival hypothesis,[46] it is surely representative of much thought on the subject. This idea of our inhabiting the body, of our agency working through the flesh and laying aside this mortal vestment at life's end - it is, I think, what most have in mind when they entertain the prospect of another life. How does this basic view accord with our moral thinking?

The idea of consciousness working through the material realm has profound kinship, I believe, with our basic convictions regarding moral activity. On this view, our choices are made, once again, in relation to a medium (principally, our neurology) that shapes our basic personality type. The conscious state of a human being, his or her general personality type, inclinations and aptitudes, all owe, in some measure, to this filtering circumstance. But again, we are not bound by this medium, which is only the vehicle through which our agency finds its present expression.

---

[46] Thus there are some, for example, who imagine that the actual mechanism of survival is not disembodiment, but *resurrection*, meaning the bodily reconstitution of an individual, either in this world or another, at some point after his or her conscious extinction. Cited in this connection are passages like *Isaiah* 26: 19, which speaks of a rising of the dead, and *Daniel* 12: 2, which tells of the day when "many of them that sleep in the dust of the earth shall awake." (See also Paul's first letter to the Corinthians, cited in chapter 7 of this volume.) It is sometimes argued that Biblical faith precludes the Greek and pagan notion of the soul's natural departure from the body at life's end, but rests instead upon a trust in God's power to raise an individual who would remain deceased otherwise. See, for example, Oscar Cullman, *Immortality of the Soul or Resurrection of the Dead?* (London: Epwarth, 1958). For a discussion of resurrection and personal identity, see chapter 15 in Hick's aforenoted *Death and Eternal Life*.

Thus the first and principal advantage of this theory, it seems to me, is that it distinguishes between agency and the medium through which it operates. For agency, on this view, is not a by-product of material events, but something distinct from it. Herein we have the prospect of *moral freedom*. While we are not, on this view, wholly independent of our material conditions (our chemistry, environment, historical situation, and so forth), we are nonetheless capable of choice with respect to them. These conditions do not determine our actions; they are, once more, a medium - they are *a part of the challenge* that we, as moral and intellectual agents, presently face.

Non-survivalist views tend, by contrast, to offer little in this regard. For typically they conceive of human beings as being material creatures, or creatures whose existence is at least grounded, in some way, in material conditions. But if indeed they are right in this, it is hard to see how action can occur apart from these conditions - how it can involve anything this is separate from material circumstance. Thus it is difficult, I think, to square such views with the common sense idea (often shared, it might be noted, by materialists themselves) that human beings are *responsible* for their actions.

The transmission theory has implications likewise for the way that we evaluate an individual's conduct and his or her moral progress over the course of time. Such conduct, we commonly suppose, is subject to evaluation by certain outward criteria. We think that these criteria can be put in terms of basic rules - that one (generally speaking) ought not to lie, to injure, or to commit theft, that one should be truthful, generous, fair-minded, and so on. We believe likewise that such rules provide some gauge of character. At the same time, we tend to think that this gauge is not perfect, that it does not tell the whole story. For there exist factors within agency, we sense, too subtle to measure in this fashion.

How does the transmission theory bear upon this line of thought? Such a theory does not require us, I think, to discard such rules, or to deny that they serve a practical purpose. It allows that they may provide a basis for the evaluation of human conduct and a guideline for civil policy. It agrees further with the idea, also basic to our instinct, that such rules are not the whole story. For our actions, by its reckoning, have a significance that outward rules cannot measure. In each case they represent action that is made, once more, not merely by choice, but in relation to a medium through which agency operates.

On a view of this kind, in fact, it is possible that no two persons can be measured, in principle, on the same scale. For perhaps no two face exactly the same challenge. One individual may contend, for example, with impulses toward violence grounded deep in his own biochemistry. Another may be spared this difficulty. If so, the outward record is not the whole story. We cannot know, under present circumstances, all that a choice involves.[47] Nor can we have, as yet, a final tally of what any given individual accomplishes over the course of this life. Perhaps he or she has come further than we imagine. We cannot be sure what progress has been made in relation to the hand that was dealt.

---

[47] A kindred observation, I believe, is found in the medieval classic *The Cloud of Unknowing*. No man in this life, writes the author, "may judge another as good or evil simply on the evidence of his deeds," even if he knows, in general terms, whether such deeds are good or evil. See William Johnston, ed., *The Cloud of Unknowing* (New York: Image Books, 1996), p. 86.

Of course, some will reply, our judgment of human behavior needs to be qualified. Materialists, they will say, do not deny this. Common sense (as reflected in many places, including the court system) acknowledges extenuating circumstance every day. Personal differences, some of them innate and some acquired, are plain knowledge. We know that some persons are strongly inclined by nature to be introverts, and some to be outgoing, that some have certain basic aptitudes that others lack. We know that not everyone has the same situation with respect to either inherited chemistry or cultural advantage.

But James' view, I think, takes us further. For by its reckoning, once again, we are *not to be identified* with these genetic packages and the tendencies to which they give rise. This distinction, again, is what offers the prospect of moral freedom in the first place. If we are to retain our ordinary notions of value, we must be able, I think, to distinguish, in some way, between human beings and the material conditions within which they operate.

A transmission view, I believe, speaks to much that is present elsewhere within human experience. Recalling discussion by Penfield and others, let us think for a moment about what is involved in certain kinds of mental effort - say, in *focusing* one's own concentration, or in *trying* to remember something. The materialist explanation (or one version of it, at least) is that such efforts are simply the electrochemical events taking place in the brain at that moment. Where, then, does the element of *will* come into this account? Is it the case that one brain event somehow *tries* to bring about another? Perhaps this is theoretically possible. But where arises, I wonder, this asymmetry, this spectacular and outrageous *difference* in the qualities of these two pieces of electro-chemistry?[48]

Consider also the attitude that we take toward our own bodies. Some persons, it is true, are closely tied to their physical aspect. Some, for example, make physique or physical condition their consuming life interest. Yet few of us, I think, wish to be identified with our flesh. Rather most of us, it seems to me, view our bodies[49] as something else, not as what we *are*, but as something that we *have* and a means by which we operate.

This attitude extends, I believe, even to the mechanism associated with consciousness itself. Take, for one - it is an example with which I am thoroughly familiar - the individual who is irked by his own absent-mindedness. It is not exactly himself, in this case, that is the object of irritation. Rather it is an accident (presumably neuro-chemical at its base) of his makeup. Or consider, as a logically similar case, the individual who faces the waning years of her life with diminished mental capacities. Does she believe herself to be *identical* with this failing apparatus, and to be diminished thereby in her own being? Or does she instead think of this event as being a *circumstance* - as something (however unfortunate) that is incidental to her own existence - *a stage of life* through which she must pass?

---

[48] The materialist view, observes Harry Emerson Fosdick, seems ever more strange as we examine it. Suppose, for example, that by looking through a fluoroscope one were able to observe one's own brain cells at work. "It would be a curious experience," he comments. "*For who would be doing the watching?* It does not seem credible that the brain cells could be cleverly looking at themselves." Harry Emerson Fosdick, *Adventurous Religion* (New York: Harper and Brothers Publishers, 1926), p. 192.

[49] The very locution 'our bodies' itself, I think, is worth note.

The latter of these conceptions, it seems to me, is the one that speaks most deeply to human sensibility. This distinction between self and mechanism speaks to the feeling that we are more than our bodies, and that we may one day transcend their present condition. Consider, as one more case, the example of an individual oppressed by severe depression. Do we take this emotional fact to be essential to his or her identity? Rather, I think, we view it as being a condition, as something to be distinguished from the individual even if it has no present remedy.

I think that a similar point can be made regarding another kind of limitation. Take the case of a person who is mentally handicapped. What do we really believe about this individual's identity? It is possible to view this individual as being essentially just what his brain chemistry makes of him at this moment. But need we see this individual in these terms? Do we see him as *being* what Down's syndrome, say, has produced? Or do we find instead, beneath this condition, some depth, some potential, that is greater?

If we suppose that we *are* our brains, it is hard, I think, to find a basis on which to make this distinction. Yet some such distinction is present, I believe, in our apprehension of human beings. On reflection we will hesitate to *identify* human beings with their present material condition. For what we find before us, it seems, is something more. Contained in this encounter is the meeting not of accidents, but of individuals. Our attitude toward other people is not an attitude toward bodies, but toward agents, toward personal entities who are something more than present evidence may disclose.

Thus the transmission view speaks more fully than does materialism, I believe, to what is present to us in human encounter. Human beings, on this view, are not exactly what we see in front of us, but something more profound. Their radiance, so to speak, does not yet have full expression. It is presently limited. It enters into this world "in all sorts of restricted forms, and with all the imperfections and queernesses that characterize our finite individualities here below."[50]

Some philosophers, as noted earlier, have maintained that belief in personal survival owes to a confused religious outlook. The real and fitting immortality, claims Hartshorne, is not a new adventure, but a lasting place in the divine omniscience. Our own experience of the world, he explains, will one day end, but there are consolations. Death is not obliteration, but the fixing of an end-page to our story.

Has this conception of eternity any advantage over the more conventional one? Hartshorne's immortality is surely different from what most religious types entertain. It is a view, he thinks, that rises above our petty and selfish tendencies, the one more in keeping with our own greater maturity.

I hold, however, that it is deficient; indeed I deny that he is talking about immortality of a meaningful kind at all. For how does eternal life, in these terms, differ truly from annihilation? We are told, on this view, that we are always a part of the (divinely remembered) history of the universe. But this comes to little more than saying that each of us, once having lived, is a part of what has happened.

---

[50] "Human Immortality", p. 17.

We have herein, perhaps, an eternity of sorts. For anything, once having existed, will forever be a part of the whole. It will always be the case that this thing has existed, even when it exists no longer. Toying some with tense and meaning, we might thus render a fairly pleasant description of what it means to have a finite life-span: Death, it is true, does not annihilate us, if by annihilation we mean our removal from the universal order. If the word 'exists' means (time-neutrally) to have a share in history, then to exist once is to exist always.

Some, perhaps, find comfort in this abstraction. I confess that I do not understand them. For an immortality of this kind offers us no conscious share in anything that lies outside the bounds of our earthly existence. A universe in which I have lived, once I am gone, is thereafter no different *for me* from one in which I have been excluded altogether. It cannot matter to me, at that point, whether I am remembered or not, whether by other time-bound mortals or by omniscience. If we wish to denote, by the phrase 'eternal life', a mere place in the history of the world, then all sentient beings (indeed things of every kind) are eternal. If we mean instead, and more commonly, ongoing conscious experience of reality, then death brings with it the end. Anyone who thinks that the first kind of survival is as meaningful as the second might ask himself if he is indifferent as to which of these shall be his in the next five minutes.

I do not deny that there is something valid, I think, in Hartshorne's account. He is right that the good of one individual, from a moral point of view, is worth no more and no less than that of some other. He is also right in thinking that moral reasoning requires us to adopt a point of view that transcends our own.

It may be worthwhile to consider for a moment how moral thought involves the adoption of this objective and neutral vantage point. The classic theorists bid us to take this point of view in various ways according to their founding principles. The founding principle of morality, argues John Stuart Mill,[51] "approves or disapproves of every action whatsoever, according to the tendency which it appears to have to augment or diminish the happiness of the party whose interest is in question." Thus the worth of an action lies in its *ultility* - its net impact upon human happiness. Each individual is to count for one, and none counts for more than one. Our own pains and pleasures are inherently no more and no less important than are the pains and pleasures of others.

Jeremy Bentham, in a related vein, argues famously that we must extend our moral vision to include not merely human beings, but sentient creatures of every kind. The day may come, he writes, when we realize that the furriness of a creature, or the number of its legs, or the termination of its *os sacrum* (tail-bone) are no more relevant to its moral status than are various differences, such as skin color, within the human species. What is relevant to a creature's moral status, says Bentham, is not its appearance, or the extent to which it may arouse our natural sympathy, but its own capacity for *pain*. Reason requires that we rise above our first tendencies if we are to have any basis for our moral thought.[52]

---

[51] See John Stuart Mill, *Utilitarianism* (London: Longmans, Green and Company, 1910).

[52] For discussion of this comment and its relevance to moral issues concerning the treatment of animals, see chapter 3 of Peter Singer's *Practical Ethics* (Cambridge: Cambridge University Press, 1993). Bentham's comment appears in his *Introduction to the Principles of Morals and Legislation*.

A similar objectivity is advocated by Kant, even though he does not accord happiness any such role in the moral scheme. The inherent dignity of each individual human being, thinks Kant, provides the basis of morality. We must extend to others (and to ourselves) the respect that this fact warrants. A proper action is one that acknowledges this worth, and so refuses to subordinate another person (or oneself) to a selfish end. Its maxim (or general rule) is one that we accept as a principle of conduct in our own society.[53] We must treat other persons as being "ends in themselves"; we cannot use them as simply a means to satisfy our own desires, nor can we make an exception of ourselves to laws binding upon human beings in general.

Thus each of these men, in his own way, testifies to the claim that moral thought is objective. The good of one individual is (all things equal) as valuable as that of another. My own good is not *inherently* more desirable than someone else's.

Hartshorne, it is clear, understands these things. He understands, as well, that true virtue requires a capacity for taking joy in the success of others - an opening outward, so to speak, that transcends self-concern. Moral action, likewise, is not *motivated* by a desire to benefit oneself. This insight finds its classic expression in Kant, who argues that there is a crucial difference between actions that are performed out of respect for the moral law and actions that (while perhaps outwardly identical) merely happen to conform to it.

---

[53] This claim, which is made in Kant's *Fundamental Principles of the Metaphysics of Morals*, is discussed in the next chapter of this volume.

Objectivity, thinks Hartshorne, is at odds with belief in survival. It is motivated, he imagines, by an excessive concern with our own fate and a failure to achieve the self-neutrality necessary to moral understanding: A better grasp of our place in the world will diminish our interest in another life. There is nothing unfair or unkind about our mortality. While it might look like a misfortune, it actually allows a kind of justice. For the higher an individual's moral development, and more generous his spirit, the richer will be his life, and the more often his occasions for happiness. Those souls less elevated will have less of this vicarious enjoyment. Those who are truly base will have none. Thus the more open one is toward others, the better one's own experience. (An individual, we might imagine, who rejoiced in the good fortune everywhere might take in a veritable eternity of happiness in the brief time that he or she is allowed here.)

Is it true, then, that a universe in which there is no survival is as morally defensible as the alternative? It is true, I think, that actions performed solely for their reward (whether the reward lies here or elsewhere) are morally impure and perhaps (as Kant insists) even morally irrelevant. But this does not mean that survival is unimportant to the moral condition of the universe in which it might occur. An individual who acts rightly out of respect for the moral law is more admirable than one who acts rightly out of fear of being punished in another world. But I am not sure how this fact is supposed to diminish *the importance of survival itself* from a moral point of view. For it is one thing, I think, to say (for example) that sacrifice without hope of reward is a noble thing, and another to say that it might as well go unrewarded.

Perhaps it will be said, once again, that truly virtuous persons will act as morality requires without hope for themselves. Or that such persons, if sufficiently elevated, will find virtue itself to be reward enough. Very well - but all the more reason, I say, why they should be rewarded! Those who choose the moral good for its own sake are thereby deserving of good in turn. It is indeed just this lack of expectation that makes reward especially appropriate. Or if it is said that notions of reward and punishment are somehow primitive or outmoded, with respect to a future life, then presumably they are outmoded with respect to this one, as well. But this hardly seems to be the case.

There is no inherent antagonism, I believe, between personal integrity and belief in another life. Hartshorne, as I have said, expresses a keen insight into the nature of moral virtue and its relationship the living of a worthwhile life. The same can be said for Lamont, who sees the pain that has entered the world through false piety and otherworldly dogmatism. But the insights of each of these thinkers, it seems to me, can be incorporated likewise into a world-view that allows personal survival. While perhaps not all belief in survival is admirable, the belief itself is consistent, I think, with sound moral judgment.

It actually accords, I believe, with much of what is right in Humanist insight - with the claim, for example, that human beings are essentially active creatures. Humanism, says Lamont,[54] disavows itself of belief in a "glorified heavenly rest-home" of passive contemplation. Perhaps residence in a glorified rest-home is not an especially high aspiration. But the fact that Lamont should put

---

[54] *The Philosophy of Humanism*, p. 210.

the case this way suggests, I think, a limitation on his own part. Belief in survival does not require any such ideal, nor need we think that the prospect is limited in any such fashion. That Lamont should characterize heaven in this manner indicates, I think, that he himself may have an inadequate conception of what the next life might involve. The claim that persons should be active, that they ought to expand their horizons, that such things as free thought and intellectual integrity ought to be cultivated - all of this, I think, accords well with belief in a future life, provided that we envision the next world as a place where such action may continue.

Our basic respect for human beings, and for their moral development, furnishes insight into the importance of their survival. How, asks famed New Testament scholar B. H. Streeter, can we make sense of a universe capable of producing heroic spirits "and then letting them perish out of existence for evermore?"[55] Streeter's line of argument emphasizes not so much reward or punishment, but divine love and the inherently precious subjects of its creation.[56] Yet its implications are much the same. Noting H. G. Wells' rejection of belief in personal survival as a product of "egotism," he observes that "if the Divine righteousness may lightly 'scrap' the individual, human righteousness may do the same."

---

[55] Burnett Hillman Streeter, "The Resurrection of the Dead", contained in B. H. Streeter, A. Clutton Brock, and others, *Immortality: An Essay in Discovery Co-ordinating Scientific, Psychical and Biblical Research* (New York: Macmillan, 1917).

[56] Cf. Hick's discussion in section # 3 of chapter 8, "Humanism and Death", in *Death and Eternal Life*.

The moral level of human beings, thinks Streeter, whether singly or as a group, is measured by the value that they place upon the lives of their fellow members - even those members less advanced in their present development. What verdict, in that case, might issue from the highest level of moral consciousness? Can we imagine that this consciousness, possessed of a love and a mercy incomparably more vast than ours, can think so little of human life as to discard it?[57] We must, says Streeter, suppose otherwise. Thus while Wells may be credited with an unselfish detachment concerning his own fate, "it would not be to God's credit were he equally content."

Hartshorne bids us, once more, to remember that *others* may succeed where we have failed. For happiness, he says, is a good thing wherever it may occur. But it is hard to square this advice with the attitude that we are bid to take toward other persons here and now. For it is just *as* inherently valuable individuals that we are supposed to treat one another in this world - as individuals, that is, whose well-being cannot be arithmetically replaced by that of others. If I cause one of my neighbors pain, for example, it is not somehow balanced by the fact that I have benefitted some other. The loss of one life is not neutralized by the salvaging of another. Nor, it seems, is the misery of one class, or one generation, made acceptable by the happiness of one elsewhere.

---

[57] "Putting the matter negatively," writes Patrick Sherry, "we might ask why a loving God would create people *not* to be immortal? For if death is the end for them, then their 'immortal longings', particularly their desire to know God and to be with Him, will be frustrated; and more importantly, their potentiality for transformation through God's grace into a likeness of Him will be unrealised." Patrick Sherry, *Spirit, Saints and Immortality* (Albany: State University of New York Press, 1984). See pp. 78-82.

This is not to say that we never make such calculations - sometimes we sacrifice the few for the many, or choose the lesser pain over the greater, feeling that it is the better choice available. But this is only the choice of less evil over more, neither of which, we imagine, is desirable in itself. From an ideal point of view, the sacrifice of past generations for the sake of future ones is senseless. The injustice suffered by one individual is a loss, as well, regardless of what happiness the cosmos may afford to sentient creatures elsewhere. Thus I fail to see consolation in the idea that other individuals, distant from us in space and time, may enjoy fulfillment when those around us do not. Death, if it is the end, is an irredeemable tragedy.

Perhaps there are other ways in which a non-survivalist account of the world can be defended. Some persons, for example think that the world is aesthetically enhanced by its inclusion of pain, as a contrast to pleasure, or that our appreciation of good requires that we have some prior acquaintance with evil. But surely such arguments are absurd. The world of human experience is not some tapestry of colors or mesh of tones to be made lovelier by its arrangement. Nor does the psychological dependence of good upon evil (if it exists) justify the gross suffering and lifelong degradation of those who endure it.

It is also said, on occasion, that the world is in our hands, to do with it what we will. If the condition of the world is unsatisfactory, then we must blame ourselves for the problem instead of finding fault elsewhere. (God, it is sometimes said, gets blamed for too much.) We should strive to improve the world, it is said, before we complain about it.

This reply is ill-conceived, I think, in several respects. In the first place, undeserved misfortune often befalls individuals through no fault of anyone, and often despite the best efforts of those around them. Persons often suffer unfairly through no human agency whatsoever. But this injustice calls for an answer whether it owes to the actions of other human beings or not. For whether such injustice is “moral” or “natural” (whether, in other words, it is attributable to human agency or to something else) from the point of view of the sufferer it is all the same. And whether the sorrows of this world are the doing of human beings or their creator is surely not an exclusive choice. God's will and human action are not antagonistic as explanations of the world's condition. That a given atrocity was freely perpetrated by human agency and was freely allowed by Providence is a consistent proposition.

It is said at times that the world's deficiencies may someday be rectified by the development of a better social structure for our descendants. So, perhaps, the errors of the past may serve as a lesson to those who come afterward. Our of this suffering may arise a higher degree of moral awareness. Thus the suffering of past generations, in the long run, may contribute to happiness. In this way it may find justification.

This answer, as I have already suggested, is inadequate, for it supposes that the happiness of future generations (should it someday occur) will somehow make up for unhappiness past. But ethics, again, is not arithmetic. This future compensation is impossible if human beings, as conscience seems to tell us, are inherently precious ends unto themselves.

It is conceded, at times, that the world is morally deficient, but it is said that this deficiency is a consequence (in part, at least) of the reality of human freedom. Such freedom, it is imagined, is a good of a very high order, one so great that its presence justifies all of the evil that may come into the world as a result. Thus while the world might be a more pleasant place under different circumstances (say, if human beings were made incapable of feeling pain, or were somehow programmed for good behavior), a higher good would be lost in the bargain. Freedom, it is thus argued, justifies the evil that comes with it.

My reply to this "free will" defense is much like the one preceding it. The freedom of transgressors in this world, I submit, is simply not worth the pain of those on whom they transgress.[58] If we say otherwise, then we fail, as before, to recognize these victims as ends in themselves. Thus I do not believe that the argument from human freedom provides an effective defense of the present world-order.

There is, I think, a decisive reply to any line of argument that purports to defend the moral condition of this world as an end in itself. For if we wish to say that the world, in its present condition (and independently of the destiny of those in it), is a good thing, then we are left with a very strange consequence, namely, that *nothing we ever shall do* can alter the fact. If the world in its present condition is justified, then my own actions, it seems, have become irrelevant.

---

[58] Cf. Dostoevsky's Ivan, who asks why we should know "that diabolical good and evil when it costs so much?" See Fyodor Dostoevsky, *The Brothers Karamazov*. Trans. Constance Garnett (New York: W. W. Norton and Co., 1976.) This quote appears in the section entitled "Rebellion". See related discussion in chapter 6 of this volume.

Whether I devote my life to good or to evil - whether I spend it in an effort, say, to combat infectious disease, or to profit by trade in child prostitution, or to anything else besides, the world will remain (as this defense would have it) a world that is acceptable. Or if not, then some reason needs to be given why my own action might one day tip the scale - why we will draw the line tomorrow when we have not drawn it before. (And what might this be? Will the sheer *amount* of suffering one day pass some crucial amount? By what reasoning is the present amount not sufficient?)

But this, I think, is tantamount to saying that significantly *bad* actions are impossible. Which is to say, morally significant choices - those that will make the world *better or worse than it might have been* - are illusory. If this world is a good world, yesterday, today, and tomorrow, then my own actions can have no bearing upon its moral condition. But if this is the case, it seems, then moral discourse itself becomes empty. It has no application in any context - even that of establishing the world's defensibility. But this seems implausible, not to mention self-defeating. Thus I do not believe that the present world-order can be defended in the way just described.

What more can be said about value and its relation to the survival issue? To this point, I have argued that belief in survival is not undermined by certain arguments that are often brought against it. I have argued likewise that belief in survival need not compromise our moral outlook. In the following chapter I will go further. I will maintain that our moral experience provides us with positive reason to think that we are immortal.

To this end I will discuss various theories concerning the nature of values, and will explain why I think that reductionist accounts (those that attempt to explain moral experience as a natural and ultimately material phenomenon) cannot be squared with our own deepest convictions. Afterward I will discuss the relationship between our present moral outlook and belief in a future life. I will argue that a serious attitude toward value involves us in a conception of reality that extends outside material bounds. I will argue likewise that this attitude involves us in a view that takes us beyond the bounds of mortal existence.

Chapter III

Moral Truth and Its Implications

Thrasymachus, don't be hard on us. If we are making any mistake in the consideration of the arguments, Polemarchus and I, know well that we're making an unwilling mistake. If we were searching for gold we would never willingly make way for one another in the search and ruin our chances of finding it; so don't suppose that when we are seeking for justice, a thing more precious than a great deal of gold, we would ever foolishly give in to one another and not be as serious as we can be about bringing it to light.

Socrates, Plato's *Republic*

I was just thinking that of all the trails in this life, there is one that matters more than all the others. It is the trail of a true human being. I think you are on this trail, and it is good to see.

Kicking Bird, speaking to John Dunbar,
in the film *Dances with Wolves*

He trusted to his strength and to the might of his hands. This is how a man who hopes to win lasting fame on the field of battle should behave, and not care for his life.

Beowulf

Much of life has to do with value - what we ought to do, what qualities of mind and character are admirable ones, what states of affairs we should strive to bring about, and so on. Our obligations, our ideals - theories abound as to where this part of reality resides and what it means.

Some philosophers imagine that our moral experience (our stirrings of conscience, our discernment of good and evil, and so forth) is a revelation. It informs us, they say, of certain timeless truths. Such truths, these philosophers suppose, have authority; they are ultimate, they represent a final court of appeal, so to speak, with regard to practical decision-making. They take rightful precedence over considerations of every other kind.

This line of thought is very old. As John Baillie[1] observes, it dates at least to Plato, who supposes that goodness is objective, and that it is moreover the foundation of all reality. *The Good*, writes Plato, is not merely a part of being, nor even its greatest feature, but "is still beyond being, exceeding it in dignity and power";[2] it is likewise "the cause of all that is beautiful."[3]

---

[1] John Baillie, *The Interpretation of Religion* (New York: Abingdon Press, 1928). See especially chapter IX, "Religion as Grounded in Our Consciousness of Value; an Historical Survey".

[2] See Plato's *Republic*. Trans. Allan Bloom (San Francisco: HarperCollins, 1968). The passage occurs in Book VI, 509 b. See also Book VII, wherein the Good is described (517 c) as being "sovereign" and as being "the cause of all that is right and fair in everything."

[3] Second *Epistle* 312 e. Trans. L. A. Post. This work is contained in Edith Hamilton and Huntington Cairns, eds., *Plato - Collected Dialogues* (Princeton: Princeton University Press, 1961). This collection is volume LXXI of the Bollingen series.

This notion of a higher order appears at various times and places in human history. The universe, by this account, is more than some dark and endless receptacle of matter and motion. It is invested with a profound meaning. Behind appearances is a something eternal, something that gives to life its rightful direction.

"He, the self-luminous," declares the *Mundaka Upanishad,*[4] "subtler than the subtlest, in whom exist all the worlds and all those that live therein - he is the imperishable Brahman." The reality of a mystic, writes F. C. Happold, "is one of a universe which is a dynamic unfolding of Spirit. There is nothing in it which is not Spirit, 'the seed of all seeds'."[5] John Keats' *Ode on a Grecian Urn* ends with the glorious (and sheerly Platonic) assertion that

> "Beauty is truth, truth beauty," - that is all
> Ye know on earth, and all ye need to know.[6]

Others, as we will see in a moment, have a different idea. They do not deny that value may seem like something high and sacred. It may impress itself on the psyche with great force. But it is, they maintain, a natural phenomenon. This alleged fact of good and evil, then, is not a real thing; or at least, it is not what certain mystic and supernaturalist types make of it.

---

[4] *Mundaka* II, ii, 1-2. See *The Upanishads*. Trans. Swami Prabhavananda and Christopher Isherwood (Hollywood: Vedanta Press, 1947). This passage is excerpted with commentary in chapter 3 of Prabhavananda's *The Spiritual Heritage of India* (Hollywood: Vedanta Press, 1980).

[5] F. C. Happold, *Mysticism* (London: Penguin Books, 1988), p. 120.

[6] John Keats, *Ode on a Grecian Urn*. This poem is reprinted in countless sources, including G. B. Harrison's *A Book of English Poetry* (London: Penguin Books, 1950).

Our notions of value are grounded, they imagine, in happenstance, in various accidents of our nature. There is no higher realm beyond what we see in front of us. Our sense of what is right or wrong, of what we ought to do, of self-transcending purpose, say these reductionists, has its source in the baseless facts of human feeling and societal development.

It remains to be asked whether either of these two conceptions of value has reasons in its favor. It must be asked, as well, what bearing this discussion may have on further issues of life and destiny. In the previous chapter, I defended belief in a future life against several charges. I maintained that a concern with survival is not selfish or misguided, as some writers have suggested, and that it is aligned indeed with the highest elements of moral sensibility. Our respect for the inherent worth of individual human beings, I have claimed, requires us to think that the universe would be an objectively better place if we did survive.

In this chapter I contend further that our respect for value gives us reason to believe in our own survival. I discuss first the effort of certain thinkers to reduce judgments of value to the natural world, and thus to deny them an objective status. Afterward I discuss the alternative view that value judgments are indeed objective, that they are timeless and beyond the realm of material nature. I explain also what I think is the advantage of this latter view over the former. Last, I discuss the relationship, as I see it, between this view and our thinking about human destiny.

The Attempted Reduction of Values to the Natural World

There are certain objections to the view that morality has any kind of absolute or trans-human basis. One is the familiar problem of moral diversity. Great differences exist, it seems, in moral views from one time and place to another. How can we take such views seriously, it is asked, when they owe so much to circumstance?

The observation that values differ across cultures was present even in ancient times. There is, for one, the celebrated story told by Herodotus in his *Histories* about King Darius of Persia, who once arranged a meeting of Greeks and Indian Callatians. The Greeks believed that the bodies of their dead fathers ought to be cremated, while the Callatians believed that such bodies ought to be eaten. The two groups, recalls Herodotus, on what seems like a wry note, were mutually horrified.[7]

Such differences, think some, undermine the notion of an objective standard of value. In our own day Bertrand Russell, for example, ridicules in the idea that human beings have insight into the realm of value, and that such insight bestows on them some elevated status. Historical notions of right and wrong, he observes,

---

[7] See section 3.38 of Herodotus' *The History* (Chicago: University of Chicago Press, 1987). The incident is cited and discussed by James Rachels in chapter 2 of his book *The Elements of Moral Philosophy* (New York: McGrawHill-Hill, 1993).

> have varied to such an extent that no single item has been permanent. We cannot say, therefore, that man knows right and wrong, but only that some men do. Which men? Nietzsche argued in favor of an ethic profoundly different from Christ's, and some powerful governments have accepted his teaching.[8]

Thus if knowledge of moral values is to be a basis for religious belief, says Russell, we must first decide, by who-knows-what means, which ethic is the correct one, and apply the argument accordingly to some individuals and not to others. In practice, he notes, it is an issue decided on the battlefield. The "better" value is the one that prevails there and is ingrained, as a result, in forthcoming generations.

The reduction of values to facts of nature has found a number of expressions in recent years. Some take as their starting point our own evolutionary origins and their impact on our conscious development. These sources stress the need to see our moral awareness from outside, as it were, and to apply this wisdom to present-day social issues. One of the most impressive of such accounts in recent years is Robert Wright's *The Moral Animal.*[9]

An understanding of our biology, believes Wright, will deeply affect our outlook on values. For certain elements of our moral constitution, he explains - among them altruism, empathy, love, conscience, and a sense of justice - have a basis in our genes. In order to think clearly about values we need to see how they have arisen.

---

[8] See once more Russell's "Do We Survive Death?", *Why I Am Not a Christian*, p. 92.

[9] Robert Wright, *The Moral Animal: Why We Are the Way We Are* (New York: Vintage Books, 1994).

Darwin, says Wright, aptly summarized this process by saying "multiply, vary, let the strongest live and the weakest die." The central tenet of evolutionary theory is that life appeared not all at once, but gradually and through a myriad of haphazard "experiments," many of which resulted in dead ends when the line perished. What allows a species or an individual to survive, in evolutionary terms, is its fitness to its environment. Thus an organism favored with sharper teeth, thicker skin, or keener eyesight than its fellows tends on average to thrive better. It tends likewise to attract more mates and to remain active longer, thus passing on its genes more abundantly to future generations. The organism less well endowed faces longer odds in this competition. Thus it happens over time that the features of the better equipped organism become features of the group. In order to think responsibly about values, Wright maintains, we need to understand them in this light.

We are in the habit of thinking that the deliverances of conscience have special authority - that they are bestowed on us, in some fashion, by a higher trans-human source. Yet observation, contends Wright, tells us otherwise. To cite one example, our sense of *justice*: We often imagine that it issues from beyond the world and informs us of some timeless reality. But modern biology enables us to see otherwise.

Our sense of justice, explains Wright,[10] is grounded in a basic *retributive impulse*, a tendency, that is, to strike back at things that threaten us. Such an

---

[10] Much of this discussion takes place in Part Four (chapters 15-18), "Morals of the Story".

impulse, he imagines, develops not because it expresses some lofty ideal, but simply because it serves the reproductive good of the individual that has it. It fosters survival. For this reason it is perpetuated.

This does not mean that the impulse is *bad*, in any particular way, but it does mean that its value is open to question. In particular, the "aura of reverence" surrounding it - the lingering sense that it embodies some higher *truth* - becomes harder to credit once this aura "is seen to be a self-serving message from our genes, not a beneficent message from the heavens." Its origin is no more heavenly than is that of hunger, hatred, or lust, "or any of the other things that exist by virtue of their past success in shoving genes through generations."[11]

We likewise imagine, says Wright, that our attitudes toward other people are grounded in principle - that when we dislike someone, for example, it is for good reason; that if we are callous to his needs, or take satisfaction in his suffering, it is because of something he did, and for which he deserves bad treatment. Hence we imagine that our attitude has some ideal justification. Yet now we are in a position to see how this attitude actually develops. And its origins do not inspire confidence. Our dislike of others may have some basis.

> But the reason, often, is that it is not in our interests to like them; liking them won't elevate our social status, aid our acquisition of material or sexual resources, help our kin, or do any of the other things that during evolution have made our genes prolific. The feeling of "rightness" accompanying our dislike is just window dressing. Once you've seen that, the feeling's power may diminish.[12]

---

[11] *The Moral Animal*, p. 339.

[12] *Ibid.*, p. 340.

This new perspective allows us to understand our moral experience not in terms of mysticism or divine command, but in terms of natural cause. Much of the story will come as bad news to those who imagine that conscience puts them in touch with cosmic authority. But science will leave them no choice.

One may want to argue, says Wright,

> with the proposition that all we are is knobs and tunings, genes and environment. You can insist that there's something ... something *more*. But if you try to visualize the form this something would take, or articulate it clearly, you'll find the task impossible, for any force that is not in the genes or the environment is outside of physical reality as we perceive it. It's beyond scientific discourse.[13]

Whatever its practical value, he explains, "there is no reason to suppose that the inherent sense of justice - the sense that people *deserve* punishment, that their suffering is a good thing *in and of itself* - reflects a higher truth." Our moral accounting system is "wantonly subjective," and informed of "a deep bias toward the self." We find our rivals morally deficient, and our allies worthy of compassion. We gear this compassion to their social status, and "ignore the socially marginal altogether." Who can look at this "and then claim with a straight face that our various departures from brotherly love possess the sort of integrity we ascribe to them?"

What of other impulses, such as that of *love*? Love, like hate, exists by virtue of "its past contribution to genetic proliferation." At the level of the gene, "it is as crassly self-serving to love a sibling, an offspring, or a spouse as it is to

---

[13] *Ibid.*, p. 348.

hate an enemy."[14] If the base origins of justice are grounds for doubting it, then why not doubt the legitimacy of love, as well?

The answer, Wright maintains, is that love should be doubted, but that "it survives the doubt in pretty good shape." By this he means that the results of love are good ones, at least in the eyes of anyone who values human happiness. Love makes us want to benefit others; it makes us want to give up something that is desirable so that others may have more of it. It also makes this sacrifice *feel* good, thus increasing the sum of human happiness all the more. While granted, love may sometimes be injurious,[15] its effects, on balance, seem to place it on the positive side of the ledger. Yet love itself, Wright maintains, is not good or bad except according to the fruits that it bears. The moral status of any impulse, be it one of love, retribution, or anything else, should be decided in the same way - "we must first clear away the window dressing, the intuitive feeling of 'rightness,' and then soberly assess the effect on overall happiness."

---

[14] *Ibid.*, p. 340.

[15] He cites the example of a Texas mother who plotted the murder of the mother of her own daughter's school cheerleading spot rival.

The Case for Supernaturalism: Why Moral Judgments Transcend the Natural World

There exist reasons, then, to doubt that values are in any sense divine or supernatural. If there exists more than one ethic, how do we know which is the right one? What reason do we have to suppose that our ideas in this arena owe to anything more than the play of material accident?

Of course, it is not obvious why mere differences of moral view, whether between cultures or individuals, provide us with any basis for moral skepticism. For diversity of opinion elsewhere does not cast doubt upon the reliability of the subject matter. Multiple views within the arena, say, of history or mathematics does not show that the inquiry is in any way subjective. What sense, then, might we make of moral differences?

Some philosophers, as I have noted, maintain that our moral experience is specially meaningful - that it *signifies* something beyond those accidents of biology or social circumstance to which naturalistic accounts aim to reduce it. They are not discouraged by the fact that beliefs about right and wrong vary from one culture or subculture to another. One such individual is C. S. Lewis, who believes that our understanding of value may benefit from attention to the process of moral development within an individual. He describes, from his own experience, what happens when one set of values encounters another, and the impact that this event may have upon a man's personal development.

> When I came first to the University, I was as nearly without a moral conscience as a boy could be. Some faint distaste for cruelty and for meanness about money was my utmost reach - of chastity, truthfulness and self-sacrifice I thought as a baboon thinks of classical music.[16]

By a stroke of mercy, he continues,

> I fell among a set of young men (none of them, by the way, Christians) who were sufficiently close to me in intellect and imagination to secure immediate intimacy, but who knew, and tried to obey, the moral law. Thus their judgement of good and evil was very different from mine.[17]

It soon became obvious, Lewis explains, that these individuals were not only different from him in this regard. They were advanced beyond him, as well. The encounter, he explains, thus provided him not only with exposure to new attitudes, but with insight *into his own defect*. It was not merely a collision of unlike habits or lifestyles. It was instead the occasion for a new awareness and a resulting change within himself.

This change, he adds, was not simply a case of now treating as "white" what was hitherto called "black." New moral judgments are not mere reversals of old ones, even if a reversal of old judgments is involved. All the while that you are in this process of change, writes Lewis, you can have no doubt as to the direction in which you are moving. The new judgments are more like good than "the little shreds of good you already had," but at the same time they are continuous with them. In this respect they are not arbitrary. Nor do they

---

[16] C. S. Lewis, *The Problem of Pain* (New York: Simon and Schuster, 1996), p. 34.

[17] *Ibid.*

represent altogether new discoveries. They involve instead the further development of a basic faculty innate in oneself, and in accord with which judgment is possible. This faculty that tells you that theft is *bad* will tell you also, in time, that charity is *good*.[18] The encounter with others more highly developed provides not merely exposure to new habits of conduct, but an attendant sense *of shame and guilt*. One is conscious "of having blundered into society that one is unfit for."

Reflection upon this experience offers an insight, I think, into the nature of moral growth. It is true, as Russell observes, that there exist varying ideas as to what is good and evil. But does this mean that there can exist no such thing as a genuine morality, or that we ourselves must remain agnostic with respect to it? Consider, for example, what happens when an individual learns honesty, or compassion, or fairness. This change of character presents itself to the learner not merely as a change, but as an *improvement*, as a change that is not merely random, but positive, as a movement in an upward direction. It seems to involve not only a difference of mental habit, but an *addition* to consciousness, a self-evident refinement of its content.

It seems, also, that the direction of this change is more or less constant across the variety of persons and cultures. That individual who moves, in his development, from cruelty to kindness, from deceit to integrity, from selfishness

---

[18] It is for this reason, says Lewis, that a move from the Confucian "Do not do to others what you would not like them to do to you" to the Christian "Do as you would be done by" is a genuine *advance*. It is the realization of the first truth that makes possible the realization of the second.

to generosity, does not move back again, as it were, in the other direction. Once seeing the world from this other vantage point, it seems, there is no return.[19]

While not all cultures have the same ethic, there is conspicuous similarity, I think, in their respect for certain elements of human character - a sense of honor, for one, and physical courage, for another.[20] There seems to exist likewise an insistence upon the real difference, in principle, between good and evil, and between conduct that is admirable and conduct that is not.

Common across cultures also is a periodic recognition from within of the need for the improvement of the culture itself. Thus the individual who challenges his own tradition is regarded, in some cases, as being not merely a non-conformist, but (depending on the quality of his message) as being a genuine visionary.[21] Cultures themselves, it appears, do not define morality as mere tradition or habit.

---

[19] I do not mean by this, of course, that no one ever changes for the worse in moral outlook. An individual may "go bad" in any number of ways, as, for example, by adopting a policy of ruthlessness toward others in place of an existing policy of restraint and compassion. But even this change, I believe, is made (whether in good faith or not) on the basis of value. Thus one may decide, in such a case, that others are *not worth* the consideration since they themselves do not extend it. Yet rarely, if ever, I think, does anyone who has seen each side believe that cruelty *per se* is on a par with kindness, or prejudice with fair play.

[20] It may happen, too, that a culture or subculture will share a powerful sense of the worth of certain virtues even when it is blind to others. For an remarkable account of criminal ethics, and of the respect sometimes accorded, even within the society of the Cosa Nostra, to such things as honor and physical bravery, see Peter Maas, *Underboss: Sammy "The Bull" Gravano's Story of Life in the Mafia* (New York: HarperCollins, 1997).

[21] Thus what good is the traditional rite of sacrifice, asks Isaiah, when it lacks concern for justice, for the fate of the widow and the orphan? (See, for example, *Isaiah* 1: 10 and following.)

Moral differences, of course, can be found within a culture in any case. And yet whatever differences we may have with our fellows, most of us treat values as if they were terribly something quite important. And we seem to have little doubt as to the objective superiority of some courses of action over others. We also seem to be more or less united in our admiration of certain traits of character. Who among us, for example, does not appreciate fairness in an employer, honesty in a retailer, faithfulness in a spouse? Who is indifferent to whether his child becomes a community leader or a dealer of drugs? (Surely, I have observed, not the dealer himself.)

In saying this I do not deny that moral awareness is shaped, in some fashion, by the environment in which it develops. In each case, such awareness bears the mark of that surrounding and characteristic sensibility. Our own culture has moral roots in several traditions, chief among them the Greeks and the Hebrews. Each of these is distinct in its conception. Neither appears all at once, but has its own historical evolution.

In Homer's day, observes Bruno Snell, the words for *virtue* and for *good*, '*arete*' and '*agathos*', were not altogether distinguished from the area of personal profit. When Homer calls a man good, *agathos*, "he does not mean thereby that he is morally unobjectionable, much less good-hearted, but rather that he is useful, proficient, and capable of vigorous action."[22] (One may, in fact, confer excellence upon a man or an instrument with the same word.) Virtue, *arete*, does not denote

---

[22] Bruno Snell, *The Discovery of the Mind*. Trans. T. G. Rosenmeyer (Cambridge, Mass.: Harvard University Press, 1953), p. 158.

a moral property quite as we think of it, but instead "nobility, achievement, success and reputation."[23] Still, as Snell explains, these words take us in a moral direction, for they designate qualities whereby a man may win the respect of his community.

The development of classical Greek thought reveals to us a sensibility that is powerfully aesthetic. The tendency of the Greeks, as William Barrett observes, is fundamentally *visual*: This tendency invests itself even in their moral awareness. Thus they conceive human excellence as a kind of moral *beauty*, as something to be admired as a fine and elevated specimen of its kind. In this they are very different from the Hebrews, who *hear*, in their prophets, the voice of God, and who conceive virtue principally in terms of *obedience*.[24]

"The kinship of the beautiful and the good," writes Paul Janet in his *Theory of Morals*, "appears at every turn in the Grecian philosophy." Often one finds the word *kalon*, fair or beautiful, where one might otherwise find *agathon*. They are even brought together, he observes, in the characteristically Greek locution *to kalokagathon*, the beautiful and the good "united by an indissoluble bond."[25] The words that Plato uses to describe virtue, or a "well-regulated soul" - *'euruthmia'*, *'harmonia'*, and the like - are borrowed from the language of music and the arts.

---

[23] *Ibid.*

[24] William Barrett, *Irrational Man* (New York: Anchor Books, 1990). See chapter 4, "Hebraism and Hellenism".

[25] Paul Janet, *Theory of Morals* (New York: Charles Scribner's Sons, 1905), p. 112.

This conception of morality is again very different from others that have shaped our civilization. In the Hebrew tradition, once more, there is Job, a man confounded, outraged, by his own misfortune, who now challenges his creator. He is answered out of a whirlwind by Yahweh, who asks, "Where wast thou when I laid the foundations of the earth?"[26] One feels here, by contrast, the personal and confrontational nature of this event. And there is Amos, a simple herdsman who cries out as a prophet against empty religious ceremony, declaring that justice should "roll down as waters, and righteousness as a mighty stream."[27] In the age of modern philosophy one finds Kant, a Christian and so an heir to this Semite tradition, who speaks of a moral law, sacred and authoritative, that excites "ever new and increasing admiration and awe" as one reflects upon it.[28]

Surely, then, there are differences in the way that the moral good has been understood across times and cultures. Yet some writers think that we may see in these phenomena a single reality - a primal truth diversely apprehended and voiced by these different traditions. Such is the thesis of C. S. Lewis' earlier noted book *The Abolition of Man*. Throughout the world, observes Lewis,[29] one finds this idea of a truth behind appearance, a mystical fount single and absolute that furnishes the basis of all legitimate judgments of value.

---

[26] *Job* 38: 4. (American Standard Version)

[27] *Amos* 5: 21-24. (American Standard Version)

[28] Immanuel Kant, *Critique of Practical Reason*. Trans. Lewis White Beck (New York: Liberal Arts Press, 1956), p. 166.

[29] See again Part I.

This source is given various names as it appears in the literature of the world. Plato, says Lewis, tells us of a *Good* that is "beyond existence."[30] Vedic Indian philosophy speaks of the *Rta*, which even the gods must obey. The Chinese tell us of the *Tao*, a reality that is "beyond all predicates," an abyss that was "before the Creator himself." This reality is sovereign; it is the principle of the cosmos and the truth to which human action must conform if life is to proceed in the right direction.

By way of abbreviation (and borrowing from Lao Tzu's *Tao Te Ching*), Lewis calls this truth the *Tao*. Its doctrine, he writes,

> is the doctrine of objective value, the belief that certain attitudes are really true, and others really false, to the kind of thing the universe is and the kind of things we are. Those who know the *Tao* can hold that to call children delightful or old men venerable is not simply to record a psychological fact about our own parental or filial emotions at the moment, but to recognize a quality which *demands* a certain response from us whether we make it or not.[31]

It is by virtue of this source, says Lewis, that some things are truly required of us, and that our actions may be measured. There is a tendency, he observes, for modern writers to dismiss any such notion of a *higher* truth as being unfounded in this age of science. What is real, they suppose, is congruent with what can be seen and tested. Lewis cites the instance of two writers, "Gaius" and "Titius", who have authored something that he calls *The Green Book*.

---

[30] *Ibid.*, p. 30. Cf. Plato's *Republic,* especially Books VI and VII.

[31] *Ibid.*, p. 31. For historical commentary on the *Tao Te Ching*, see Arthur Waley's translation and appended essays in *The Way and Its Power* (New York: Grove Weidenfeld, 1958).

The book purports to be a instruction in English reading and writing for the upper division of public school. In it is contained the illustration of two persons who observe a waterfall. One calls the sight *sublime*, the other calls it *pretty*.[32] What we learn from this example, believe the writers, is that value is subjective. Thus whenever we speak of the *worth* of an object, while we may appear to be saying something about the object itself, in reality we are only saying something about our feelings toward it.

It seems like an innocuous statement, says Lewis. But such an attitude, should it carry over, will destroy the soul of the individual and the culture that adopt it. For if we accept what Gaius and Titius tell us, we will have no basis left on which to believe anything about value - about beauty, for example, or good and evil, or the rightful direction of our own lives.

The intended strategy of this *Innovator*, Lewis explains, is to reduce judgments of value ultimately to judgments about the material world. In so doing, such a theorist keeps his analysis within the realm of nature and so (he imagines) within the bounds of rationality. Thus he purports to offer an advance in human understanding.

But in order for us to retain any serious notion of value, explains Lewis, we must go beyond the world of nature. For facts of nature, after all, are silent about what *ought* to be the case. By themselves they tell us only how things are, and not how they should be.

---

[32] The example is taken from a discussion by Samuel Coleridge, who (like Lewis) endorses the first judgment, and is dissatisfied with the second.

The Innovator, says Lewis, may imagine that he has uncovered the ground of values in some natural *instinct* - one that inclines us, say, to share with others, or perpetuate the race, or further the cause of "society." But how, he asks, can this analysis furnish us with any direction? The bare fact that I have an instinct (if such is the case) to share, or to produce a new generation, or to benefit society, cannot tell me *what to do with the instinct itself*. (The presence of some further guiding instinct, he adds, will be of no help. For how should I regard *it*?)

Lewis' discussion speaks directly to naturalistic accounts noted above. The reduction of values to nature, says Lewis, is self-defeating. For if we accept its principal thesis (i. e., that our moral experience issues ultimately from natural events), then whatever else we may say about good and evil, we must suppose, are but the expression of our own ungrounded emotions. On what basis, then, can our own policies be defended?

This does not mean, I think, that naturalists themselves are amoral, or that they lack moral insight in regard to particular issues. There is much to admire, for example, in Lamont's philosophy. Consider, for one, his view that we should promote the blessings of science and social justice. Surely this seems true enough. Consider also the Humanist attitude toward sexuality. The sexual impulse, Lamont believes, is not evil. At the same time he recognizes the need for "a high standard" of conduct in this arena of human relationship. Each of these views again seems right to me. An impulse itself, I must think, is not evil, though possibilities of good and evil may arise with respect to it. And there exists, I believe, such a thing as a high standard of conduct in sexual relations.

But what is it, I ask, that makes a given standard a *high* one? A general code of respect for members of the opposite sex is superior, it seems to me, to one of exploitation. But how can nature itself provide us with any basis for such a claim? A Humanist may say that some policies, some actions, conduce to the general human happiness, while others do not. But where does *human happiness* or *the general welfare* derive its moral status in the first place?[33] Perhaps Lamont will say that there is no such ideal written in the heavens, or decreed by providence, but that it is simply the way in which more humane, more enlightened individuals view the matter. Human happiness, he may say, is just what more highly developed persons want to bring about.[34]

But this invites the same question. It is true, perhaps, that a society mindful of the common good will be, on the whole, a happier and more progressive one. But as Lewis points out,[35] this does not furnish an any given individual with a reason why *he* should be the giver. Suppose, to take one case,

---

[33] Lamont does say, in the course of his discussion, that such a good is "relative" (*Philosophy of Humanism,* p. 194). But what he means by this, it appears, is simply that an action may be useful or humane in one context and not in another. The general principle of concern for the greater welfare seems to hold, in his mind, as a valid ideal throughout the discussion. While he calls this principle is an "assumption" (p. 207), he treats it as being a desirable one nonetheless.

[34] A view of this kind seems to be expressed by Kai Nielsen. "Secular morality," he writes, "starts with the assumption that happiness and self-awareness are fundamental human goods and that pain and suffering are never desirable in themselves. It may finally be impossible to prove that this is so, but if people will be honest with themselves they will see that in their behavior ... they subscribe to such a principle." See Nielsen's *Ethics Without God* (London: Prometheus Books, 1973), p. 58.

[35] See discussion in *Abolition of Man*, Part II.

he is told that his effort on the battlefield may confer some benefit on others and their posterity. Perhaps indeed, says Lewis, it will. But on what basis, given materialist assumptions, can this individual prefer to take the risk?

Every appeal to such things as pride, honor, or shame is excluded. For these things, again, have no objective basis. They are, by the hypothesis, mere accidents, quirks of the psyche grounded in material happenstance. It may be that I do have some impulse to lay down my life for certain things - for my family, for the cause of democracy, or whatever. But what of it? It remains, on the reductionist hypothesis, an open question as to what I ought to do.

Lamont says that anti-intellectualism should be eradicated. This view, I think, is right and admirable. Such things as unfounded dogma and entrenched superstition, it seems to me, ought not to impede human progress. I myself am wholly persuaded that biologists, astronomers, anthropologists, and others, should be able to conduct their investigations without being stifled as they often have been.[36] But on what grounds can a materialist hold that this progress, and the open-mindedness that conduces toward it, is an *intrinsic* good?

Consider also Wright's discussion. It, too, expresses concern for human welfare without appeal to extra-natural principle. Our values, he imagines, arise from our chemistry. By understanding this, we can begin to emancipate ourselves from accidents that have hitherto "conned" us into maintaining certain policies.[37]

---

[36] See, again, a number of Russell's related essays in his *Religion and Science*.

[37] See Wright's footnote, p. 340.

Thus there are, on Wright's view, no higher values to which we must conform. This, he imagines, does not leave us adrift, for within nature itself we may find our moral bearings. To do this, we must examine our instincts, and subject each one to the test of how it bears on the common good. We ought then to employ our insight to create for ourselves a happier and healthier environment. The concern that lies at the heart of most moral positions, he believes, is that of human welfare - of what will bring about pleasant experiences, and will avoid painful ones, for those who are affected by our actions.[38] A knowledge of our origins will help us to better understand ourselves and to determine social policies.

Nature itself is not prescriptive. It does not supply us with principle. Thus our retributive impulse, once again, does not tell us how we ought to behave (either singly or as a society) toward others. We need not respect it just because it is *there*. Or else we commit the fallacy, says Wright, of deriving an *ought* from an *is*[39] - of inferring a judgement of value from some fact about the natural world.

---

[38] We may, he suggests, consider other factors besides human happiness in determining the moral equation, but no one, Wright contends, regards this consideration as being irrelevant. Even such non-utilitarian ideals as fairness and liberty, he imagines, tend to rely, in the end, upon human happiness for their plausibility. When pressed in argument, he notes, "you probably have a tendency to justify your trump cards in utilitarian terms," as, for example, by claiming that a widespread habit of cheating would lead to chaos and overall human detriment, and that if liberty is denied to some, no one will feel secure (p. 332 and following).

[39] It is a mystery, writes Hume, how writers manage to leap from statements of empirical fact to judgments of value. An author, he notes, "proceeds for some time in the ordinary way of reasoning ... when of a sudden I am surpriz'd to find, that instead of the usual copulations ... *is*, and *is not*, I meet with ... *ought*, and *ought not*. This change is imperceptible; but is, however, of the last consequence. For as this *ought*, and *ought not*, expresses some new relation ... 'tis necessary that it shou'd be observ'd and explained." (*Treatise*, p. 469)

Wright is correct, I believe, in his claim that the presence or absence of an instinct does not supply us with moral directive. (Lewis, it may be recalled, has said the same thing, albeit while steering the argument elsewhere.) But where do we find such a directive if we remain within the natural sphere? It is quite likely, once again, that a society of persons who care about one another fares better, on the whole, than one comprised of persons who do not. It is probably true, as well, that if I am perceived as being a decent individual, I stand to reap certain social rewards that I might not reap otherwise. But why should I think human happiness, or the general good, has any worth unto itself?[40]

Perhaps it will be said that I *should* want to benefit it - that any sound and healthy individual can see that it is better to help human beings than to harm them. Quite possibly they are right - that one should help others may be intuitively self-evident. But what sort of truth is it? We cannot, as Wright himself admits, look to the intuition itself, for it is merely a fact of nature without prescriptive content. We must instead maintain that this instinct (unlike certain others) is worth respect - that it leads us in the right direction. But the claim that such an intuition has this property - that it not only exists, but *reveals* to us something - goes beyond the realm of nature. Claims about what we ought to do involve not merely science, but principle - truth, in other words, concerning our rightful stance toward the world that science reveals. Such claims thus require

---

[40] It is worth adding that Wright himself seems to notice this problem, for he acknowledges that some would question the unconditional worth of human happiness. Yet such an ethic, he believes, can withstand this challenge, though space, he adds, does not permit "the dissertation-length defense" that such a claim requires. (p. 334)

an ontology (an accounting, or an inventory, so to speak, of what is real) wider in scope than the one that science provides.

But all of our moral experience, some will say, is ultimately grounded in our genes. All of it is thus merely the by-product of biological accident. And so it does no good to go outside of nature to understand value. I think, however, that this line of argument begs the question. It may be true, as Wright suggests, that such experience has certain biological prerequisites. (A human being, after all, typically has such experience, while a snail does not.) But this observed relationship between experience and genetic constitution does not mean that value is a merely biological phenomenon.

The fact that a given level of organic development precedes an experience says nothing as to the nature of its object. The presence of the optic nerve, for example, is a prerequisite of seeing light, but this does not make light any less real. Perhaps conscience, too, has a referent, albeit of a different kind. Certain developments of the brain are presumably necessary likewise for the event of conscience. But this by itself tells us nothing as to how conscience ought to be interpreted. It may be that this prerequisite structure provides the occasion for *knowledge*. Perhaps it allows us not only to feel *as if* something (say, justice) is real, but to see its reality.

Moral value, observes Janet, is a species unto itself. It is not like the value of money or pleasure. It cannot be derived either, from any set of sensory facts. From the standpoint of sensation, nothing can be more important than the preservation of life itself, which is needed for experience of any kind. Yet from a moral standpoint, it seems, we find things even more valuable - such things, for example, as honor, truth, and justice, that may on occasion take precedence over all else.[41]

Our ordinary common-sense convictions about value, Janet argues, require an outlook that takes us beyond natural limits. We commonly suppose that some things are better than others, that one thing may exceed another in its quality. Thus we think that friendship is better than selfishness, that nobility of character is higher than servility. We imagine also that nature may evolve from lower goods to higher ones, as in the development of human intelligence from the intelligence of lower life forms.

We suppose, for all practical purposes, that these relations are "absolute," that they are as real as those, say, in the disciplines of material science or mathematics. But if reality, explains Janet, has in it "only physical laws" (if, in other words, materialism is true), then such claims have no basis. If there were, he writes,

> a purely physical order of things - that is to say, one in which all phenomena could be brought under physical and mechanical laws, in which life, thought, will, liberty, and love were merely chemical combinations - on what ground, I ask, could one affirm that certain things are *worth* more than others; that one act is more excellent and noble than another; that love is worth more than selfishness, science than gluttony, the beautiful than the voluptuous, nobility of soul than base flattery; in a word, that the goods of the soul are superior to those of the body, and the happiness of a man is superior to that of an animal?[42]

---

[41] *The Theory of Morals*, p. 121.

[42] *Ibid.*, pp. 123-24.

From the standpoint of nature, one thing is worth as much as any other. For within this scheme every event, every action and outcome, occurs in conformity with the same laws and is equally necessary. Each thing is made of the same stuff; it shares the same source and the same basic nature. When you say, on the other hand, that one thing is truly better than another, "you can do so only because you attribute to one something more than to the other - because you discover in one something that is lacking in the other." But what sort of thing must this be? If everything is reduced to material chemistry, what is it, asks Janet, that "makes a privileged character of some actions, and leads us to declare them of a superior order?"

Materialists, he writes, explain the ascending degrees of nature and the progressive development of faculties in terms of more and more complex material *forms*. But complexity does not seem to be the same thing as value. A complicated imbroglio is not *per se* superior to a Grecian tragedy. Copernicus' view of the cosmos seems better, for its simplicity, than that of Ptolemy.

> If complexity is not perfection; if the number and the complication of elements do not suffice to give to one combination any more value than belongs to another; if, relatively to the primitive laws of matter, all combinations are merely resultants having no mutual relations of excellence and of dignity - then how can physico-chemical philosophy explain the idea of good?[43]

The notion of an objective value, of something that ought to be done for its own sake, is thus at its heart metaphysical. It requires an account of the truth that goes beyond the world disclosed by the senses. The human organism, of

---

[43] *Ibid.,* p. 125.

course, is a natural entity - a subject for disciplines like biology, medicine, and anthropology. But what can one say, within these confines, about a thing like *the inviolate nature* of the human personality? This, says Janet, "is not a fact like any other, for it involves right and duty; that is to say, *that which is not*, but *which ought to be!*" And how can such a thing as *that which ought to be*, he asks, be anything material?

If everything were reducible to material causes, then there could be no law other than "the law of that which is." In the physical order, Janet explains, that which is, should be, and everything that can be, is. If so, then morality assumes the reality of some order beyond the physical, one that is ideal, and that the free will endeavors to serve amidst the challenge of material circumstance. To the extent that we take such an idea seriously, we must suppose that the human being belongs to "two orders, to two kingdoms." If man's feet are plunged in the physical order, his head rises to an order that is "intelligible and divine."[44]

Moral Demand and Its Relationship to Human Destiny

Our acceptance of value is a basis, then, for certain inferences about the nature of reality. To say that good and evil exist, that something has value, that some things are truly required of us, requires us to suppose that there is more to the universe than material particles or the laws that govern them.

---

[44] *Ibid.,* p. 129.

On occasion it is said that moral experience provides us with a basis for other inferences - for belief, say some, in a supreme being.[45] It provides a ground, as well, some maintain, for belief in a future life.

Morality, I say, is thought to provide *a basis* for such beliefs. Rarely is it claimed that morality *proves* them. For moral experience is open to more than one theoretical interpretation. It may be that the reductionist account is correct; it may be, for all we know, that this phenomenon of conscience is merely a biological accident. It is possible that the moral impulse thus reflects nothing beyond itself.

Yet I have argued, by the same token, that this reductionist account does not square with the attitude that we take toward values in daily life. This account, I maintain, cannot provide us with a morality that speaks to us with authority. Our acceptance of morality as absolute (in other words, as objective and unconditionally binding) demands from us an implicit rejection of such an account if we are to be consistent.

Morality, believes Kant, is instructive. We cannot have, he says in *The Critique of Pure Reason*, theoretical assurance of such things as moral freedom,

---

[45] Thus Cardinal John Newman, to cite one example, maintains that our experience of shame in transgressing the voice of conscience provides us with evidence of a supernatural object toward which these feelings are directed. See J. H. Newman, *A Grammar of Assent*. Ed. C. F. Harrold (New York: David McKay Co., 1947), pages 83-84. This book had its first printing in 1870. The argument is cited and discussed by John Hick in his *Philosophy of Religion* (Englewood Cliffs, New Jersey: Prentice-Hall, 1990). See chapter 2, "Arguments for the Existence of God". As Hick notes, Newman's argument tends to overlook the naturalistic alternatives to his interpretation of conscience.

God's existence, and the survival of the soul.[46] Yet he argues later, in his *Critique of Practical Reason,*[47] that we have a basis for believing in them. Our justification, he explains, lies in our moral experience. In the remainder of this chapter I will discuss Kant's several formulations of this argument along with a few of its interpretations. I will also sketch, as I see it, the central line of argument that emerges from his discussion.

There are certain things, says Kant, that we must believe if we accept the moral law as binding upon ourselves. These things, again, cannot be rationally demonstrated (even if history contains many efforts in this direction). They are instead propositions that we must accept, for practical purposes, as being true in order to remain consistent with our moral convictions. These postulates, as he calls them, are those of freedom of the will, personal immortality, and the existence of God.

We must suppose ourselves to be free, thinks Kant, if we believe that the moral law has any claim upon us. For such a belief assumes the reality of a demand to which the will is subject, and by which it can abide (or not) as it chooses. If the will lacks sovereignty - if it is determined instead by forces of nature - then this choice is an illusion. If we accept the moral law as being real, we must assume that the will is independent of the world of the senses and can

---

[46] Immanuel Kant, *Critique of Pure Reason.* Trans. Norman Kemp Smith ((New York: St. Martin's Press, 1965). See especially Part II of the Transcendental Dialectic.

[47] Immanuel Kant, *Critique of Practical Reason.* Trans. T. K. Abbott (Amherst, New York: Prometheus Books, 1996). See especially chapter II, Part 6.

conform itself to "the law of an intelligible world."[48] We must believe, in other words, that human beings are capable of acting *upon principle* and are not bound by laws that govern nature.

Furthermore, we are morally required to achieve the condition of "the highest possible good." We are required, in other words, to bring about a state of affairs that is the best possible from a moral point of view. This state of affairs, which Kant names the *summum bonum*, is nothing less than a community of morally perfect individuals enjoying pure happiness. Since we are required to achieve this state of affairs, its realization must be possible. But this means that the requisite condition of our own moral perfection - that is, *holiness*, or "the perfect accordance of the will with the moral law" - must likewise be possible, since it is "contained in the command" to bring about this good in its entirety.[49]

And yet holiness, reasons Kant, is a thing of which no rational being in this world is "at any moment of his existence" (in other words, in any finite amount of time) capable. Thus it can be attained only in an endless progress toward the goal. We are obliged, then, to think that our own existence is unlimited in time in order to allow this progress. We are obliged, in other words, to postulate the immortality of the soul.

We are obliged also, thinks Kant, to postulate the reality of a supreme being. For if we believe that this moral scheme is real, we must suppose that there exists a means by which this higher state of affairs can be brought into

---

[48] *Ibid.,* p. 159.

[49] *Ibid.,* p. 148.

being - "a cause of all nature, distinct from nature itself, and containing the principle of this connection ... of the exact harmony of happiness with morality."[50] We must suppose, in other words, that there exists a power in whose sovereign hands happiness is conjoined with deservedness of its enjoyment.

Kant's argument, as one might imagine, has given rise to a great deal of discussion. It is perhaps worth noting, before going further, some of the ways in which his argument has been treated by hostile critics.

Kant, says Bertrand Russell,

> invented a new moral argument for the existence of God, and that in varying forms was extremely popular during the nineteenth century. It has all sorts of forms. One form is to say that there would be no right or wrong unless God existed.[51]

The implicit premise, in this case, is that right and wrong in some obvious way do exist, in which case God (and so also the judgment hereafter) must exist as well. Surely, as Russell contends, this argument is naive. But Kant himself, as we have seen, does not argue in this way. He does not maintain that God's existence is what makes possible the existence of right and wrong. Rather he argues that *if we accept* the moral law as binding upon us, then we must suppose that its obligation can be met. And this, as noted, requires the assumptions that make such an obligation coherent. Belief in our own existence hereafter is required in order to achieve rational consistency with the belief that we must achieve moral perfection.

---

[50] *Ibid.*, p. 151.

[51] See Russell's "Why I Am Not a Christian", the title essay in Russell's earlier cited volume *Why I Am Not a Christian*, p. 12.

This, as explained earlier, is not a proof of God's existence, or of the soul's eternity; rather it is an argument to show that our acceptance of the moral law (the acknowledgment, in other words, that this law is binding upon us) carries with it certain practical implications. It is not a proof, I say, because we cannot prove the existence of this obligation. But this does not mean that we must remain agnostic. For if we acknowledge the presence of this demand in daily life, we ought to consider further what conditions would make it possible.

Further on Russell says that there exists

> another very curious form of moral argument, which is this: they say that the existence of God is required in order to bring justice into the world. In the part of this universe that we know there is great injustice, and often the good suffer, and often the wicked prosper, and one hardly knows which of those is the more annoying; but if you are going to have justice in the universe as a whole you have to suppose a future life to redress the balance of life here on earth.[52]

This reading of the argument, incidentally, is not confined to humanist thinkers. It seems to be the one, for example, that David Lorimer has in mind in a book that elsewhere makes a case of its own (though not on moral grounds) for personal survival. Lorimer says of Kant that while he is

> unable to assert the immortality of the soul on empirical grounds, Kant claims to be able to do so on practical grounds. He argues that it is clear that the individual does not receive the just deserts of his conduct in this world, therefore, given the assumption of the justice of God ... there must be another life which balances the accounts of this one.[53]

---

[52] *Ibid.,* p. 13.

[53] David Lorimer, *Survival? - Body, Mind and Death in the Light of Psychic Research* (London: Routledge and Kegan Paul, 1984), p. 106.

It is, as Russell observes, a strange line of reason. Does the moral deficiency of this world provide us with reason to expect an improvement elsewhere? Normally, and as a working inductive rule, one does better to infer, from a given sample, more of the same. So if one opens a crate of oranges, for example, and sees the top ones gone bad, one does not expect the others to be good for the sake of balance. More likely the box just contains bad oranges.

I think that Russell's criticism of this argument is a fair one, but the argument (as Russell himself may realize) is quite different from the one offered by Kant. For Kant does not take the injustice present in this world to be *evidence* for justice in another. Rather, he says that if we recognize the need to conform our actions to the moral law - and ultimately, then, to achieve holiness - then we must believe the universe to be such as to allow our eventual success. If we prize justice, thinks Kant, we must accept it as our goal. We must likewise believe that this goal is reached.

It is sometimes said that moral arguments involve a presumptuously high estimate of human worth. Reflecting on Kant's discussion, Corliss Lamont says that the argument reduces itself to the claim "that men's moral aspirations are so excellent and noble that there must be an immortality which will allow their complete fulfillment."[54]

Here again, I think, the intended criticism misses the point, for Kant does not argue for immortality from any starting point of human excellence or nobility. He begins instead with the claim that we as moral beings face a valid claim upon

---

[54] *The Illusion of Immortality,* p. 163.

our lives. This involves no assumption about human excellence *per se*; it presupposes only that such a thing as excellence exists, and that we are subject to its standard. The validity of the standard, and the extent to which any given human being respects it, are separate questions. Our moral status is determined by our response to the challenge. There is nothing inherently noble or elevated in our condition, other than to the extent that we ourselves willfully determine it. This is not to say, of course, that human beings are worthless. We must recognize the inherent value of others (and of ourselves) as free and rational agents if we are to act morally at all. But such action does not presuppose any presently fixed moral excellence in human nature.

Kant's argument has inspired sympathetic discussion, as well. One of the most memorable examples is contained in Hastings Rashdall's two-volume masterpiece *The Theory of Good and Evil*. Our consciousness of morality, says Rashdall,[55] requires of us certain assumptions about ourselves and the world in which we live if we are to make sense of it. The first of these is that the self is real and enduring, and that it is the real cause of its own actions. If we are to retain our moral convictions, writes Rashdall, then we must suppose that these actions are "the work of a single self which has a definite character of its own, a spiritual character which expresses itself in those actions, and which is susceptible of spiritual changes and amenable to spiritual influences."[56]

---

[55] Hastings Rashdall, *The Theory of Good and Evil* (London: Oxford University Press, 1907). Two volumes. See especially volume II, Book 3, "Man and the Universe".

[56] *Ibid.*, vol. II, p. 200.

If selfhood is an illusion, if it can be splintered into some empty succession of moments, or reduced to the status of material accident, then the true origin of our actions lies elsewhere. In which case, all talk of value and responsibility, it seems, is an illusion. If instead such things are real, then the self must be a substantial thing; it must endure through time as the subject of deliberation, choice, and responsibility - so we must believe, if we are to retain our moral beliefs. When we have admitted, argues Rashdall,

> that knowledge is not mere subjective feeling or passive experience, that the self is as real as or more real than any 'thing' of which Physical Science can tell us, and that the self causes certain events which are commonly spoken of as its actions, then we are able to recognize the reality of duty, of ideals, of a good which includes right conduct.[57]

Investigation, says Rashdall, reveals more. We say oftentimes that the moral law has a real existence, that there is "something absolutely true or false in ethical judgements" whatever the prevailing human opinion. We commonly say, for example, that courage exceeds cowardice, that justice is worthy of our commitment. We believe such things strongly enough to act on them, even at cost to ourselves. If we want to retain this outlook, says Rashdall, we ought "to face the question *where* such an ideal exists, and what manner of existence we are to attribute to it."

Our moral conviction thus takes us, once again, outside of the material world. For on materialistic assumptions, the moral ideal cannot be regarded as a real thing. It may exist in the imagination, and may play a role, perhaps even a

---

[57] *Ibid.*, vol. II, p. 206.

powerful one, in the motivational process. But it cannot *compel respect* when we lack the inclination to abide by it.

An absolute moral law, writes Rashdall, "cannot exist *in* material things." Such a law does not exist, either, within the mind of any given human being. It must then reside in a source that is not subject to such limitations; it must exist, in other words, in a source from which all reality is derived. Thus the notion of an objective morality, writes Rashdall,

> implies the belief in God. The belief in God, if not so obviously and primarily a postulate of Morality as the belief in a permanent spiritual and active self, is still a postulate of a Morality which shall be able fully to satisfy the demands of the moral consciousness. It may conveniently be called the secondary postulate of Morality.[58]

Such a belief takes us still further. For morality, says Rashdall, cannot be merely a thing known or envisioned by some greater intelligence. There can be, he explains, "no meaning in the idea of Morality for a being who is mere Thought and not Will." If our own morality (that is, our own limited moral consciousness) is a revelation, in some degree, of the truth, then it tells us something about *the nature of the end* toward which reality is moving. If our own conception of *good* has its counterpart in the divine mind, then the universe

> is itself governed by the same Mind which is the source of our moral ideas, and must be ultimately directed towards the end which the true moral ideal, disclosed however imperfectly in the moral consciousness of man, sets us up as the goal and canon of human conduct.[59]

---

[58] *Ibid.*, vol. II, p. 213.

[59] *Ibid.*

The universe itself, in other words, must have an end that commends itself to this mind, and thereby to all genuine moral understanding. Our own judgment, so far as it is valid, thus gives us some indication of its direction. It must be an end that the best human judgment, seeing it in its entirety, would pronounce to be good.

How does this bear on the question of human survival? If the end revealed to our own consciousness is the end of God, it is likewise the end of the universe. This end must be such "as to make the being of the world better than its non-being." Otherwise the world has no justification.

What must this end involve? Let us suspend, for a moment, the issue of another life and render our verdict on the world before us. Can anyone, Rashdall asks, imagine that the world, in its present condition, is a legitimate end? It is only, he maintains, when we think of this life as a means to something beyond itself that we have the prospect of an answer. This end cannot be merely, say, the advantage gained by future generations from the errors of those before. That the pain of one generation will be rectified by the pleasures of another has no basis in ethics and none in history, either. There is as little empirical justification for an optimistic view of the future of humanity "as for an optimistic view of its past or its present."[60]

Only, it seems, if we suppose that this life "has an end which lies in part beyond the limits of the present world order" can we find an explanation. If, says Rashdall,

---

[60] *Ibid.*, vol. II, p. 215.

> human life be a training-ground and discipline for souls wherein they are being fitted and prepared for a life better alike in a moral and a hedonistic sense than the present, then at last we do find an adequate explanation of the willing of such a world by a Being whose character the moral consciousness at its highest presents to us as Love.[61]

It is not just the balance of good and evil that makes it difficult to justify this world. The problem, as much as anything, is its *distribution*. Our common thinking about reward and punishment is instructive, in this regard, for it expresses the realization that moral goodness and happiness ideally belong together. Virtue by itself cannot be the whole good, for justice demands that it be accompanied by a proportionate happiness. If the universe does not have this direction, its character is defective. In this life, Rashdall observes, "nothing but the roughest and most general tendency to such a coincidence, if even that, can possibly be discerned." Justice is not realized in present human experience.

Our moral sensibility may itself bring pain into the world that is undesirable from a moral point of view. Consider, says Rashdall, the features of a developed moral consciousness - the pain that comes with sympathy, the anxiety of a scrupulous conscience, the discomfort that comes with failure to fully attain one's own moral ends. There is thus little correspondence in this world between virtue and happiness. The relationship between these two things may even be inverse.[62]

The deeper our faith in the rationality of the universe, "the stronger becomes our unwillingness to believe that such an order can be final and

---

[61] *Ibid.,* vol. II, p. 216.

[62] Indeed Christendom, he writes, finds its highest ideal "in a man of sorrows." (p. 217)

permanent." It is for this reason that "a sincere theism has nearly always carried with it a belief in Immortality." Such a belief, in whatever culture it appears, seems to have an intensity proportionate to that culture's moral strength. A belief in immortality, Rashdall concludes, is a warranted postulate for all those who find the present constitution of things to be unfitting of a being whose nature and purpose is revealed "in our own moral consciousness."

A more recent discussion is found in C. S. Lewis' *Mere Christianity*.[63] There are, Lewis writes, two odd things about the human race. First, they are "haunted" by the idea of some sort of behavior that they ought to practice - what you might call "fair play," he writes, "or decency, or morality, or the Law of Nature." Second, they do not always practice it. These facts are of use in knowing something about the kind of universe in which we live.

Herein is an essential difference, says Lewis, between human beings and the rest of the world. In the case, say, of a stone or a tree, no one supposes that this thing *ought* to be in any particular condition. It may be said that the stone is the wrong shape for a given purpose (say, its use in a rockery), or that a tree is bad in that it does not yield the crop desired. But no one actually blames the object for its shortcomings. Words like 'wrong' and 'bad', in this context, mean just that the thing is not suitable for the purpose one has in mind.

When one uses the word 'law' in connection with material objects, there is no element of prescription involved. One says that the stone obeys the law of

---

[63] C. S. Lewis, *Mere Christianity* (New York: Touchstone Books, 1980).

gravitation, but it is not as if the stone had it in mind to do something else, or that it moves as it does by some willful choice. So-called laws of nature, as Lewis observes, only mean "what Nature, in fact, does." There is no reason to entertain the existence of an ideal, in this regard, over and above the actual events.

But *the law of decent behavior* is a very different thing. For in this case, we refer not merely to "what human beings, in fact, do." Some human beings act in ways quite contrary to this law, and indeed no human being obeys it altogether. A law of gravity tells us how stones behave when we let go of them; a law of human behavior tells us, by contrast, how human beings ought to behave whether they comply with it or not. In other words, says Lewis, when dealing with human beings "something else comes in above and beyond the actual facts" of observation.

Efforts to translate this latter kind of law into something plain and ordinary, he observes, never seem to capture what is in it. Sometimes we hear, for example, that good behavior is just behavior that tends to benefit human beings on the whole. Persons see, it is claimed, that they cannot live safely in a society without certain rules. Thus they devise rules of their own making that will safeguard the common good.

Does such an explanation suffice to make sense of our present moral experience? It is true, of course, that human beings fare better in societies where they are kind to each other. But suppose that someone asks, "Why ought I to be unselfish?" The answer, presumably, is that unselfishness is good for society. But why should I care what happens to society?

The only answer to this, says Lewis, is that one *ought* to care, that one ought to be unselfish. This, he explains, is the logical stopping point. And so it should be. One need not go further. The moral law is not simply a fact about human nature, as the law of gravitation is a fact about the nature of material objects. And neither is it a mere fancy, for "we cannot get rid of the idea," and most of what we think about human beings would turn into nonsense if we did. Nor is this law simply an expression of how we would like others to behave for our own sake. In some cases we approve of behavior that runs contrary to our own interest, and disapprove of behavior that might serve us quite well.

This law, says Lewis, presents itself to us as "a real thing - a thing that is really there, not made up by ourselves." And yet it is not a fact "in the ordinary sense," as an observable thing (like our actual behavior) is a fact. Perhaps, then, we shall have to admit that *there is more than one kind of reality*, that there is something real beyond ordinary fact, and that we find "pressing on us."[64]

There have been, Lewis observes, two broad views long present regarding the nature of the universe in which we live. The first of these is the *materialist* view. By this account matter and space "just happen to exist," and have always existed. They have happened, by some coincidence, to produce creatures like ourselves capable of thought and reflection. Somewhere along the way something hit our sun and made it produce the planets, and by the same happenstance, the chemicals needed for life, and the right temperature, and so on, with the eventual result being the world as we now have it.

---

[64] *Ibid.*, p. 30.

The second of these, by contrast, is the *religious* view. According to this view, the governing force of the universe is ultimately "more like a mind than it is like anything else we know." It is conscious and has purposes, and prefers one thing to another. It made the universe, and made it partly, at least, for the sake of creating sentient beings in some measure like itself.

Which of these views is the more reasonable? One cannot, says Lewis, appeal to science for this answer. For science can only tell us how things happen in the visible sphere; as to whether there exists something behind this phenomenon, something itself invisible and yet governing the world as a whole, it cannot say. Even if science could one day answer every question about what exists in the universe, further questions would remain - why, after all, is there such a universe in the first place, and what is its real meaning?

This does not mean that we are condemned to complete uncertainty about such things. For there is one thing in the universe that we know about from within, and know more intimately than anything we know by way of sensation. This one thing is man. On this subject we are not mere observers. For we do not merely see humanity; it is what we *are*. With respect to ourselves, we are "in the know"; we have an inside information that we do not have about other kinds of reality. And what we discover when we attend to the facts is that we are under a law that is not of our own making, one that we cannot forget, and one that we truly ought to obey.

This, Lewis insists, is not empirical knowledge. It is not something that we gain by outward or scientific observation. We gain it from the immediate facts of experience. An outside investigator, studying us in the way that we study such things as electricity or the chemistry of life, could not detect such a law no matter how long he continued the task. For this observation would provide him only with facts about what we do, and not about what we ought to do.

What does moral experience tell us about the universe? If, writes Lewis, there were a controlling force outside the universe, it could not show itself to us as one more fact about the universe itself ("no more than the architect of a house could actually be a wall or staircase or fireplace in the house"). In this respect we are in the same boat as the outside observer. But it could reveal itself, on the other hand, as an influence within consciousness, telling us something about how we are meant to behave. I cannot know what, if anything, controls the movement of inanimate nature, but I can know, from the inside, that there exists a power that has an interest in my behavior. Whatever is the particular nature of this power is a question perhaps not answerable, or at least not at this point of the inquiry. But surely physical matter itself cannot have such an interest.

In the past century, Lewis notes, there has appeared a seeming third alternative to the two views just discussed. It is sometimes known as a Life-Force philosophy, or as the view of Creative or Emergent Evolution. According to this line of thought, the events by which life has evolved on this planet are due not to mere chance, but to the "striving" or purposiveness of a force of some kind.

What kind of force might this be? Is it, asks Lewis, something with a mind, or is it something else instead? If it is the former, then perhaps it is a god of some kind, after all. And if not, then what is meant by attributing *striving* or *purpose* to it? This alleged third view thus seems to collapse, on closer look, into one of the two others.[65]

We are left, in any case, with the question of what we will do with this persistent voice within us - a voice that tells us that some courses of action are truly better than some others, and that we are being called upon to make the choice.

Kant's argument, then, has inspired much reaction. His account of ethics, in fact, is perhaps the most deeply influential of the past two hundred years. It expresses a powerful awareness of the reality and seriousness of the moral demand, and of the connection between this demand and the rest of our outlook on reality. In returning to his discussion, we might look for a moment at his conception of this demand, as brilliantly expressed in his work *Fundamental Principles of the Metaphysics of Morals*.[66] There is nothing, he writes, in all of reality that can be called good *without qualification*, except a good will. The

---

[65] This view, which Lewis attributes to such figures as George Bernard Shaw and Henri Bergson, is very likely generated, he thinks, by a kind of wishful thinking. For it gives one "much of the emotional comfort of believing in God and none of the less pleasant consequences. When you are feeling fit and the sun is shining and you do not want to believe that the whole universe is a mere mechanical dance of atoms, it is nice to think of this great mysterious Force rolling on through the centuries and carrying you on its crest. If, on the other hand, you want to do something rather shabby, the Life-Force, being only a blind force, with no morals and no mind, will never interfere with you like that troublesome God we learned about when we were children." (p. 35)

[66] The edition from which I cite is that translated by Thomas K. Abbott in *Kant's Ethics or Practical Philosophy* (London: Longmans, Green, Reader and Dyer, 1873). The relevant portions are reprinted with commentary in Peyton Richter and Walter Fogg, eds., *Philosophy Looks to the Future* (Prospect Heights, Illinois: Waveland Press, 1978).

goodness of this will is determined by its respect for the moral law. Such a will is thus not good because of what it brings about, but by the quality of its motive. Even, he writes,

> if it should happen that, owing to special disfavour of fortune, or the niggardly provision of a step-motherly nature, this will should wholly lack power to accomplish its purpose, if with its greatest efforts it should yet achieve nothing, and there should remain only the good will ... then, like a jewel, it would still shine by its own light ...[67]

We can best understand value, thinks Kant, by reflecting upon certain choices that we find in actual life. One such example involves generosity. To help others when we can is a duty. There are, moreover, some individuals so constituted that they derive, apart from any sort of vanity or self-interest, an enjoyment out of promoting the good fortune of others. Thus it may happen, for example, that some man or woman gives great sums of money to charity without even a thought for what personal advantage (say, publicity) might be gained in return. Yet an action of this kind, Kant maintains, however amiable it may be, however much affection it may have or may generate, has in it no moral worth. In value, it is on a level with other inclinations.

It is, in other words, something that one *feels* like doing, and for this reason (and no matter how much it may happen to benefit others) it is essentially self-serving. While surely it is not *im*moral (for it is consistent with what duty prescribes), it is not performed out of respect for the moral law. Moral worth, Kant maintains, is found only in those cases where duty and inclination are

---

[67] *Philosophy Looks to the Future*, p. 215.

opposed, where an individual thus suppresses his own desire and acts for the sake of duty itself.[68]

Kant's refusal to attribute any moral worth to generosity of the kind just described strikes many contemporary readers as being itself rather uncharitable. Can it be that an individual who enjoys, say, making sizeable contributions to community enterprises of art and education is doing nothing of moral consequence? Consider, by contrast, the person who reluctantly abstains from molesting a small child. Has this individual done something more admirable? Kant's attribution of worth to the latter action, and not to the former, has seemed implausible, if not outrageous, to many. Kant insists, however, that the difference between such actions is crucial.[69] Suppose, he writes,

> that the mind of that philanthropist were clouded by sorrow of his own, extinguishing all sympathy with the lot of others, and that while he still has the power to benefit others in distress, he is not touched by their trouble because he is absorbed with his own; and now suppose that he tears himself out of this dead insensibility, and performs the action without any inclination to it, but simply from duty, then first has his action its genuine moral worth.[70]

---

[68] Likewise, he explains, moral action "always costs the subject some sacrifice and requires self-compulsion, i. e., an inner constraint to do that which one does not quite like to do." (*Critique of Practical Reason*, p. 86) Our finite and natural condition, Kant believes, insures that there will always exist some tension between moral law and our own inclination.

[69] Kant, of course, does not mean by this that the benefactor and the would-be molester are *on the same level* in terms of their moral evolution. The latter individual, he thinks, has indeed done something admirable in resisting his present inclination, but he is also (all things equal) presumably in an inferior condition, and has yet to progress by his choices to the level of the other.

[70] *Philosophy Looks to the Future*, pp. 216-17.

And similarly,

> if nature has put little sympathy in the heart of this or that man ... if nature had not specially framed him for a philanthropist, would he not still find in himself a source from whence to give himself a far higher worth than that of a good-natured temperament could be?[71]

It is a powerful insight. Even if we do not share Kant's outlook in its entirety, this example strikes within us a chord of recognition. To see its point we must put ourselves, in mind's eye, in the position of this individual just described. What does such a choice involve? We all know what it is like to perform an act of charity, or justice, or honesty, when we have no particular aversion. But what is it like to perform such an action when it goes against our grain, when we really would prefer to do something else, and *its inherent goodness* is all that now recommends it?

A moment's reflection allows us to see the difference. There is indeed a special worth, perhaps even a heroism, in an action of this latter kind. It is this quality, Kant maintains, that invests such an action (independently, again, of its consequences) with a worth that surpasses all of the conditional goods (pleasure, comfort, knowledge, freedom, or whatever) that may exist in the universe.

Moral experience, believes Kant, puts us in contact with a different order of reality.[72] Herein, he thinks, we have insight into the universe and its real

---

[71] *Ibid.*, p. 217.

[72] The universe that I observe with my senses, he writes, all but annihilates my own importance. The moral world, by contrast, "infinitely elevates my worth as an *intelligence* ... in which the moral law reveals to me a life independent on animality and even on the whole sensible world ..." (*Critique of Practical Reason*, p. 191)

meaning. Let me cite here another of his arguments, one simple and yet telling, I think, in its force. It is contained in his *Lectures on Ethics*, under the heading of "Natural Religion". In this section, he speaks of the importance of morality as a foundation of higher religion.

Morality, says Kant, is an ideal that needs religion to imbue it with "vigour, beauty and reality." If we are to do justice to it, we must connect it in some way with a reality that transcends this sphere altogether.

> We are obliged to be moral. Morality implies a natural promise: otherwise it could not impose any obligation upon us. We owe obedience only to those who can protect us. Morality alone cannot protect us.[73]

In order for the law to exert its claim upon us, it must offer a certain promise. Clearly it does not promise our safety in this world. This much is obvious. Acceptance of its demand may cost us our security, our well-being, even our very existence, with respect to this life. Its promise instead concerns the greater scheme of which this life is a part. And it must be a genuine promise if this demand is real. This law can impose its obligation only if it does so in the name of final justice for all those who are subject to its command.

Morality, for this reason, cannot be a passive ideal having no connection with the actual course of human destiny. It must promise a return on all that has ever been done in the pursuit of its realization. If this rectification is not contained within the present world-order, it must occur elsewhere. Moral obligation, then, carries with it the implied promise of survival.

---

[73] Kant, *Lectures on Ethics*. Trans. Louis Infield (New York: Harper and Row, 1963), p. 81.

Kant expresses a similar thought in his *Lectures on Philosophical Theology*.[74] Here he observes that there must exist a life hereafter wherein "a creature ... who has made himself worthy of happiness through morality will actually participate in this happiness." For otherwise, he explains, "all subjectively necessary duties which I as a rational being am responsible for performing" (i. e., those obligations I perceive myself to have) will "lose their objective reality" (i. e., will turn out not to be genuine obligations after all).

Why, asks Kant, should an individual make himself "worthy of happiness through morality" if there is no being who can finally bestow that happiness upon him? A morality on its own, so to speak, and having no connection with destiny is a curious thing, for it is unworthy of respect. Thus, Kant says, without the prospect of this reward hereafter, "I would have to deny my own nature and its eternal moral laws." [75]

To see what he means, let us try to imagine, to the contrary, a universe containing moral demand but not survival. Let us then imagine a world inhabited by beings like ourselves, with impulses and tendencies (moral, religious, and otherwise) of the same general kind. Let us suppose that these beings are mortal, that their consciousness (while they may not realize it) ends once and for all at death. Thus whatever the quality of an individual's activity in this world, he or she comes at last to the same end - to extinction.

---

[74] Kant, *Lectures on Philosophical Theology* (Ithaca: Cornell University Press, 1978). These lectures come quite late in Kant's career, and may well express his most mature thought on the subject.

[75] *Ibid.*, p. 110.

Let us suppose, however, that these beings perceive themselves to be subject unconditionally to a moral law. Thus they find themselves, from time to time, in situations where they feel required to put duty ahead of self-interest. These situations, we may imagine, involve at times great risk and even sacrifice. Some of these individuals, let us suppose, respond admirably, on the whole, to the call, while others do not. Often the nobler ones suffer great losses as a result, while others profit by their baseness.

By now, let us imagine, this race has vanished to the grave. In looking back, what does it mean to say of these persons that they were ever *obligated* to choose a given course of action? Let us look, in particular, at those who suffered losses as a result of their integrity. Surely *justice itself* was not a product of their heroism, if only because they themselves met (albeit nobly) with an undeserved bad fate in the process. What, then, has commanded them to make these choices that *themselves* have produced such injustice? To what have these individuals owed their allegiance?

Perhaps it will be said that morality itself does not owe these individuals anything. For it is, some will say, an ideal, and not a promise at all. It offers no reward, but must be obeyed for its own sake. That worthy individuals should thus suffer is tragic. But this, it may be said, has no bearing on whether or not there exists moral demand in the first place.

Surely, I agree, we admire the individual who chooses the right course of action for its own sake and without expectation. But is there not something strange about a universe that provides the setting for such choices and extracts, with perfect indifference, this price? In such a universe, the moral law itself, it seems, produces the rankest injustice of all.

Let us turn now to an episode in our own world. Consider Viktor Frankl's concentration camp experiences during the second world war as recounted in his book *Man's Search for Meaning*.[76] As conditions worsened with time, explains Frankl, the test of integrity in these camps became greater. There were, in fact, two kinds of moral selection going on in this situation. First there were the Capos - prisoners themselves, in the role of trustees, given special privileges and chosen for their brutality.

At the same time,

> there was a sort of self-selecting process going on the whole time among all of the prisoners. On the average, only those prisoners could keep alive who, after years of trekking from camp to camp, had lost all scruples in their fight for existence; they were prepared to use every means, honest and otherwise, even brutal force, theft, and betrayal of their friends, in order to save themselves.[77]

The end of this passage is haunting. "We who have come back", he continues, "by the aid of many lucky chances or miracles - whatever one may choose to call them - we know: the best of us did not return."

Kindred examples abound in the pages of our own history. Consider, to cite one famous case, those one hundred and eighty-odd volunteers at a mission in San Antonio who made their stand for thirteen days in 1836 against thousands

---

[76] Viktor Frankl, *Man's Search for Meaning* (New York: Washington Square Press, 1984).

[77] *Ibid.*, pp. 23-27.

of Mexican troops for the cause of Texan independence.[78] The sacrifice that is inherent in certain kinds of heroism sometimes puts virtue and earthly fortune at drastic odds. The best action may sacrifice the agent.

To what end? Again, I say, we should admire an individual who faces duty, who goes even "above and beyond" it, for the sake of principle. All the more so, one must think, when his or her very life lies in the balance. But let us note also that the situation wherein such an individual chooses heroically *is itself* an atrocity when all is tallied. And, ironic as it may seem, a choice of this kind is often the very thing that contributes most to its offensiveness - to the gain of the most ruthless and to the loss of the most decent. It is this very choice that insures, for example, that the bravest among us will be least apt to survive in a situation of the kind that Frankl describes. We must then ask *what principle it is* that prescribes a choice productive of this outcome.

We commonly suppose, as a principle of conduct, that the moral law makes a valid claim upon our lives. Wherein resides its worthiness? Not, I submit, in the *result* of our obedience, if this world is the measure of it. The point of arguments offered by such philosophers as Kant and Rashdall, I believe, is that the story of the universe is not complete until justice is done. If we do not live in such a universe, then there is something tragically and morally wrong with this very situation in which we are called upon.

---

[78] For what may be the definitive account of this event and its principal figures, see William C. Davis, *Three Roads to the Alamo* (New York: HaperCollins, 1998). Alleged and graphic eyewitness accounts of the battle are contained in Timothy M. Matovina, *The Alamo Remembered* (Austin: University of Texas Press, 1995).

The essence of the argument, as I see it, is not that duty should be performed for the sake of reward, but that recognition of duty for its own sake presupposes ***a moral source worthy of obedience***. It thus presupposes that the arena within which this war is waged is one in which justice is sovereign. The law can only make its claim if it makes it righteously; only, that is, if this situation wherein we see and respond to this law is itself a righteous thing. But it can only be so if it is ultimately part of a greater course of events in which justice is realized.

This argument, as I conceive it, does not require us to suppose (although Kant does suppose it) that we must progress unto eternity to achieve our moral end. Nor does it require us to frame any precise theoretical account of the law itself (whether it is definable, say, as the command of a supreme being, or as some other thing instead). It requires centrally the belief that we are, at given times, faced with the task of conformity to its ideal - of responding to certain demands that cannot, as John Hick explains,[79] be rightfully set in the balance with any other interest whatsoever. The particular nature of these demands (those calling, in given cases, for such things as courage, honesty, fairness, and the like) will vary with their context. Their common characteristic, across each set of circumstance, is their authority.

It is possible, I acknowledge, that this law is an illusion - that it is ultimately a product of such things as genetic accident and influences of the

---

[79] See again John Hick, ed., *Classical and Contemporary Readings in the Philosophy of Religion*. For a particularly effective statement concerning moral demand and religious belief, see Appendix IV, "The Moral Argument", pp. 531-32.

environment upon the developing psyche. Or it may be the sacred and authoritative thing that we often imagine it to be. We have no theoretical basis to decide the case either way, and science, I think, must indeed remain neutral. Yet this does not mean, as I see it, that our choice in this matter is arbitrary. For the moral law has a primacy in our experience that overrides practical doubt. We are, at times, as sure of our duty as of any fact that sense perception discloses about the natural world.

The senses, it may be said, are better guides - for they deal in what is *tangible* - in what can be seen and tested. Yet there is nothing, so far as I can tell, that requires us to think that only tangible things are real, or that the moral faculty is any less reliable. Thus it means nothing, I think, to say that belief in an absolute value is unproven or "unscientific." That science should operate within the realm of the observable does not mean that only observable things are real. If we perceive ourselves to be subject to the moral demand - if this is evident to us, as evident as the fact that we are in the world at all - then this perception may reasonably be included within our world-view. It is as worthy of inclusion as is belief of any kind whatsoever.

If we accept the testimony of conscience, I contend, we are rationally bound to accept whatever else may help us to make sense of it. For it is contrary to reason to respect this source, to honor it in practice, while denying it in theory. Our acceptance of the moral law as binding upon us involves us implicitly in a view of reality, and thus also of our own destiny, that exceeds the bounds of this world.

In ending this chapter, a brief word of summary may be in order. These past three chapters have dealt, in general terms, with the theoretical possibility of survival and with the connection between survival and our present moral experience. In subsequent chapters I will examine the work of three different philosophers, those, I believe, who have made outstanding contributions over the past hundred years to the survival issue. The first of these is Frederic Myers, who helped to found the Society for Psychical Research in London in the late nineteenth century. In following chapters I will discuss two others, after which I will offer a discussion of the possible character of the next world itself.

Chapter IV

Empirical Evidence of Survival: The Case of Frederic Myers

> **If you wish to upset the law that all crows are black, you mustn't seek to show that no crows are; it is enough if you prove one single crow to be white. My own white crow is Mrs. Piper.**
>
> **William James, "Address of the President" before the Society for Psychical Research**

> **I receive, I transmit. I don't *create*.**
>
> **Keith Richards, veteran Rolling Stones guitarist on the subject of songwriting**

Frederic Myers was born in 1843. A Cambridge classicist, he devoted the latter part of his life to the question of human survival. In the process he became a psychologist and philosopher of the first rank. His two-volume work *Human Personality and Its Survival of Bodily Death* is counted by many the preeminent work of the psychical research movement. Myers taught at Cambridge for some years before becoming a government school inspector. He lived until 1901.

The Development of Psychical Research

The nineteenth century was a time of change. The past few hundred years had seen the rise of the sciences, culminating in the theory of natural evolution. With this rise had come a whole new perspective on our own origins and cosmic place. Empirical science, it seemed, was on its way to understanding all of reality, human beings included.

It was also a time when neither religion nor science, as each was presently constituted, seemed quite satisfying. On the one hand was a tradition that looked to the Bible - one that found in it an inerrant record of such things as the age of the earth and the origin of the race. On the other was a view that offered no room in its account for human spirituality. The former of these alternatives offered an answer that no scientifically informed person could accept; the latter made of human beings a kind of organic machinery without rhyme or purpose. The former view was untenable, while the latter made a fiction of much that seemed real in human experience.

Were these the only choices? Conventional religion, to be sure, was losing its hold. But there was more to human life, believed some, than materialists made of it. For experience contained, it seemed, even if only in rare instances, some inkling of a reality beyond the senses.

There were, said some, those odd cases in which one mind impinged on another by means of "thought-transference." There were sightings of apparitions, and seeming communication, in some cases, between this world and the next. And there were persons who claimed in perfect sobriety to have left this world and to have visited another. Were any of these cases genuine? Surely fraud would account for some. And if not fraud, then self-delusion, or error of some kind. But what if some of these episodes were real? There were some who supposed that they were, and that it was possible furthermore to subject them to investigation.

"In about 1873," writes Myers in the introduction to his *Human Personality*,

> - at the crest, as one may say, of perhaps the highest wave of materialism which has ever swept over these shores - it became the conviction of a small group of Cambridge friends that the deep questions thus at issue must be fought out in a way more thorough than the champions either of religion or of materialism had yet suggested. Our attitudes of mind were in some ways different; but to myself, at least, it seemed that no adequate attempt had yet been made even to determine whether anything could be learnt as to an unseen world or no ....[1]

This inquiry, as Myers envisioned it, would proceed not from religious tradition, nor from metaphysical speculation, but simply instead from experiment and observation - the same methods of "deliberate, dispassionate, exact inquiry" that yielded our knowledge of the natural world. The working hypothesis of such an inquiry, he states, is "that *if a spiritual world exists, and if that world has at any epoch been manifest or even discoverable, then it ought to be manifest or discoverable now.*"

---

[1] Frederic Myers, *Human Personality and its Survival of Bodily Death* (Salem, New Hampshire: Ayer Company, Publishers, Inc., 1992,) vol. I, p. 7. This edition duplicates the 1903 London publication of Longmans, Green, and Co.

Myers, as Suzy Smith observes,[2] undertook his project in an age when materialism ruled, a time when the alleged discovery of "man's soul-less descent from the apes" held center stage. It showed daring, at the time, to express the belief that man has a soul and to suggest that he survives his earthly demise. Myers, writes Smith, was a pioneer in the field of psychical research when virtually all pioneering around him headed in another direction.

If Myers was an analyst, warm blood still flowed in his veins. He was, said those who knew him, a lover of life, and not abstractions. His initial interest in survival was occasioned, Smith explains, by a personal relationship. In 1873, when Myers was 30 years of age, he fell in love with Annie Hall Marshall, the wife of his cousin Walter James Marshall, who lived at Hallsteads, Cumberland. The marriage was, for her, a reasonably happy one, yet unromantic. The proud and sensual young Myers, writes Smith, was passionately in love with her, though it appears, she adds, from what can be discerned, that Annie returned this love "only as far as was compatible with complete loyalty to her husband." Frederic and Annie walked together and talked ardently there in the valley at Hallsteads.

Annie died suddenly on August 29th, 1876. Her death, writes Smith, was a shattering blow to Myers, yet "the intensity of his feelings convinced him that they and their love could survive the death of the body."

---

[2] See Smith's editorial preface to her own edition of Myers' *Human Personality and Its Survival of Bodily Death* (New Hyde Park, New York: University Books, Inc., 1961).

From that time forward, observes psychical researcher W. H. Salter,[3] he had "a faith that satisfied his emotions, his intelligence and his moral sense in a way that he had not found possible in any of the phases of belief through which he had previously passed." Prior to that time Myers had developed an interest in the alleged phenomena of such things as mediumship and telekinesis, but had been unimpressed, on the whole, with purported demonstrations. In 1873, a few years prior to Annie's passing, he had come across his first convincing experience with mediumship. Some years later, notes Smith, a communication from Annie, through a medium, confirmed once and for all his belief in survival.

The *Magnum Opus*: Human Personality

Mediums, thought-transference, glimpses of another world - it all sounds quite sensational. This area, on the current view, is *paranormal*; it lies, in other words, outside the bounds of established reality. For this reason it tends to raise suspicion. Yet if this business of other worlds and special abilities seems odd to us, observes Brian Inglis,[4] we might bear in mind that our own tradition takes us deeply into its territory.

---

[3] Smith, preface. The quotation comes from Salter's "Our Pioneers", an article contained in the *Journal* of the Society for Psychical Research, volume 39, September, 1958.

[4] Brian Inglis, *Natural and Supernatural: A History of the Paranormal* (Dorset: Prism Press, 1992).

In Moses, for example, one finds "the archetype of shamanism." His vocation "is made clear to him by signs and wonders - the bush that burns but is not consumed by the flames; by clairaudience - the voice of the Lord sounding as if it came from the midst of the bush; and by the discovery that he can work magic."[5] The early literature of the Greeks abounds in references to oracles and seance-activity.[6] Interest in such things, Inglis explains, has not ceased with the progress of rational inquiry, but has endured through the middle ages, the Renaissance, and the Age of Reason to the present.

And yet no one, it seems, entertains the thought of subjecting these ideas to systematic inquiry. In the long story, writes Myers, of our effort to understand our own environment and to govern our own fate, there is one omission. It is, he observes, an omission so odd, so singular, that its statement is a paradox. We have never applied, to those problems that concern us most, the methods that have proved most useful in attacking all other problems in which we have an interest.

---

[5] *Ibid.*, p. 46. For related discussion, see Part I (chs. 1 - 4), "Historical", of James Hyslop's *Contact with the Other World* (New York: The Century Company, 1919). Concerning the reference to Moses, see for example *Exodus* 3: 1 and following.

[6] *Ibid.*, pp. 52-58. For more on the subject of oracles, see the essay "Greek Oracles" written by Myers. It is contained in his *Essays - Classical* (London: Macmillan, 1888). For a more recent discussion of oracles, see Robert K. G. Temple, *Conversations with Eternity* (London: Rider and Co., 1984). Temple's account stresses the probable role of drug use and hallucination in this activity. For an extensively researched account of unusual claims in ancient times, uncommitted but open in its assessment to the possibility of genuine paranormal occurrence, see E. R. Dodds' "Supernatural Phenomena in Classical Antiquity", contained in Dodds' *The Ancient Concept of Progress and Other Essays on Greek Literature and Belief* (London: Oxford University Press, 1973).

And what question stands above all others? It is, Myers explains, the question of whether or not the soul is immortal, or if not deathless to eternity, then capable, at least, of surviving the body. In this direction "have always lain the gravest fears, the farthest-reaching hopes, which could either oppress or stimulate mortal minds."[7]

In Myers is the fusion of scientist and classical scholar. *Human Personality* is at once a work of stupendous research and distinctly human sensibility. It aims at bringing together these unusual yet persistent data[8] of visions, premonitions, genius abilities, thought-transference, and what are today called "near-death" experiences under some rational unity of organization. It is seminal, and one feels its influence in practically every discussion in the field since. Myers himself, with characteristic modesty, maintained that the best test of its worth would be its rapid supersession by a better one. A century later, this remains perhaps the only respect in which the book might be said to have failed.

Central to Myers' thesis is the idea of what he calls a "subliminal" (*sub-limen*, "beneath the threshold") self, a reservoir, as he imagines, under the ordinary waking consciousness, one with strengths and capacities that now and then break through in highly interesting ways to the surface. It is this hidden source, he believes, that makes sense of these fleeting and diverse phenomena.

---

[7] Myers, *Human Personality*, vol. I, p. 1.

[8] A good many of the examples are drawn from an earlier work co-authored by Myers and two of his colleagues. See Edmund Gurney, F. W. H. Myers, and Frank Podmore, *Phantasms of the Living* (London: Kegan Paul, Trench, Trubner, and Co., Ltd., 1918). The book had its first printing in 1886.

If this notion of a hidden mind seems again fantastic, it is not completely foreign to experience. Indeed it is familiar to those who have studied conventional psychology, where its place is established. Our observation of human beings, notes psychiatrist Charles Brenner,[9] tells us that there is more to them than is present on the surface.

Some of this observation is clinical in its setting. Take the case where an individual is hypnotized, and while in the trance is told that he will do something after he has awakened. (For example, he is told that when the clock strikes two, he will get up from his chair and open a window.) Before being awakened, this subject is also told that he will have no recollection of the time that he is "under." Afterward he will carry out the instruction, says Brenner, without knowledge of what has impelled him to do it, either saying that he does not know or offering some rationalization. He is not conscious, at this time, of the reason for his behavior, nor can he find it by a simple act of memory or introspection. Thus we have an example of how an unconscious mental process has a dynamic effect upon behavior.

Related examples abound, some of them quite common. Consider, says Brenner, the case (famously noted by Freud) of "slips" - of conspicuous little errors of tongue, or pen, or memory. One has the feeling that these events are not just omissions, that they owe to more than mere lapses of the waking consciousness. Thus a young woman left waiting by her suitor, for example, may resent his

---

[9] Charles Brenner, *An Elementary Textbook of Psychoanalysis* (New York: Anchor Books, 1974).

neglect as much as if it had been planned.[10] We find cases, too, where an individual's real motives are more evident to others than to himself. (Consider, says Brenner, a "pacifist" ready to quarrel violently with anyone who contradicts his view, and who harbors a deep wish to fight, though his conscious attitude condemns it.)

Myers develops his conception of a subliminal self with wide-ranging observations concerning the nature and potential of the mind, some of which are well known to specialists in related fields. The data of psychopathology, for example, contain significant material. In the disintegration of the personality, notes Myers, we find cases in which whole new complex *persona* sometimes emerge and disappear. In these cases separate and thoroughly different identities seem to surface, at times with traits and capacities that exclude one another. While these may be unusual, they suffice to show that the mind has depths and capacities far in excess of what we normally imagine.[11]

---

[10] Brenner cites also the example of a patient whose session with a therapist was canceled on short notice for the therapist's convenience, and who ended up later, in trying to wile away the time, practicing on a field with an antique dueling pistol he had recently purchased. There seems, he says, to be a detectable aggression in this patient's behavior - of shooting at a target when he would otherwise be spending that time with the therapist!

[11] See vol. I, chapter 2, "Disintegrations of Personality" in *Human Personality*. Myers cites in this chapter numerous cases in which distinct persona alternately emerge within a single subject, often with mutually exclusive abilities. It some cases, it appears, these divisions of personality are associated with extraordinary perception. Myers cites (p. 64) the case of "Molly Fancher", who was rumored to have known, on occasion, the contents of letters in sealed envelopes. (See also pp. 352-54 of this volume for further discussion of the same case in the appendix to this chapter.)

In the data of genius, Myers believes, is contained another clue. Prodigies, he says,[12] show us depths unplumbed by conventional science. Genius, he thinks, involves not merely an imbalance or lack of completeness in development, but "a power of utilising a wider range than other men can utilise of faculties in some degree innate in all." It is a power, he maintains,

> of appropriating the results of subliminal mentation to subserve the supraliminal stream of thought; - so that an "inspiration of Genius" will be in truth a *subliminal uprush*, an emergence into the current of ideas which the man is consciously manipulating of other ideas which he has not consciously originated, but which have shaped themselves beyond his will, in profounder regions of his being.[13]

In this phenomenon, says Myers, there is no departure from normality, or none, at least, of a degenerative kind. Rather there is "a fulfilment of the true norm of man, with suggestions, it may be, of something *supernormal*; - of something which transcends existing normality as an advanced stage of evolutionary progress transcends an earlier age."[14]

Consider, for one, mathematical prodigies. An acquaintance of Myers named Edward Blyth supplies an account of his brother Benjamin, who demonstrated at an early age the ability to give answers to incredibly complex problems of mathematics. "When almost exactly six years of age," writes Blyth,

---

[12] In this regard Myers again goes against the mainstream. See, for example, his reference to Lombroso and others who suppose that genius is merely an aberration, a want of balance, as Myers puts it, involving "an over-development of one side of their nature; - helpful or injurious to other men as accident may decide." (vol. I, p. 71)

[13] *Ibid.*

[14] *Ibid.*

> Benjamin was walking with his father before breakfast, when he said, "Papa, at what hour was I born?" He was told four A. M.
> *Ben.* - "What o'clock is it at present?"
> *Ans.* - "Seven fifty A. M."
> The child walked on a few hundred yards, then turned to his father and stated the number of seconds he had lived. My father noted down the figures, made the calculation when he got home, and told Ben he was 172,800 seconds wrong, to which he got a ready reply: "Oh, papa, you have left out two days for the leap-years - 1820 and 1824," which was the case.[15]

Myers cites also the case of Vito Mangiamele, who at ten was taken to an academy in Paris after it had been discovered that he was able to solve problems normally requiring an extended knowledge of mathematics. As a test of his powers he was asked to give the cube root of 3,796,416. In about half a minute Mangiamele answered correctly that the number was 156. He was asked what number is such that its cube plus five times its square is equal to 42 times itself increased by 40.[16] In less than a minute he produced the answer of five, again correct.

There is something uncanny, says Myers, about ability of this kind. It is found at times in persons of average or even sub-average general intelligence. It may come mysteriously and may depart, as well, without any obvious reason. What is yet stranger, *it seems not to involve a calculating process* of the kind by which one might ordinarily gain the answer. On the whole, writes Myers, these prodigies seem to be unaware of "any continuous logical process" in arriving at

---

[15] *Ibid.*, vol. I, p. 81.

[16] Mangiamele was asked, in other words, to provide an solution to the equation $x3 + 5x2 - 42x - 40 = 0$. According to the account, he also produced, on a second try and in remarkably little time, the correct solution of 7 to the even more difficult equation $x5 - 4x - 16,779 = 0$. (vol. I, p. 84)

their answers. In some cases, "the separation of the supraliminal and subliminal trains of thought must have been very complete."[17]

In sometimes happens incredibly that individuals who excel in this fashion are deficient otherwise in mathematics itself. Myers cites the case of a man named Dase, a subject of considerable talent who appeared to be "singularly devoid" of any grasp of numerical processes, and who tried in vain for weeks to understand basic principles of arithmetic and geometry. In addition, it is noted, he could not comprehend a single word in any language but his own.

How then, are the answers obtained? Luck, one must think, is out of the question. We might say that they do it by "instinct" or "intuition," but this seems to be little more than another way of putting our ignorance. The more we ponder what is involved in solving problems of mathematics the "regular" way, in fact, the more mysterious the phenomenon becomes. Myers' answer is that these solutions owe to sudden bursts of insight from another and wider level of consciousness. Other faculties, such as premonition and mystical insight, he thinks, may owe to this same source.

The phenomenon of sleep, thinks Myers, merits similar attention. Sleep, he explains, ought not to be defined merely in *negative* terms. It is not, as some persons might imagine, merely an absence of waking faculties, but something more. It needs to be approached in positive fashion, as a phase of the personality co-ordinate with the waking state. Out of slumber comes "each fresh arousal and

---

[17] *Ibid.*, vol. I, p. 83.

initiation of waking faculties."[18] In sleep, some agency is at work that surpasses the efficacy of the waking state. It is a fact, albeit unexplained, that the regenerative quality of sleep "is something *sui generis*, which no completeness of waking quiescence can rival or approach."[19] A mere bowing of the head, if consciousness should cease for a second, may change a man's outlook on the world. At such moments, one feels that what has happened has been in some sense discontinuous, as if there has been "a break in the inward *regime*," involving more than just the cessation of outward stimulation.

In sleep is creativity. Some persons report, for example, the experience of images when passing into or out of it, images that exceed in vivacity what the conscious mind can willfully produce. Myers cites the experience of Robert Louis Stevenson,[20] who was able, by self-suggestion beforehand, to secure a vividness in his dreams that furnished him with material for his stories.

In sleep, we find on occasion the wellspring of "intellectual work of the severest order." There exists an analogy between the achievements of sleep and those of genius; in each there is "the same triumphant spontaneity, the same sense of drawing no longer upon the narrow and brief endurance of nerves and brain, but upon some unknown source exempt from those limitations."[21]

---

[18] *Ibid.*, vol. I, p. 122.

[19] *Ibid.*, vol. I, p. 123.

[20] *Ibid.*, vol. I, p. 126. Myers cites the "Chapter on Dreams" in Stevenson's *Across the Plains*.

[21] *Ibid.*, vol. I, p. 135.

It is worth noting, he adds, that the notion of "wanderings of the spirit" in the dream-state is practically universal across times and cultures. In the Stone Age, he imagines, one would find scarcely one skeptic venturing to deny it. And if this "palaeolithic psychology" has drifted from center stage of late, we might do well to take it seriously once again.

The lasting result of some dreams, thinks Myers, suffices to show that the dream has not been a mere entanglement of past waking experiences, but that it has "an unexplained potency of its own," drawn "from some depth in our being which the waking self cannot reach."[22] He cites instances of dreams that involve the acquisition of knowledge that cannot be accounted for by ordinary means. "Sometimes," he notes,

> there is a flash of vision, which seems to represent correctly the critical scene. Sometimes there is what seems like a longer gaze, accompanied, perhaps, by some sense of *communion* with the invaded person. And in some few cases - the most interesting of all - the circumstances of a death seem to be symbolically *shown* to a dreamer, as though by the deceased person, or by some intelligence connected with him ...[23]

There is, to cite one minor case, the case of two brothers named Warburton, one of whom had an uncannily accurate dream (correct even in its details of the setting, with which he was otherwise unacquainted) of the other's falling accident, at which time the latter brother was thinking of him. In reviewing the details of such testimony, says Myers, one gets the feeling that "a jerk were given to some delicate link connecting the two brothers" at some deep level.

---

[22] *Ibid.*

[23] *Ibid.*, vol. I, p. 137.

This *telepathy* (*tele-pathos*, "distant feeling"), as Myers calls it, is relatively common; it seems also to extend across the line to cases in which the "sender" has already departed this world. He cites the case of a Mrs. Storie, a woman known well to Myers' colleagues Edmund Gurney, Henry Sidgwick, and others, and who was in their estimate "a witness eminently deserving of trust."[24]

Storie describes in her account a disturbing dream in which it appeared that her husband William was killed at the edge of the tracks by a passing train. In this dream there seemed to be an added voice communicating information. Among the things revealed by this voice was the presence on board the train of a Reverend Johnstone, whom she saw in the vision before being told, "He's here."

About a week later, Storie received the news that indeed her husband had been killed in the manner (down to detail) that she had perceived. This episode, thinks Myers, is noteworthy in its features, including that of the Reverend, who was in fact present on the train though Storie could not have known it otherwise.[25] It suggests also, he thinks, communication from the other side.

Another relevant phenomenon is that of so-called motor automatism. It includes events of transmitted speech and writing that one encounters, for example, in the activity of seance-mediumship.[26] Myers and his colleagues

---

[24] *Ibid.*, vol. I, p. 144.

[25] *Ibid.*, vol. I, pp. 144-47.

[26] Myers classes these phenomena separately from those of "sensory" automatism, under which heading he places such things as inward voices and visions suggesting the direct influence of one mind upon another. For an enumeration of motor phenomena, see vol. II, p. 115.

conducted painstaking investigations of a number of mediums. Perhaps the outstanding subject was Mrs. Leonore Piper, who provided evidence over a number of years of contact with another world. Piper's mediumship, Myers notes, involved a form of "possession," during which her ordinary consciousness was suspended and her speech and writing were seemingly controlled by discarnate spirits using these motor faculties for communication.

Most of Piper's mediumship during the earlier period of her activity (roughly that of 1884-91) involved the communication of a curious entity who called himself *Dr. Phinuit*, and who claimed to have once been a French doctor. Phinuit's communication seemed to involve a mixture of the serious and the silly - in most cases, it is noted, whatever he could offer of value was given in the first portion of the trance, after which his communication degenerated into a trivia of "fishing questions and random assertions."[27] Some thus think it likely that "he" represented nothing more than a stratum (albeit an extraordinary one) of Piper's own consciousness.

Be this as it may, Phinuit many times demonstrated knowledge that neither Piper nor any of those present at a sitting could have acquired by ordinary means. On more than one occasion he predicted, for example, the deaths of persons who were known by the sitters. There seems to be no way to attribute this insight to Piper, or to anyone else of earthly residence. Myers cites several examples of this, including the following report from a sitter who is identified as Miss E. G. W.

---

[27] *Ibid.*, vol. II, p. 239.

> In the spring of 1888, an acquaintance, S., was suffering torturing disease. There was no hope of relief, and only distant prospect of release. A consultation of physicians predicted continued physical suffering and probably mental decay, continuing perhaps through a series of years. S.'s daughter, worn with anxiety and care, was in danger of breaking in health. "How can I get her away for a little rest?" I asked Dr. Phinuit, May 24, 1888. "She will not leave her father," was his reply, "but his suffering is not for long. The doctors are wrong about that. There will be a change soon, and he will pass out of the body before the summer is over."[28]

The father's death, concludes the report, occurred in the following month.

Another case, provided by Piper visitor Mrs. "M. N.", is as follows.

> About end March of last year I made her a visit (having been in the habit of doing so, since early in February, about once a fortnight). She told me that a death of a near relative of mine would occur in about six weeks, from which I should realise some pecuniary advantages. I naturally thought of my father, who was advanced in years, and whose description Mrs. Piper had given me very accurately some week or two previously ... My wife, to whom I was then engaged, went to see Mrs. Piper a few days afterwards, and she told her (my wife) that my father would die in a few weeks.

"About the middle of May," she continues,

> my father died very suddenly in London from heart failure, when he was recovering from a very slight attack of bronchitis, and the very day that his doctor had pronounced him out of danger. Previous to this Mrs. Piper (as Dr. Phinuit) had told me that she would endeavour to influence my father about certain matters connected with his will before he died.

---

[28] *Ibid.*, vol. II, p. 622. (This report originally appeared in the *Proceedings* of the Society for Psychical Research, vol. VIII, page 34. Detailed reports from the *Proceedings* of the Piper mediumship are reprinted with commentary on pp. 599-624 of vol. II of *Human Personality*.)

"Two days after I received the cable announcing his death," this account continues,

> my wife and I went to see Mrs. Piper, and she [Phinuit] spoke of his presence, and his sudden arrival in the spirit-world, and said that he (Dr. Phinuit) had endeavoured to persuade him in those matters while my father was sick. Dr. Phinuit told me the state of the will, and described the principal executor, and said that he (the executor) would make a certain disposition in my favour, subject to the consent of the two other executors, when I got to London, England.[29]

Three weeks afterward, reports this man, he arrived in London, and found the executor himself to fit the description that Phinuit had given. He found that the will, too, was substantially just as said. "The disposition," he concludes, "was made in my favour, and my sister, who was chiefly at my father's bedside the last three days of his life, told me that he had repeatedly complained of the presence of an old man at the foot of his bed, who annoyed him by discussing his private affairs."

It is, again, hard to know what to make of Phinuit, who never provided any real conformation of his earthly existence and never did establish his credentials as a French doctor. There is little record of Piper's first trances, notes Myers, and so it is unclear when this entity made his appearance. But the fact remains that Mrs. Piper was able to provide remarkably accurate information about a number of subjects to sitters over a period of many years - so much so, thinks Myers, that we have reason to suppose that this communicator does represent an independent intelligence.

---

[29] *Ibid.* (Quotes on p. 623; from *Proceedings*, vol. VIII, p. 120.)

As for the oddness of Phinuit's personality, Myers cites as one possible explanation the statements of a communicator named "Imperator", according to whom, he observes,

> Phinuit was an "earth-bound" or inferior spirit, who had become confused and bewildered in his first attempts at communication, and had, as we say, "lost his consciousness of personal identity." That such an occurrence is not uncommon in this life is plain from the cases to which I have drawn attention ... and we cannot prove it to be impossible that profound memory disturbances should be produced in an inexperienced discarnate spirit when first attempting to communicate with us through a material organism.[30]

After several years, Phinuit's communication trailed off and the dominant communicator became a individual named "G. P.", an entity who gave powerful evidence of being the deceased George Pelham (so-called), a friend and associate of several of the researchers prior to his death. Pelham himself, explains Richard Hodgson, was a young man who had met his death accidentally, and probably instantaneously, by a fall a few years earlier (in 1892) in New York. He was a lawyer by trade, but devoted himself to literature and philosophy.

Pelham, it appears, was a bright and energetic individual with a strong interest in the survival issue. He had published two books, each of which had received high praise. He was an associate of the Society, his interest being explicable "rather by an intellectual openness and fearlessness characteristic of him than by any tendency to believe in supernormal phenomena."[31]

---

[30] *Ibid.*, vol. II, p. 240.

[31] *Ibid.*, vol. II, p. 609. This discussion is reprinted from the beginning of Hodgson's "History of the G. P. Communications", contained in *Proceedings* vol. XIII, pp. 295-335.

He and Hodgson had engaged in several long discussions, recalls Hodgson, on various topics of philosophy, including one, perhaps two years before Pelham's death, on the subject of a possible future life. Pelham, a staunch skeptic, had maintained that such a life was not only impossible, but also inconceivable, while Hodgson had thought that it was at least conceivable. At the end of the discussion, Hodgson says,

> he admitted that a future life was conceivable, but he did not accept its credibility, and vowed that if he should die before I did, and found himself "still existing," he would "make things lively" in the effort to reveal the fact of his continued existence.[32]

Did Pelham keep his promise? The G. P. communication had a quality that separated it from many others on record. For one thing, it was not erratic, as had been the case with Phinuit. It was also highly impressive in its details. Myers provides a summary from the record of Hodgson,[33] written some years later, of its content. In it Hodgson attests to the detailed knowledge of the G. P. communicator with respect both to Pelham's actual friends and personal incidents concerning them. One example, to which Hodgson alludes, involved G. P.'s recognition (Phinuit being an intermediary in this instance) of one of a pair of studs worn by a Mr. Hart,[34] an acquaintance of Pelham who was present at an early sitting.

---

[32] *Ibid.*

[33] *Ibid.*, vol. II, pp. 242-42. Hodgson's account is taken from *Proceedings*, vol. XIII, pp. 328-30.

[34] "Mr. Hart" was a pseudonym, the sitter's real identity being concealed from Mrs. Piper, as was commonly the case, in order to keep her own knowledge of those persons involved in the sittings to an absolute minimum.

When asked by Hart "Who gave these to me?", G. P. replied, "That's mine ... I gave that to you." [Hart: "When?"] "Before I came here. That's mine. I gave you that." [Hart: "No."] "Well, father then, father and mother together. You got those after I passed out. Mother took them. Gave them to father and father gave them to you. I want you to keep them. I will them to you." Hart knew that Pelham's father had given the studs to him as a remembrance of his son. Only later did he ascertain that Pelham's stepmother had taken them from the body and had suggested to Mr. Pelham that they might make an appropriate response to Hart's request to be sent something as a keepsake.

There is not space here to cover all the details. By Hodgson's reckoning, the communicator demonstrated an extensive awareness of personal details of the lives of Pelham and those who knew him, and did not fail a single time in his recognition of Pelham's friends or events associated with them. At various sittings, notes Hodgson, G. P. made "appropriate comments concerning different articles presented that had belonged to G. P. living, or had been familiar to him." He also made inquiries about other personal articles not presented, and showed "intimate and detailed recollections of incidents in connection with them."[35]

In all, reports Hodgson, the G. P. communications

> have exhibited the marks of a continuous living and persistent personality, manifesting itself through a course of years, and showing the same characteristics of an independent intelligence whether friends of G. P. were present at the sittings or not.[36]

---

[35] *Human Personality*, vol. II, pp. 242-43.

[36] *Ibid.*, vol. II, p. 243.

"I learned of various cases," he continues,

> where in my absence active assistance was rendered by G. P. to sitters who had never previously heard of him, and from time to time he would make brief pertinent reference to matters with which G. P. living was acquainted, though I was not, and sometimes in ways which indicated that he could to some extent see what was happening in our world to persons in whose welfare G. P. living would have been specially interested.[37]

The Pelham case constitutes one of the most impressive on record of seeming communication across two worlds. Despite instances of this kind, however, occasional errors and oddities and the sometimes "dream-like" quality involved in much of trance-mediumship are taken by some as an indication of the invalidity of the entire enterprise. It does appear, on occasion, that the "messages" of mediums reflect not independent communication, but mind-states of the sitters present. This fact has persuaded many investigators to think that thought-transference among the living accounts for at least some of the material. It has been suggested also that mediumship, even when it is genuine, involves at times the added influence of the conscious or unconscious mind of the medium.[38]

There may exist, say some, other complicating factors besides. For what if there exist difficulties "over there" in making contact? It may be, suggests Hodgson, that communication from that side is an art, that it requires a certain gift, much like the earthly activities of painting or mathematics (or mediumship itself).

---

[37] *Ibid.*

[38] For a detailed and very balanced discussion of mediumship and its interpretation, see Alan Gauld, *Mediumship and Survival* (London: Paladin Books, 1983).

It may also be, he observes, that difficulties exist owing to the sheer change that death involves. "If my own ordinary body," he writes,

could be preserved in its present state, and I could absent myself from it for days or months or years, and continue my existence under another set of conditions altogether, and if I could then return to my own body, it might well be that I should be very confused and incoherent at first in my manifestations by means of it.[39]

"How much more would this be the case," he continues,

were I to return to *another* human body. I might be troubled with various forms of aphasia and agraphia, might be particularly liable to failures of inhibition, might find the conditions oppressive and exhausting, and my state of mind would probably be of an automatic and dreamlike character. Now, the communicators through Mrs. Piper's trance exhibit precisely the kind of confusion and incoherence which it seems to me we have some reason *a priori* to expect if they are actually what they claim to be.[40]

There is, in this regard, one other "G. P." item worth note. In a written communication of February 15th, 1894, he writes,

Remember we share and always shall have our friends in the dream-life, *i. e.*, your life so to speak, which will attract us for ever and ever, and so long as we have any friends *sleeping* in the material world; you to us are more like as we understand sleep, you look shut up as one in prison, and in order for us to get into communication with you, we have to enter into your sphere, as one like yourself, asleep. This is just why we make mistakes, as you call them, or get confused and muddled.[41]

G. P. was also able to produce information, unavailable to any of the sitters and only later confirmed, of the personal activity of his own father and of other parties in the sitters' acquaintance. Those present, says Myers, found it

---

[39] *Ibid.*, vol. II, pp. 253-54.

[40] *Ibid.*, vol. II, p. 254.

[41] *Ibid.* (Cited again from Hodgson's material.)

impossible to resist the belief that they were communicating with Pelham himself, who displayed in his ongoing messages not only knowledge of key facts, but "all the keenness and pertinacity which were eminently characteristic of G. P. living."

The enterprise of psychical research, and particularly that of mediumship, Myers realizes, is apt to raise eyebrows. There are many, he says, who will think such notions outmoded in today's civilized world. Talk of disembodied spirits, they will maintain, is better placed within the "medicine man's wig-wam" than within the forum of science. And yet how far advanced are we, asks Myers, in the affairs of the spirit over those in materially less developed cultures?

We are guilty, he thinks, of an absent-mindedness concerning the subject of our spirituality. The average man, even if he has an inclination toward things unseen, "has contented himself, like the mass of mankind, with some traditional theory, some emotional preference for some such picture as seems to him satisfying and exalted."[42] Herein he fails the test that he demands of himself elsewhere.

The primitive believer, says Myers, speaks of happy hunting grounds and animal companions. His picture may seem to us not ethereal enough to have credence. Yet if this savage, he adds, has assumed too little difference between this world and the next, the philosopher has assumed too much. He has supposed *a priori* that the gulf is unbridgeable; "he has taken for granted too clean a sweep

---

[42] *Ibid.*, vol. II, p. 251.

of earthly modes of thought."[43]

Whatever the difficulties with mediumship, thinks Myers, one can scarcely overestimate its importance. For here, he believes, we are actually witnessing, on at least some rare occasions, "the central mystery of human life, unrolling itself under novel conditions, and open to closer observation than ever before." Here we are seeing a *mind* use a *brain*. We are thus gaining an insight into the nature of each entity that we might not have otherwise.

Transworld communication, says Myers, has immense importance to the subject of religion. With further progress in psychical research will come discoveries more exciting, more joyous, than any yet imagined. In the age of Thales, he writes, Greece delighted in "its first dim vision" of cosmic law. In the age of Christ, Europe felt "the first high authentic message from a world beyond our own." In our own age, we find that such messages may become continuous

---

[43] *Ibid.*, p. 252. An instance of the American Indian conception of a future state is provided by George Catlin in his 1841 classic *The Manners, Customs and Condition of the North American Indian*. "Our people," reports one Choctaw subject, "all believe that the spirit lives in a future state." The good, he explains, live in continual cloudless day and green wood, with continual breezes, where "there is one continual scene of feasting, dancing and rejoicing - where there is no pain or trouble, and people never grow old, but for ever live young and enjoy the youthful pleasures." The place of the wicked, by contrast, is one of nightmare hardship. See George Catlin, *North American Indians*. Ed. Peter Matthiessen (New York: Penguin Books, 1989), p. 404.

If this portrayal of heaven is wanting (I myself am not so sure), it does nonetheless have in it a moral element that parallels those of religions closer to our own acquaintance. Catlin emphasizes also (pp. 472-73) the universal recognition in the North American Indian of an "intuitive knowledge of some great Author of his being" who passes judgment upon his actions and who rewards or punishes "according to the merits he has gained or forfeited in this world." For a succinct account of pre-European ethics and spirituality in the culture of the plains Indians, see also Charles Eastman's noted 1911 work *The Soul of the Indian* (Lincoln: University of Nebraska Press, 1980).

and progressive.[44] Our outlook upon life, both present and future, is thus transformed. That individual who finds his present life a burden may see his situation differently now. An evolution "gradual with many gradations," and extending vastly into as-yet unknowable heights - such is the life now revealed to us. For the first time, says Myers, a human being may feel truly *at home* in the universe. The worst fear - that of spiritual isolation and death - is over, and true security has been won.[45]

Motor automatism, Myers notes, is especially valuable - more so, in one respect, than others, such as apparitions. For it provides us with something public and enduring. And its material, in some cases, is quite convincing. But there remain questions as to the "ethical" and "religious" aspects of this activity. Might it, as some conservative types warn, bring us into play with demonic forces?

If we respect the evidence, says Myers, we will reject this hypothesis. Mediumship does not seem to involve communication with demons. "Haunting phantoms," he observes, "incoherent and unintelligent, may seem restless and unhappy." But as they rise into definiteness and intelligence, these phantoms "rise

---

[44] *Ibid.*, vol. II, p. 281.

[45] Myers offers likewise a pertinent comment on the question of whether or not desire for immortality is selfish. Concern with a future life, and effort to establish it, he observes, sometimes faces this charge. Yet it seems to come from those very individuals "who declare themselves most eager to promote the terrestrial welfare of their fellows." Why, asks Myers, is it philanthropic to desire the lesser good for mankind and not the greater? There is no reason to suppose that such concern is selfish, he explains, unless we suppose that "the genuine philanthropist is forbidden to aim at any common benefit in which he himself may expect to share." Frederic W. H. Myers, "Science and a Future Life", contained in Myers' *Science and a Future Life* (London: Macmillan and Co., 1893), p. 48.

also into love and joy."[46] The most vivid cases of communication, it seems, yield the most encouraging results. In no case within his acquaintance, he maintains, has there turned up this identifiable combination of *intelligence* and *wickedness* that anti-spiritualists imagine. The "world-old conception of Evil Spirits, of malevolent Powers, which has been the basis of so much of actual devil-worship and of so much more of vague supernatural fear" - all this, says Myers, "insensibly melts from the mind as we study the evidence before us."[47]

The terror that shaped primitive theologies still tinges us. But need this feeling be our guide? The transmutation of fear into curiosity, says Myers, "is of the essence of civilization." In all of life's encounter, he contends, on this plane or another, "I can find nothing worse than living men." What we find in mediumship is not "an intensification but a disintegration of selfishness, malevolence, pride."

Psychical research, Myers concludes, provides us with reason to extend our conception of the universe and the conduct of our inquiry. Once we are within its domain and acquainted with its phenomena, survival of death becomes "an almost inevitable corollary."[48] If indeed we give fair hearing to the evidence for such things as telepathy, apparitions, and automatism, we must suppose that discarnate sprits are not only real, but that they are active and have an interest in ourselves here below.

---

[46] *Ibid.*, vol. II, p. 78.

[47] *Ibid.*

[48] *Ibid.*, vol. II, p. 274.

We now stand, thinks Myers, a moment of critical importance. For at last, the spiritual world is beginning to act upon ours in a systematic fashion. There is no reason to think that this action has begun only in recent years and with our first disciplined inquiry. Very likely it has always existed, in some irregular fashion. But now, and with the benefit of our own rational effort, there is the prospect of more.

The indication of psychical research to date, thinks Myers, is that dwellers on earth, themselves spirits, "are an object of love and care to spirits higher than they."[49] There could be no greater boon bestowed upon them than "knowledge as to their position in the universe, the assurance that their existence is a cosmic and not merely a planetary, a spiritual and not merely a corporeal, phenomenon."[50] This truth seems to have been apprehended from time to time by certain highly developed souls in this world. Yet until now there has not been the prospect (from our side or theirs) of direct and sustained communication. There has not been the possibility of real comprehension of our place in the universe.

Beyond us still, writes Myers, is mystery;

> but it is mystery lit and mellowed with an infinite hope. We ride in darkness at the haven's mouth; but sometimes through rifted clouds we see the desires and needs of many generations floating and melting upwards into a distant glow, "up through the light of the seas by the moon's long-silvering ray."[51]

---

[49] *Ibid.*

[50] *Ibid.*, vol. II, pp. 274-75.

[51] *Ibid.*, vol. II, pp. 276-77.

Questions, of course, persist regarding psychical research and the basic integrity of its enterprise. Interest in the occult is associated at times with such things as deceit, mental depression, and basic unsoundness of mind. There are some, no doubt, who will think that such interest is inspired by these things. Might any summary response be made to such types? I can find none better than the one offered by William James, who writes,

> When I hear good people say ... that dabbling in such phenomena reduces us to a sort of jelly, disintegrates the critical faculties, liquefies the character, and makes of one a gullible fool generally, I console myself by thinking of my friends Frederic Myers and Richard Hodgson. These men lived exclusively for psychical research, and it converted both to spiritism ... Myers' character ... grew stronger in every particular for his devotion to these inquiries. Brought up on literature and sentiment, something of a courtier, passionate, disdainful, and impatient naturally, he was made over again form the day when he took up psychical research seriously. He became learned in science, circumspect, democratic in sympathy, endlessly patient, and above all, happy. The fortitude of his last hours touched the heroic, so completely were the atrocious sufferings of his body cast into insignificance by his interest in the cause he lived for. When a man's pursuit gradually makes his face shine and grow handsome, you may be sure it is a worthy one.[52]

---

[52] William James, "The Final Impressions of a Psychical Researcher". The essay is contained in James' *Memories and Studies* (New York: Longmans, Green, and Co., 1911), and is excerpted in Suzy Smith's Preface to the 1961 edition of Myers' *Human Personality* (New Hyde Park, New York: University Books, Inc.).

Myers' Legacy: The Mind as Mystery and Miracle

Myers' work has influenced many authors, among them Evelyn Underhill, whose *Mysticism* ranks as one of the finest studies ever made of the phenomena of altered states of consciousness. There exist profound affinities, observes Underhill, between the experiences of mystics and those of other gifted individuals. In those types whom we identify as geniuses, she notes,

> we seem to detect a hint of the relations which may exist between these deep levels of being and the crust of consciousness. In the poet, the musician, the great mathematician or inventor, powers lying below the threshold, and hardly controllable by their owner's conscious will, clearly take a major part in the business of perception and conception. In all creative acts, the larger share of the work is done subconsciously; it emergence is in a sense automatic.[53]

This element, says Underhill, is present before us in mystics, artists, philosophers, rulers, and discoverers. In each is an element of genius that comes from outside the bounds of ordinary thought. The characteristic insight, the invention, she maintains, owes always to "some sudden uprush of intuitions or ideas for which the superficial self cannot account." It issues from a level so deep that it seems to the subject himself to "come from beyond." This, she explains, is *inspiration*, "the opening of the sluices, so that those waters of truth in which all life is bathed may rise to the level of consciousness."[54]

---

[53] Evelyn Underhill, *Mysticism* (New York: New American Library, 1974), p. 63.

[54] *Ibid.*

Within us, it seems, is something extraordinary. Indeed it is only our constant acquaintance with the mind, say some, that keeps us from seeing its wondrousness. The "feel" of mind, writes Huston Smith, "as we encounter it awake is so familiar that we overlook the mystery that it parades in broad daylight."[55] No theory counting solely upon material fact, he contends, can fathom its active processes. No theory of perception, for example, can remove the miracle of our visual experience. How indeed does this neural spasm - this interaction of eye and wavelength - explain such things as the *sparkle* of a mountain stream, or the brilliant *red* upon the throat of a ring-necked pheasant? When we move, says Smith, from perception to such processes as imagination and abstract thought, the mysteries only compound. "If physiological psychology ever gives the impression of explaining these phenomena we should not be misled: it removes their mysteries in the way daylight banishes stars."[56]

The feeling of many is that there exists within us a source whose power exceeds the bounds of nature - a source, it seems, that is irreducibly spiritual. Our consciousness, writes Sir William Barrett,[57] is the fundamental thing of which we are aware. It is also the thing of greatest mystery. Think of what is involved in common experience. This experience consists in a series of states, no two of which are quite the same. Yet these states combine to produce a sense of *self*.

---

[55] Huston Smith, *Forgotten Truth* (San Francisco: HarperCollins, 1992), p. 69.

[56] *Ibid.*, p. 70.

[57] Sir William F. Barrett, *On the Threshold of the Unseen* (New York: E. P. Dutton and Co., 1918).

When the stream is interrupted, as in sleep, we recognize the continuity of this waking self with the one before. So, throughout our life, we are aware of our sameness even as the materials of body and brain are swept away and renewed.

Hence our personality is more than a loose "bundle"; no mere succession of discrete experiences can *fuse* itself into a single consciousness. Barrett describes this succession in terms of the production of a film image. Everyone is now familiar with the rapid presentation of still photographs whereby one obtains, for example, the image of a man running in continuous motion. But the photographs, he notes, remain distinct from one another. Thus something *external* to the pictures must account for this unifying process. By the same token, something more than our individual conscious episodes must explain their organization into a coherent whole. Even if these episodes are, as some imagine, a by-product or "epiphenomenon" of the brain, we require some further and transcending principle to explain their experiential unity. We require, in other words, "something which *gives a meaning to and holds together* the stream of manifold ideas."[58]

---

[58] Cf. Kant: "The thought that these presentations given in intuition belong one and all to me is ... tantamount to the thought that I unite them, or at least can unite them, in one self-consciousness ... only because I can comprise the manifold of the presentations in one consciousness, do I call them one and all *my* presentations. For otherwise I would have a self as many-colored and varied as I have presentations ..." It is for this reason, thinks Kant, that one cannot dissolve selfhood, as Hume suggests, into a mere series of individual perceptions. I cannot have experience, as I presently have it, of a world-order apart from myself otherwise. My successive perceptions of an object must somehow be *united* into perceptions of a single and enduring reality if they are to represent something that exists in its own right. See Immanuel Kant, *Critique of Pure Reason*. Trans. Werner S. Pluhar (Indianapolis: Hackett Publishing Company, 1996), pp. 178-79.

Consciousness is furthermore selective. Of the multitude of impressions constantly being made upon us, we are aware of a relatively small portion. Some element, operating in accord with what attracts or interests us, determines our focus. Thus there is a sense, writes Barrett, in which *choice* determines *experience*. Much of what impinges on our senses is excluded from conscious notice. And yet again, these passing impressions can later make their mark upon us, as evidenced, for example, in hypnosis and automatic writing.

Our being, then, is not merely co-extensive with those things of which we are conscious. This much is not our entire self, any more than the visible face is the whole moon. Our normal consciousness, says Barrett, acknowledging Myers,[59] might well be compared to the visible spectrum of sunlight. Beyond it on either side is a tract imperceptible to the eye, yet crowded with radiation. Just as the light from the sun embraces both the visible portion and these ultra-marginal areas, so does each human personality embrace both a conscious and an unconscious self. And just as experimental physics has shown the existence of such things as ultra-violet and infra-red portions of the light spectrum, so is experimental psychology demonstrating the reality of the self beyond the conscious threshold.

Further, says Barrett, as "the bright light of day quenches the feebler light of the stars, so the vivid stream of consciousness in our waking life must usually be withdrawn or enfeebled" before certain faint impressions, such as the

---

[59] Barrett takes this illustration from Myers. Cf. related discussion in chapter 1 of *Human Personality*.

telepathic impact of another mind, can become apparent.[60] A state of *passivity*, he notes, is favorable to the emergence of the subliminal consciousness, as in the case of mediumship. Often, in cases of automatic writing, lengthy and coherent messages are given while the medium is disengaged from activity at hand. But if attention is directed to the writing itself, "the spell is broken."[61]

This secondary or subliminal self, writes Barrett, cannot be identified with that of the waking state. Nor can its activity be explained in terms of bodily mechanism. Indeed in some cases, it seems, this extended activity may be attributable to the presence of an actual invader, a consciousness foreign to the subject whose mechanism is being used. The demonstration of knowledge, in certain cases, by a purported spirit[62] lends credence to the idea "that occasionally a human body may be the seat of a real invasion from the spirit world."

---

[60] *On the Threshold of the Unseen*, 133.

[61] A similar fact, he notes, obtains in cases of telepathy, where the intrusion of the will seems to have destructive effects upon the communication that is desired. Those well-meaning individuals, writes Barrett, who tell a subject "to try earnestly" to guess the thing or message thought about are liable to defeat the object in view.

[62] Such is the case presumably with mediumship. Barrett cites also the case of Lurancy Vennum, an American girl who, at the age of 14, seemed to have become controlled by the spirit of Mary Roff, a neighbor's daughter, who had died at 19 when Lurancy was 15 months old. The two families had lived, for the most part, far away from one another, and had never developed more than a passing acquaintance, yet Lurancy, in her "new" personality, called the Roffs her parents, recognized and knew by name the Roffs' friends and acquaintances, and demonstrated knowledge of trivial incidents in Mary's own life. (Cf. Myers, vol. I, chapter 2, "Disintegrations of Personality", and the appendix to this chapter in the same volume, pp. 360 and following.)

Human personality, concludes Barrett,[63] is a mystery. Within each of us are potentialities that outstrip ordinary intelligence and transcend its limits. The "dark continent" within is not merely a hidden record or lower store-house of experience, but something that has *higher perceptual ability*; something that "links our individual life to the Source of that life, and to the ocean of universal life." He cites the claims of a number of famous figures, among them Kant[64] and the neo-Platonist philosopher Plotinus, who say that a human being belongs at once "to the visible and to the invisible world," that men are "amphibia" who live, whether they realize it or not, at two levels.

As the roots of a tree are hidden in the earth, so do our own roots extend past visible reach. Consider, says Barrett, a primitive organism. We know, of course, that reality exists beyond its perceiving threshold. In the progress from lower forms of life to higher ones, this barrier has shifted, each time "with a corresponding exaltation of consciousness." The perceptual apparatus of an oyster, for example, shuts out from it the greater part of our own world; in like manner, says Barrett, the organism of man may form "a threshold which separates him from the larger and transcendental world of which he forms a part."[65]

But the threshold is not immovable. For occasionally, in rapture, in dream, in hypnotic trance, it is shifted, if only for a moment, and the soul moves in worlds

---

[63] See chapter 22, "The Mystery of Human Personality".

[64] The preceding quotation is taken from Kant's early work *Dreams of a Spirit-Seer*.

[65] *On the Threshold of the Unseen.*, 282.

not ordinarily realized. In some cases it is shifted further, and a higher intelligence emerges. This intelligence, as research will attest, is extraordinary. Its operation, it seems, is hindered by our present bodily organism. It may fare better, thinks Barrett, when freed from this "muddy vesture" of limit. At that time, he imagines, the new dawn may rise gently upward, awakening us to a wider reality.

This notion of a multi-storeyed existence is considered by philosopher and Society member H. H. Price in his earlier-cited essay "Survival and the Idea of 'Another World'".[66] Price, once again, believes that we might think of the next life (or one stage of it, at least) as involving *images* - dream-like sensations, the raw materials of which are gained from our present experience. Our experiences in the next world, he suggests, may be fashioned in some manner by these sensations and by our own moral condition.

If there are other worlds, he continues, perhaps *we inhabit them at the present time* with some stratum of our personalities. This, he says, may be the source of certain peculiar doctrines in the history of philosophy, such as the claim that the reality is nothing except conscious experience.[67] It may be, thinks Price, that certain philosophers have actually given us an accurate description of one level of reality while thinking that they describe another.

---

[66] See chapter 2. The essay is reprinted in John Hick, ed., *Classical and Contemporary Readings in the Philosophy of Religion*, cited in previous chapters of this volume.

[67] See, as perhaps the most famous example, George Berkeley's *Three Dialogues Between Hylas and Philonous*. The dialogue has many printings and is contained in its entirety in Joel Feinberg's *Reason and Responsibility* (Belmont, Cal.: Wadsworth Publishing Company, 1978).

The science of depth psychology, as noted earlier, has unearthed much information about unconscious processes. There is Freud, for example, who maintains that certain impulses are censored - dropped, as it were, through the trap door - because they cannot be consciously tolerated. How does Myers' view compare with that of psychology's best-known pioneer?

A marvelous statement in this regard is made by Aldous Huxley[68] in his Foreword to a more recent edition of *Human Personality*. Is the *house*, asks Huxley, "a mere bungalow with a cellar"? Or does it have an upstairs, as well? Freud, he writes, inclined toward the former view. This, he says, is to be expected. Freud, after all, was a doctor, and was concerned in his professional activity more with sickness than with health. Thus his primary concern, explains Huxley, was with "the subterranean rats and black beetles, and with all the ways in which a conscious ego may be disturbed by the bad smells and the vermin below the stairs."

Myers, by contrast, who was born fifteen years before Freud and predeceased him by forty, was a classicist. He was decidedly otherworldly in his inclination. He was also free to pay more attention to the positive aspects of his subject. Myers knew, says Huxley, that the cellar has its vermin, but he was more interested in what goes on in those rooms above the street level - in the treasures, he explains, "of the *piano nobile*, in the far-ranging birds (and perhaps even angels) that come and go between the rafters of a roofless attic that is open to the sky." If his account is excessively "spiritual" to some tastes, it is superior,

---

[68] Huxley's Foreword is contained in Suzy Smith's one-volume edition.

says Huxley, in at least one respect. It pays attention to the full range of fact. It is also superior, he thinks, to other accounts of the more esoteric kind, in that it is stronger in its concrete documentation and is less encumbered with speculation.[69]

A splendid account of psychical research and its conception of selfhood is offered by G. N. M. Tyrrell in his book *The Personality of Man*.[70] Few as yet realize, says Tyrrell, the significance of the fact that "the conscious mind does not exhaust the personality." We may not see much in this at first, but reflection shows us more and more of its implications, until at last our whole perspective begins to change.

Take, for one, a dancer. This individual, says Tyrrell, performs an exercise of amazing complexity without taking conscious note of its many successive movements. Yet something must be responsible for this coordination. Consider also dreams. They reveal "a quasi-mental element" that is not identical with the conscious self. It is not obvious how we might explain them. Who or what is it that "constructs the dream which seems so strange and surprising to the dreamer?"

In the nineteenth century, Tyrrell notes, there was much talk of "unconscious cerebration," a process determined by "well-worn paths" in the brain

---

[69] Thus Carl Jung, for example, is like those German scholars, says Huxley, who "dive deeper and come up muddier" than any others. Myers, he contends, dives no less deeply into that psychic world, and comes up with a minimum of mud on him.

[70] G. N. M. Tyrrell, *The Personality of Man* (Middlesex: Penguin Books, 1960).

circuitry. Any sort of teleological explanation, one involving a *direction* of some kind, was dismissed as being too mythical, too fantastic, to merit consideration. Today, no one speaks of unconscious cerebration, but it was a starting point for the discovery of "reaches of personality stretching beyond the conscious threshold."

Myers, writes Tyrrell, understood that personality contains a gold mine as well as a rubbish heap. His account of such phenomena as genius and inspiration receives corroboration in the testimony of figures in science, philosophy, and literature. Such testimony, in fact, is present in some of the oldest material on record. There is, for one, Socrates, who says, "I soon found that it is not by wisdom that the poets create their works, but by a certain natural power and by inspiration, like soothsayers and prophets, who say many fine things, but who understand nothing of what they say."[71] And there is Shelley, who insists that poetry "is not like reasoning, a power to be exerted according to the determination of the will. A man cannot say 'I will write poetry.' The greatest poet even cannot say it."

Poets, artists, writers, Tyrrell observes, attest one after another to the fact that their work comes from beyond the threshold. This stuff of inspiration is not ground out by the work of conscious intention. It does not come passively floating to them; rather it is imperious, dynamic, and willful. Thus Blake says of his *Milton*, "I have written this poem from immediate dictation, twelve or

---

[71] Tyrrell draws here from Plato's *Apology* 22c. All of the quotes immediately following are given by him without citation in chapter 2, "Inspiration and Genius".

sometimes twenty or thirty lines at a time, without premeditation, and even against my will." Keats maintains that his description of Apollo in *Hyperion* came "by chance or magic," as something given to him. He was not aware, in many cases, of the beauty of a particular thought or expression until he had written it down. He was then astonished by what he had produced, feeling even that it had been produced by someone else.

Goethe, Dickens, Wordsworth, Eliot, Kipling - they all refer in some way, says Tyrrell, to a source outside of their own conscious activity. He quotes Dostoevsky, who reports, "I ... write every scene down at once just as it first comes to me and rejoice in it; then I work at it for months and years." And again there is Robert Lewis Stevenson, mentioned earlier, who attributes much to his "little people" who do half his work for him while he is asleep - and perhaps do the rest while he is awake and taking the credit.[72]

This capacity of some persons to create, to compose, to formulate key hypotheses, seems to involve not so much step-by-step effort as a sudden intuitive flash. Sir Francis Gaulton, notes Tyrrell, maintained that he thought without the use of *words*, a fact that created serious problems in his effort to convey his ideas in writing. "It would be in vain," states Tchaikovsky, "to try to put into words that immeasurable sense of bliss which comes over me directly a new idea awakens in me and begins to assume a definite form." Says Mozart, "Nor do I hear in my imagination the parts *successively*, but I hear them, as it were, all at once ... What a delight this is I cannot tell!"

---

[72] Cf. Myers, vol. I, pp. 91 and 126.

Genius, insists Tyrrell, involves more than labor. Carlyle may say that genius is "an infinite capacity for taking pains." But taking pains will not by itself bring inspiration. The idea, it seems, must seep into consciousness from without, after which the subject will labor to express it. Technical skill by itself may produce a flawless piece of work, but it cannot produce greatness. This only comes as a gift.

Tyrrell is right, I think, in saying that we have not yet come to theoretical grips with this deeper resource within ourselves. What must be its nature if it can yield results like those noted in this chapter? Perhaps we can dismiss the phenomenon by giving it a name - saying, again, that it is a product of "intuition," that it is "unconscious," or whatever, and letting it go at that. But the thing that we see remains no less astounding. For herein are not only hidden processes, but *a source of intelligence*, as well. Surely, at least, we would think such results (like those mathematical problems) to be the product of intelligence were they rendered by ordinary means.

Can we say this phenomenon is merely the result of the material structure of the brain? Some, no doubt, will choose this option. But why should this organ be structured in such a way as to produce *accurate results*? Why should it render likewise beauty and creative magnificence? The hypothesis of chance, as I have said, is out of the question.[73] Nor can I imagine any natural explanation (say, in

---

[73] Consider, again, the performance of those individuals who could determine, say, the cube root of a very large number or the logarithm of a number to seven or eight places. See again relevant material in chapter 3 of *Human Personality*.

evolutionary terms) of cognitive ability stupendously far removed from daily need. In reflecting upon these findings we are encouraged, I believe, to think of consciousness as being something more than a material accident.

The results of psychical research point us dramatically in this other direction. Among these are the data of thought-transference, or telepathy. Such cases, says Tyrrell,[74] make it difficult to explain the mind in terms of any conventional theory. The question arises, however, as to whether we might account for them in material terms, as for example by some kind of radiation. Perhaps, some imagine, telepathy is thus explicable within a sufficiently widened materialist view.

Yet there are several reasons, argues Tyrrell, why it is difficult to explain telepathy in this way. In the first place, such radiation would have to be generated by a material transmitter of some kind, one presumably located within the brain or body of the agent. Since telepathy is known to take place over long distances, this transmitter would have to be a very powerful one, able to send messages over thousands of miles. This, thinks Tyrrell, would make it unlikely that it were quite small, say, of microscopic dimensions. Its existence should be evident. Yet no such transmitter has been found within the human body, nor has any receiver.

All known radiation, furthermore, says Tyrrell, obeys the law of the inverse square connecting intensity with distance (i. e., the former diminishing

---

[74] He cites various examples in chapter 4, "The Problems of Telepathy and Foreknowledge". The Interpretation of such cases is discussed in chapter 7, "What does Telepathy Imply?"

with the latter). There is no evidence that telepathic action is bound in this way. If it were, an individual who could transmit a message across the ocean, for example, would produce a much more powerful effect across a table. Yet this does not seem to be the case. Physicists possess a variety of instruments for detecting different kinds of radiation. They have not turned up anything that appears to be associated with telepathy.

There is yet another objection, Tyrrell continues, to the hypothesis that telepathy works by physical means. For in every case where ideas are naturally transmitted from one party to another, use has to be made of a *code*. Unless such a code exists and is shared by each party, no information can be transmitted. Thus spoken language, for example, is a code, as is written language. So is a conventional system of dots and dashes. Even facial and bodily gestures are codes, of sorts, that depend upon mutual understanding. Every code, to be effective, must be consciously applied and interpreted. Where, then, is the one associated with telepathy? Until radiation-theorists can answer such questions as these, they cannot hope to offer a plausible account of the phenomenon.

If telepathy does resist interpretation along physical lines, there are interesting consequences. Individual A, it seems, can be in communication with individual B without any connecting physical link. Yet how can a mental event occurring at one place influence one occurring at another if nothing travels the intervening space? The answer, thinks Tyrrell, is that telepathy may be a relation between the subliminal portions of two personalities, and that the question of space is actually irrelevant. The subliminal personality may have no spatial characteristics - no shape, size, or location.[75] Telepathy is important, Tyrrell concludes, because it reveals a deeper part of the human personality at work. It shows that things happen in the subliminal region very differently from the way in which they happen elsewhere.

Another example of the mind's seemingly trans-natural character is suggested by certain cases of multiple personality. Myers, as Colin Wilson notes,[76] was particularly interested in the phenomenon. Certain instances of its occurrence, he adds,[77] make it difficult to account for consciousness in solely in terms of the nervous system.

Consider, for one, the case of Christine Sizemore, whose story was made famous in *Three Faces of Eve*. Sizemore was allergic to nylon, but when an alter-ego surfaced, the nylon rash disappeared. Further, she herself was shortsighted, but another persona could see perfectly well without glasses. On one occasion, notes Wilson, Sizemore was under an anesthetic, but an alter-ego took over and was unaffected by it.

If such things happen, he reasons,

---

[75] It may be objected, says Tyrrell, that A's subliminal self is simply where A is at any given moment, but this implies something that we need not accept, namely that A is identical with that body with which A is currently associated. The fact that A experiences the world from a particular viewpoint owes to the fact that his sensory apparatus has that location and so takes in reality from that specific vantage point, much as a person may seem, by analogy, to be in the place depicted on a television screen owing to his viewing sensations.

[76] Colin Wilson, *Afterlife* (Garden City, New York: Doubleday and Co., 1987). See especially chapter 5, "Recovering a Masterpiece", which is devoted to Myers' *Human Personality*.

[77] *Ibid.*, pp. 143-4. Cf. once more chapter 2 of *Human Personality*.

> then our usual assumption that 'personality' is somehow dependent on the body may be a misunderstanding. The body may be an instrument that responds to the demands of the personality - in the same way that a car responds to its driver, but to a far greater extent. This in turn suggests that physical illness may depend on the personality, not on the body - that when a person is bent and decrepit and feeble, it is the personality that is bent and decrepit.[78]

It is worth mention, in concluding this chapter, that Myers may have made yet other contributions to psychical research after his passing. For he is credited in some quarters, notes Suzy Smith,[79] with giving, from the other side, some of the most impressive evidence ever obtained of survival and transworld communication. The ostensible method by which this communication is delivered is called "cross-correspondence".

The idea of cross-correspondence, as explained by Raynor C. Johnson,[80] is as follows. Imagine that a bit of material appears in an automatic script suggesting the communication from some given individual - say, Myers - on the other side. It may be claimed by a sceptic that this material has been drawn from the medium's own subliminal mind, or that she has derived it by some form of telepathy from those who knew Myers in this world. Suppose, however, that Myers, working from the other side, divided his message into phrases and fragments, sending some of these through one automatist and some through another. These fragments, by themselves having no distinct meaning, do not

---

[78] *Ibid.*, p. 144.

[79] See again Smith's preface to her edition of *Human Personality*.

[80] Raynor C. Johnson, *The Imprisoned Splendour* (New York: Harper and Brothers, 1953). See pp. 287-88. Johnson is cited by Smith.

seem to be the sorts of things that would exist on their own and avail themselves to a medium's extrasensory ability. Thus when connections are found to exist between them, believes Johnson, they indicate the existence of an independent intelligence at work.

Evidence that such an effort was being made began to appear in scripts from 1907 onward. At around this time, four women[81] who were deeply interested in psychical research began to develop facility in automatic writing. Those who studied the scripts came to think that Myers was indeed responsible.

In addition, notes Smith, there is a related incident. Myers, it seems, had left a message in a sealed envelope with the hope that a medium might one day give a report of its contents by means of his influence. Shortly after his death a message was received through the automatist Mrs. Verrall, which read, "I have long told you of the contents of the envelope. Myers' sealed envelope left with Lodge. You have not understood. It has in it the words from the SYMPOSIUM - about Love bridging the chasm."

The envelope was then opened, and the message read, "If I can revisit any earthly scene, I should choose the *Valley* in the grounds of Hallsteads, Cumberland." It was first thought that the experiment had failed. But several members of the Society, after studying other documents, came to the conclusion that while these messages were not identical, they bore a rather curious relationship.

---

[81] These, notes Smith, were Mrs. A. W. Verrall, her daughter Helen (the future Mrs. Salter), Mrs. Holland (a pseudonym for Rudyard Kipling's sister) who lived in India, and the noted Mrs. Leonore Piper in the United States.

In 1893, it turned out, Myers had printed a short booklet called *Fragments of Inner Life*. Copies were sent to old friends with the understanding that they should be opened after his death.[82] The references to Plato in the last chapter of this booklet show that there was a definite association in Myers' mind between the valley at Hallsteads and the account of love given in Plato's *Symposium*. Thus it is surmised by some that a real connection exists between the two messages.

Years later came another development. In 1932 there appeared a book penned by a young Irish woman named Geraldine Cummins. It was entitled *The Road to Immortality* and it purported to deliver, *via* automatic writing, Myers' own communication. This book described the various stages of growth through which a soul passes on the other side. It was, in the estimation of fellow psychical researcher Oliver Lodge, strongly characteristic of Myers, and bore a noticeable relationship, in its content, to some of Myers' own ideas. (I briefly cite this material in chapters 6 and 7.)

---

[82] A portion of this booklet, notes Smith, was republished by Myers' widow under the title *Fragments of Prose and Poetry* in 1904. See related discussion of this incident in Colin Wilson, *The Psychic Detectives* (San Francisco: Mercury Books, 1985), pp. 75 and following.

Chapter V

Survival as Life's One and Final Question: The Case of Miguel de Unamuno

> If it is nothingness that awaits us, let us make an injustice of it; let us fight against destiny, even though without hope of victory; let us fight against it quixotically.
>
> Miguel de Unamuno, *The Tragic Sense of Life*

Miguel de Unamuno was born in 1864 in the Basque city of Bilbao. He studied classics and philosophy at Madrid and came to Salamanca in 1891 as professor of Greek at the local university. He was appointed rector of the university in 1901 and was later named rector for life in 1934. In 1924 Unamuno was deported for some time to the Canary Islands for his constant attack upon the totalitarian policies of General Primo de Rivera. Far and away his greatest work is *The Tragic Sense of Life*, which appeared in 1913.[1] He lived until 1936.

Unamuno, it may be said at the outset, offers a challenge all his own. It is not easy to summarize his most famous work, throughout which are strewn

---

[1] All quotations in this chapter come from Miguel de Unamuno, *The Tragic Sense of Life*. Trans. J. E. Crawford Flitch (New York: Dover Publications, 1954).

fierce comments upon life, the soul, and the history of human thought. In it one finds not just fact and argument, but anguish, paradox - scorn, at times, for his own discipline, and searing vision into the strengths and weaknesses of philosophers themselves. Unamuno does not just address ideas. He addresses men.

The question of our personal destiny, he believes, lies at the heart of all real philosophy and all human hope. Yet in trying to answer it, he maintains, we are pulled in two directions. Always there are reasons, the reasons of the head, as he calls them,[2] why we ought not to believe. Yet again there are intimations of hope, moments in our experience that beckon beyond. *The Tragic Sense of Life* is a reflection upon this internal warfare. It ranks, I believe, as one of the most valuable books ever written.

---

[2] Cf. Blaise Pascal, whom Unamuno quotes, and who shares Unamuno's view regarding the seriousness of the survival question. The knowledge of God, writes Pascal (*Pensees # 280*), "is very far from the love of Him." Elsewhere Pascal maintains that the heart may have reasons that the head does not understand. Blaise Pascal, *Pensees and the Provincial Letters*. Trans. W. F. Trotter and Thomas M'Crie (New York: Modern Library, 1941).

The Hunger for Immortality

Unamuno was none too happy with the going outlook of his day. Discoveries of science, it seemed, were fast swallowing up any vestige of hope in conventional religion. Philosophy was becoming largely an exercise in the analysis and dissection of ideas. Unamuno cites the example of positivism, which counts both religion and metaphysics as useless (albeit historically necessary) stages on the way to science.[3] He would be scarcely happier with developments since.[4] One can only wonder what he might have said about activity in the field today, which consists largely of technical exchanges that separate even members of the same university departments.

The result of pure analytic investigation, contends Unamuno, is that reality is pulverized, reduced, as he says, to a *dust* of facts. Its "truths" are but truth-fragments with no bearing on the life-enterprise. Each real man, by contrast, is a man of flesh and bone, who addresses other men of flesh and bone like himself. And each, did he confess it, is infinitely concerned about his own destiny.

---

[3] See August Comte's *Introduction to Positive Philosophy* (Indianapolis, Indiana: Hackett Publishing Company, Inc., 1988). Frederick Ferre, translator.

[4] About twenty-five years after the writing of *The Tragic Sense of Life* there appeared, for example, a "logical" positivism, a view that dismissed claims about souls, gods and other worlds as being outright nonsense. The central tenet of this doctrine is that an expression must be either (1) analytic (true by virtue of the definitions of its terms) or (2) empirically verifiable (confirmable by the senses), if it is to be meaningful at all. See, as an introduction, A. J. Ayer's 1936 classic *Language, Truth and Logic* (New York: Dover Publications, 1952).

A human soul, writes Unamuno, is worth all the universe. Not, he adds, a human *life*, something vain and transitory, but an eternal soul. There is an inversion of values, he observes, in those who lack this insight. The less they comprehend eternity, the more they exaggerate the worth of this life.[5] A man should not want to die, but it is the death of the soul that holds the real terror.

The prospect of eternity, he thinks, outweighs infinitely any other. We understand this, at some level, he insists, even if we do not admit it. The thought possesses us even if we cannot confirm its reality. The philosopher who believes in immortality may find a "proof," but it is his will that produces it.

Kant, observes Unamuno, was a ruthless critic of attempts to establish such things as God or eternity on rational grounds. Thus in his *Critique of Pure Reason*, for example, he refutes the claim that God's existence follows logically from His own limitless nature or that the indestructibility of the soul is demonstrable by reason.[6] Yet in his subsequent *Critique of Practical Reason*, sees Unamuno, Kant overthrows with his heart[7] what he has established with his head.

---

[5] This ultimate concern with the present life is the source from which springs (p. 12) "all that effeminate, sentimental ebullition against war." He returns to this theme, as I will note, in his later chapters.

[6] Thus in Book II, Chapter III, section 4 of his Transcendental *Dialectic*, for example, Kant criticizes Descartes' claim that God's *existence* is necessarily a part of His limitless essence. Existence, writes Kant, is not one more attribute that a thing may have or lack; it is not a property, as Descartes imagines, in addition to others, rather it is the prior fact that the notion of a property presupposes. Nor, thinks Kant, is the existence of an enduring and substantial *soul* something that reason can establish. (See, for example, Book II, Chapter I of this section.)

[7] See related discussion in chapter 3 of this volume.

It is not mere reason that produces such an event. The real source of this affirmation lies instead in the tragic fight of a man to save himself, to quench his craving for life without end. At bottom it is a fight for consciousness. If consciousness, writes Unamuno, is - as some *inhuman* thinker has said - "nothing more than a flash of light between two eternities of darkness, then there is nothing more execrable than existence."[8]

The mainstream of philosophy, he observes, has taken Aristotle's conception of man as the rational and political animal as its starting point. But man, he insists, is as much a feeling animal as a thinking one. If we are to truly know philosophy, we must first have a better sense of who we are that undertake it. In so doing we will realize that we are more than reasoners, and that life's greatest truths are to be known not with the head but with the whole being.

Unamuno's work is typically classed as being *existentialist* in its approach, meaning roughly that it takes as its starting point the individual human condition and the wilful response that it demands. Life, he reminds us, is not a puzzle, but a challenge, a confrontation facing us from the time that we enter it.

Unamuno's writing fairly bleeds with this urgency. In it is expressed his astonishment, his indignation, with the way in which philosophers themselves approach their task. In most purported histories, he observes, philosophical systems are presented to the reader as if they grew from one another - as if, in other words, philosophy were an event of logic, flowing by the dictates of reason. The philosophers themselves are pretexts whose inner lives are but incidental.

---

[8] *Tragic Sense of Life*, p. 13.

A good many of us have indeed forgotten who we are. A friend, he recalls, with whom he talked on many occasions, once confessed to Unamuno that he had no sense of *himself* as something irreplaceable and distinct from the rest of things.

> On a certain occasion this friend remarked to me: "I should like to be So-and-So" (naming someone), and I said: "That is what I shall never be able to understand - that one should want to be someone else. To want to be someone else is to want to cease to be he who one is. I understand that one should wish to have what someone else has, his wealth or his knowledge; but to be someone else, that is a thing I cannot comprehend."[9]

Thus it is often observed, says Unamuno, that a man who has suffered misfortunes prefers to be himself, even with those misfortunes, than to be someone else without them. In so doing they think rightly, for what this means is that they prefer misfortune to nonexistence. As a child, he continues,

> I remained unmoved when shown even the most moving pictures of hell, for even then nothing appeared to me quite so horrible as nothingness itself. It was a furious hunger of being that possessed me, an appetite for divinity, as one of our ascetics has put it.[10]

There is a sense, Unamuno writes, in which philosophy is closer to poetry than to science. By this he does not mean that philosophy (or poetry, for that matter) lacks objective truth. He means rather that each individual's philosophy is a concrete and unique expression of his being - that it comes out of the depths of his soul, not as mere inference, but as vital song. It wells out of a depth that he himself may not fully apprehend.

---

[9] *Ibid.*, p. 9.

[10] *Ibid.*

Man himself is not an abstraction but a *thing* - something that is "concrete, unitary, and substantive."[11] There is a sense in which a truly conscious individual must be self-absorbed, even self-obsessed, if he is to understand what is at stake in philosophy. An individual may undergo changes in his personality, but within a process of action and memory that retains his continuity. To become something utterly different from what one is, he reminds the reader, is to cease to exist. And anything is to be preferred to this. Perhaps another person could do certain things better than I. But this, he adds, would not be I.

> "I, I, I, always I!" some reader will exclaim; "and who are you?" I might reply in the words of Obermann, that tremendous man Obermann: "For the universe, nothing - for myself, everything."[12]

And if this view seems excessively self-centered, writes Unamuno, we would do well to remember Kant's famous dictate each human being is an end, and not a means. All civilization addresses itself to each man, to each single I. Certain reformers, it is true, may think that individuals are quantities to be expended for the cause of progress. But what is this idol *Humanity*, to which the individual may be given? To what end do I sacrifice myself to my children, or nation, or to the next generation, who presumably must sacrifice themselves in turn?

---

[11] *Ibid.*, p. 6.

[12] *Ibid.*, p. 11. Unamuno cites an early nineteenth century work by the French author Etienne Pivert de Senancour (1770 - 1846). It is, explain editors Martin Nozick and Anthony Kerrigan, one of Unamuno's favorite novels. See Unamuno's *The Tragic Sense of Life in Men and Nations*. Trans. Anthony Kerrigan (Princeton: Princeton University Press, 1972), pp. 381-82. This translation constitutes Volume IV of his collected works in the Princeton Bollingen series.

We are mortal. Confronted with this tragedy, we seek any pathetic consolation. Consider that one, says Unamuno, who says to a father who has lost his son in the young man's prime of life, "Patience, my friend, we all must die." Such an axiom is an offense, to which may be given the reply,

Para pensa, tual cu, solo es preciso, no tener nada mas que inteligencia.[13]

There are some who think wholly with the head, which is to say, who are rational creatures, capable of articulation, but who lack all sense of value or direction. Such persons become definition mongers; they become "professionals" of thought. Were they truly conscious they would think instead with body and soul, with the blood, with the marrow - with life.

Think, says Unamuno, of a professional boxer. This individual has learned to strike with such economy that he brings into play just those muscles necessary to the task at hand. He can knock out his opponent with a specialization of effort. A blow delivered by a non-professional, on the other hand, will not have this same efficiency, yet it will more greatly vitalize the man who throws it. The one is the effort of a professional, the other that of a man.

Just so do many make a profession of philosophy. It is for them a *skill* - a thing to be honed and displayed. The cost of this pose is truth. Their words cease to express what is real and become instead a self-serving performance. A philosopher, if he is not first a man, is anything but a genuine philosopher. He may succeed in becoming a pedant, but as such he is a caricature.

---

[13] "To be lacking in everything but intelligence is the necessary qualification for thinking like you."

> All this talk, we must realize,
>
> of a man surviving in his children, or in his works, or in the universal consciousness, is but vague verbiage which satisfies only those who suffer from affective stupidity, and who, for the rest, may be persons of a certain cerebral distinction. For it is possible to possess great talent, or what we call great talent, and yet to be stupid as regards the feelings and even morally imbecile. There have been instances.[14]

There are many who suffer from this deadness of sensation. They tell us that the pursuit is useless. Do not delve, they say, into the unknowable. It is as if one should say to a man who has lost his leg that it will not help him to think about it. A pedant saw Solon weeping for the death of a son and asked him why he wept, when it avails nothing. Solon's reply was that he wept just for this reason - because it availed nothing! Weeping, says Unamuno, may in fact avail something, if only the release of stress. But there is another and deeper truth, he imagines, in Solon's reply. The sanctity of a temple is that it provides a place for men to weep in common. A *miserere* sung in common by a multitude has as much value as a philosophy. Perhaps we must learn to weep.

There is, writes Unamuno, what for lack of a better name is *the tragic sense of life*, which has within itself a whole conception of life and the universe. It is shared by some individuals and by some peoples. This sense does not so much flow from ideas as it *determines* them. It is from this starting point that real philosophy may proceed.

---

[14] *Tragic Sense of Life*, p. 16.

Despair and Resolution

"Whence do I come and whence comes the world in which and by which I live? Whither do I go and whither goes everything that environs me? What does it all mean?"

Such, says Unamuno, are the questions that we ask when freed from the task of sustaining our mortal existence. And if we look closely, he says, we will find that what they seek is not so much the *why* as the *wherefore* - not the *cause*, but the *end*. If we wish to know whence we came, it is in order to know where we are going.

The history of philosophy is one of failure. At the heart of this failure is dishonesty. Descartes, for example, writes his *Meditations* and *Discourse on Method* by emptying himself (so he says) of all but intellect. He then "proves" such things as that God exists, that knowledge is certain, and that he himself is distinct from his material body. How many persons, Unamuno wonders, would rest their lives upon such conclusions? Surely, he thinks, not Descartes himself. The real man is not an abstraction, but a man of flesh and bone, "the man who does not want to die." *Cogito, ergo sum* ("I think, therefore I am"), writes Descartes. Yet "the primary reality," writes Unamuno,[15] "is not that I think, but that I live." Descartes believes in his heart that he is immortal. It is the man beneath this performance who thrusts himself into it and decides its course.

---

[15] *Ibid.*, p. 35.

The soul does battle within itself. Once conscious of itself, it cannot cease to want to live. In certain moments it may apprehend its own triumph, its destined eternal place. But there are again moments of doubt.

> When I contemplate the green serenity of the fields or look into the depths of clear eyes through which shines a fellow-soul, my consciousness dilates, I feel the diastole of the soul and am bathed in the flood of the life that flows about me, and I believe in my future; but instantly the voice of mystery whispers to me, "Thou shalt cease to be!"[16]

There may be individuals, admits Unamuno, untouched by these feelings. But he does not pretend to understand them. If consciousness returns at death to the unconsciousness from which it sprang, and if a like fate befalls humanity, then is our toil-worn race "nothing but a fatidical procession of phantoms, going from nothingness to nothingness, and humanitarianism the most inhuman thing known."

What, he asks, is this earthly *joie de vivre* of which some persons speak? Our thirst for God, for life without end, will always stifle the enjoyment of this time that evaporates with the hours. It is the frenzied love of life, the love that would have life be unending, that makes us, in contrary fashion, long for death. For if I am one day to die utterly, to be annihilated, and the world for me will be finished, then what is the good of living? Perhaps we will be told that this feeling is selfish, that it is pessimistic, that our longing to live on is in some way incoherent. It is better, they may say, to enjoy this one chance that we are given. But this longing cannot be appeased by any amount of such argument.

---

[16] *Ibid.*, p. 40.

> I do not want to die - no; I neither want to die nor do I want to want to die; I want to live for ever and ever and ever. I want this "I" to live - this poor "I" that I am and that I feel myself to be here and now, and therefore the problem of the duration of my soul, of my own soul, tortures me.[17]

I am the center of my own universe. So it should be. Where else might I reside? And what, in any case, is more universal than the individual? We should put aside our interests, we are sometimes told, for the sake of others. Perhaps so; but sacrifice, thinks Unamuno, cannot be the basis of life. If I sacrifice my interests to those of others, to whom do I offer the gift, but to those presumably as much concerned for their welfare as I for mine? *Love thy neighbor as thyself* - this very ethic, says Unamuno, presupposes that we love ourselves in the first place. And yet there is a sense, he believes, in which we do not know how to love ourselves.

All problems of philosophy derive their importance from this concern with self if they are problems at all. There are some among us concerned with the issue of *God's existence*. How so? Unamuno tells of the time[18] that he talked with a peasant about how there might be a God, a governing "Consciousness of the Universe", but that nonetheless the soul of the individual man might not be immortal. Whereupon the man cried, "Then wherefore God?" The same thought lies deep in each believer, even if he does not say it outright.[19]

---

[17] *Ibid.*, p. 45.

[18] *Ibid.*, p. 5.

[19] For most of us, writes James, religion "*means* immortality, and nothing else," and God is its producer. William James, *The Varieties of Religious Experience* (New York: Macmillan, 1961), p. 406. (Cf. Unamuno, p. 5.)

Nor are these odd and specious versions of survival so often dreamed up by philosophers of any help. Such examples abound.[20] Always they are shameless counterfeits. We are told, for example, that "not the least particle of matter is annihilated, not the least impulse of energy is lost." And there are some who pretend to be consoled.

The answer lies not in efforts to establish survival on rational grounds. Such has Catholicism attempted[21] without success. The intellect not only fails to support this belief; it works in the other direction. It is all too obvious the extent to which consciousness is dependent upon the physical organism - how it comes to develop as the brain receives impressions from the outside world, how it is temporarily suspended in sleep and in swoons and accidents, and how all such facts lead us naturally to suppose that death brings with it the end.

---

[20] One such example is surely Santayana, who maintains in his *Reason in Religion* (New York: Dover, 1982) that reason "lifts a larger or smaller element in each man to the plane of ideality." He who lives in the ideal, and who expresses it in some fashion in society, says Santayana, enjoys a kind of double immortality, for the eternal "has absorbed him while he lived, and when he is dead his influence brings others to the same absorption." This kind of analysis, thinks Unamuno, amounts to a kind of double-talk, and even to outright lying.

He would think little better, I am sure, of the discussion offered by Paul Tillich. Our popular notion of immortality, writes Tillich, owes in part to our attempt to escape from the inevitable. This belief, he explains, wishes to continue one's finitude, one's having to die, "infinitely, so that actual death never will occur." This, says Tillich, is an illusion, and even a contradiction in terms. "It makes endless what, by definition, must come to an end." The so-called immortality of the soul is thus but "a poor symbol for the courage to be in the face of one's having to die." (p. 169) The individual, by contrast, who participates in God, Tillich says, "participates in eternity." But it is not obvious what this means in terms of this individual's actual destiny. See Tillich's *The Courage to Be* (New Haven, Conn.: Yale University Press, 1980).

[21] See discussion in chapter 4, "The Essence of Catholicism".

Rationalism,[22] the method that abides solely by reason, is necessarily antagonistic to belief in another life. Such belief requires a duality, a distinction between oneself and the world that science describes. Yet the impulse of rationalism is monist. Its goal is to explain the universe, to understand it as a coherent whole. For this purpose the notion of another reality, of something outside its theater of sight and sound, is unneeded.

Efforts to ground the belief in survival upon rational premises, writes Unamuno, are but wishful thinking at best. We have no clear sense of what it means for the soul to be "simple" or "incorruptible," or to be a pure "substance," as some metaphysicians maintain. It is our deeper wellspring of faith that precedes such ruminations and gives them their force. Nor does the alternative of pantheism hold promise. To say that God is everything, or that He contains all things in Himself, means that we were somehow in God before we were born. If in dying we return to this condition, then it is the same as extinction.

Yet there is a remedy, claims Unamuno, if we have the courage to accept it. It is "to consider our mortal destiny without flinching, to fasten our gaze upon the gaze of the Sphinx." For it is thus that "the malevolence of its spell is discharmed." From the depth of this unhappiness springs new life. It is only by "draining the lees of spiritual sorrow" that we can at last taste "the honey that lies at the bottom of the cup." Anguish thus leads to consolation. In the abyss of skepticism, "reason encounters the despair of the heart," and from this encounter is born the possibility of genuine faith.

---

[22] See discussion in chapter 5, "The Rationalist Dissolution".

In the depths of the abyss, the despair of the heart meets face to face with the skepticism of reason, and the two embrace like brothers. Out of this embrace of despair and scepticism is born a new awareness, a new sensibility. It is not a guarantee of eternal life, but it is a basis for hope. Were we to have certainty either way - either the perfect demonstration of our mortality, or that of our endless survival - life would become impossible. Thus we retain before us each of these prospects, however we might want it otherwise.

> In the most secret chamber of him who believes himself convinced that death puts an end to his personal consciousness ... there lurks a shadow, a vague shadow, a shadow of shadow, of uncertainty, and while he says within himself, "Well, let us live this life that passes away, for there is no other!" the silence of this secret chamber speaks to him and murmurs, "Who knows!"[23]

He may not admit to hearing it, may not be altogether sure that he does hear it. But it is there nevertheless. The materialist cannot know that his view is correct. And doubt, by the same token, is there in the mind of the most fervent believer. If there are men structured otherwise, they are exceptions to the rule. Belief about some things (say, the proposition that a triangle contains within itself the sum of two right angles) may be all or nothing. But belief in this case is not so simple. There can exist contradiction, even warfare, within a single soul.

Witness, says Unamuno, the man who comes to Jesus with a son possessed by demons[24] and is told that all things are possible for one who believes. He responds by saying, "Lord, I believe, help thou mine unbelief!"

---

[23] *Ibid.*, p. 118.

[24] *Mark* 9: 19 and following.

It is, on the face of it, a contradiction. For if he believes, how can he be asking Jesus to help him in his lack of faith? Yet it is this contradiction that gives to the father's cry its profound human value. It is a faith based upon incertitude, rather like that of the heroic figure Don Quixote - a madman, thinks Unamuno, but not a fool, and "the prototype of the vitalist whose faith is based upon uncertainty."[25]

When we have arrived at the bottom of the abyss, we are left with these enduring elements of reason and vital feeling. We are then faced with the task of accepting the conflict and living by it. The task may be difficult, it may cause us anguish. And yet there is something good, something intensifying and revelatory, in a life of this kind. Men love one another with a spiritual love "only when they have suffered the same sorrow together, when through long days they have ploughed the stony ground bowed beneath the common yoke of a common grief."[26] It is then that they know, then that they feel, one another. To love, he writes, is to pity. If bodies are united by pleasure, souls are united by pain. But in this latter kind of union is revelation.

Never is this union more powerfully felt than in one of those tragic loves doomed to contend with "the diamond-hard laws of Destiny" - a love, perhaps, born out of due time and season, or one not of the kind that the world welcomes. The more barriers this destiny imposes, the more forcefully do these lovers cling together. In this condition,

---

[25] *Tragic Sense of Life*, p. 120.

[26] *Ibid.*, p. 135.

> they establish their love beyond the confines of the world, and the strength of this poor love suffering beneath the yoke of Destiny gives them intuition of another world where there is no other law than the liberty of love - another world where there are no barriers because there is no flesh.[27]

Unamuno and paradox! We gain faith in another world by the impossibility of our love coming to fruition in this one. Maternal love, at its heart, is compassion for the defenseless infant who craves the comfort of her breast. Sexual love, thinks Unamuno, is something akin. The man who extends love to his neighbors is kindled by the depth of his own misery. As love grows, it embraces what is sees, and pities what it embraces. Turn inwards, penetrate more deeply into yourself, and you will discover more and more your own limitation. In finding this, you will have a whole-hearted pity for yourself, and will burn with a sorrowful self-love.

This love may be called egotism, but it is the furthest thing, insists Unamuno, from egotism as commonly defined. This pity, this self-despair, bred of the consciousness that just as once you were not, so one day (so far as this world is concerned) you will cease to be, will lead you to love all of those with whom you tread the path - "these unhappy shadows," he writes, "who pass from nothingness to nothingness, these sparks of consciousness which shine for a moment in the infinite and eternal darkness." This compassion for other folk will expand into a love for all living things, perhaps even, at last, for those very stars in the heavens that one day will shine no longer. In looking at the universe and feeling all things that have traced their painful impression, you will arrive, he

---

[27] *Ibid.*, p. 136.

explains, *at the abyss of the tedium*, not merely a tedium of life, but of existence - at the bottomless pit, as he calls it, of this vanity of vanities. In so doing you will arrive at universal love.

There arise movements within philosophy, writes Unamuno, that try to do away with notions like these. Such is positivism, for example, which tries to lead us from primitive impulse into reason. But life, he insists, never surrenders. He cites the example of Aristophanes' Strepsiades, who, when told by Socrates that it is not Zeus who sends the rain, but "an atmospheric whirligig," replies in surprise that he had not been acquainted with Zeus' son Whirligig.[28] We all do something of this kind, for we cannot rid ourselves of the conviction that *our relationship to the universe is ultimately personal*. Nor should we think that reason will somehow lead us away from it. Philosophy does not deal merely with the senses, but with the sum total of our experience.[29]

We formulate religious proof, but never with a satisfying result. Standard arguments for God's existence, for example, are never adequate. For in the first place, they are generally open to objections. Thus the argument, for example,

---

[28] See Aristophanes' *The Clouds*.

[29] Although Unamuno does not try to justify this tendency intellectually, I am reminded of an especially provocative passage within Huston Smith's classic *The World's Religions*, in which he describes the evolution of theism among the ancient Hebrews. It is easy, he writes, to smile at the anthropomorphism of these folk, "who could imagine ultimate reality as a person walking in the garden of Eden in cool of the morning." (*Genesis* 3: 8) But when we make our way through the poetic concreteness of this notion, he writes, to its underlying claim - namely, that reality is ultimately *more like a person than a thing*, we ought to ask ourselves, first, what is the evidence against this claim, and second, is such an idea "intrinsically any less exalted" than its alternative? (page 273)

that no amount of random printing over time would ever produce *Don Quixote*[30] is met by the reply that something might be composed that would be just as impressive to those who were there to observe it. The claim that belief in God is justified by its frequency among various peoples is no better. (Does common assent, after all, justify a belief? Think, says Unamuno, of the popularity of the pre-scientific belief that the earth goes round the sun.) But whether or not we see the defect of such an argument, it fails to move our souls.

The real basis of faith, Unamuno believes, is not theory, but the life-blood of experience. Religion, he explains, "consists in the simple feeling of a relationship of dependence upon something above us and a desire to establish relations with this mysterious power."[31] This relationship furthermore is one between persons. It cannot be one of being lost and *submerged* in God as some mystics would have it. For any such event would mean the virtual loss of oneself, a "dreamless sleep of *nirvana*," which is to say, the loss of existence altogether. Unamuno cites, in this connection, the words of Jesus, who, when asked by Peter, "Behold, we have forsaken all and followed thee; what shall we have therefore?", replied not that they should be somehow absorbed in the Father, but that they should sit upon thrones, judging the twelve tribes of Israel.[32] Religion is not the longing for annihilation, but the longing for *completion*.

---

[30] The argument thus alleges that the world could not have arisen by chance.

[31] *Tragic Sense of Life.*, p. 217.

[32] *Matthew* 19: 23-6.

This insistence on the distinctness of oneself from God has a parallel within the tradition of India. The point is made with marvelous succinctness by Huston Smith, who recounts in *The World's Religions* the various strands of Vedic religious thought. There seem to be, Smith observes, two basic conceptions of the divine in this tradition, one that conceives liberation as literal non-dividedness (*a-dvaita*) with God, the other as a "qualified" non-dividedness (*vishisht-a-dvaita*) that views self and God to remain eternally distinct from one another.

This difference is reflected in the different practices of *yoga* (cognate with the English words 'yoke' and 'union'). Among its classic forms, Smith notes, are those of *jnana* (knowledge) and *bhakti* (love). The former of these is a *yoga* that tends toward abstraction, toward impersonality in its conception of the divine. It proposes a literal identification of *atman* and *Brahman* - of self and ultimate reality. The latter is the *yoga* of a more emotive constitution, one that expresses its impulse primarily in love. In summarizing its rationale, Smith writes,

> as healthy love is outgoing, the bhakta will reject all suggestions that the God one loves is oneself, even one's deepest Self, and insist on God's otherness. As a Hindu devotional classic puts the point, "I want to taste sugar; I don't want to be sugar."[33]

---

[33] Huston Smith, *The World's Religions* (San Francisco: HarperCollins, 1991). Smith quotes the Song of Tukaram, translated by John S. Hoyland in *An Indian Peasant Mystic* in 1932. (Reprinted by Prinit Press of Dublin in 1978). The song contains such lyrics as, "Can water quaff itself? Can trees taste of the fruit they bear? He who worships God must stand distinct from Him, So only shall he know the joyful love of God ... " An excellent summary of Indian thought is contained in Sarvepalli Radhakrishnan's two-volume *Indian Philosophy* (London: George Allen & Unwin Ltd, 1923). For a detailed account of non-dualist and qualified-non-dualist traditions, see also Surendranath Dasgupta's five-volume work *A History of Indian Philosophy* (London: Cambridge University Press, 1922). See especially volumes I and III, which discuss, respectively, the outlooks of the philosophers Shankara and Ramanuja. (See also chapters 6 and 7 ahead.)

Those who are closest to God may speak of their absorption in Him. Yet even in this flight of the mystic, if we think about it, "the consciousness of self is preserved, the awareness of distinction from God with whom one is united." If we read St. Teresa[34] carefully, notes Unamuno, we shall notice that the *sensitive* element, "the element of delight," and hence the element of personal consciousness, is never excluded. In truth, the soul allows itself to be absorbed in God "in order that it may absorb Him," in order that it may acquire consciousness of its own divinity.

It is the individual, solitary and discrete, that has primacy in Unamuno's thought. The real gist of religion, he emphasizes, even theistic religion, is not the longing *that there be a God*. Rather it is the longing for our own being, "for the permanence, in some form or another, of our personal and individual consciousness." No individual who knows himself, who has a strong and enduring sense of who he is, can claim otherwise. The questions of metaphysics gain their weight from our concern for our own destiny. It is from their bearing upon this one question that they derive their value. If they do not bear upon it they are idle.

If we are truly conscious of ourselves, we will not let go. We will be unable to refrain from speculating about the next life even if we cannot form an exact idea of its nature. Belief in God and belief in our own survival thus come at last to the same thing. For what, after all, can belief in God mean if it does not involve us? How can we subtract ourselves from this eternal picture?

---

[34] A recent edition of Teresa's sixteenth-century classic *Interior Castle* is published by Doubleday (New York, 1989). E. Allison Peers, translator.

This inveterate spiritual tendency is expressed in the renewed currency of such things as spiritualism and belief in the transmigration of souls. These things may be pronounced dead, proved untenable, time and again. Always we can be sure that they will flower anew. For man, by his nature, will never willingly give up this attempt to form a concrete representation of the other life.

We cannot rest content, either, with common platitudes about a *beatific vision* - a loving contemplation, it seems, wherein the soul is absorbed in its creator. If we are honest, we will admit that there is little in this idea to distinguish it from infinite boredom. Man's highest pleasure lies in *acquiring and intensifying consciousness*.[35] His purest delight is allied with the act of learning, of "getting at the truth of things", and actively gaining a greater understanding.

Unamuno recalls the story[36] of an aged Spaniard who ascended a peak in Darien from which the Atlantic and Pacific oceans were visible. On beholding the two great bodies, he writes, the man fell to his knees and thanked God for not taking him before allowing him this sight. But if he had stayed there very long, Unamuno continues, this sight would have lost in wondrousness and his joy would have diminished. His joy was fundamentally that of discovery. Thus it may be that our joy hereafter lies not the whole instantaneous truth (something, says Unamuno, that we probably could not bear in any case), but continual discovery ongoing. The eternity that is like an eternal present, without memory and without

---

[35] *Tragic Sense of Life*, p. 229.

[36] *Ibid.*

hope, is indistinguishable from death.[37] There is thus a sense in which even purgatory is preferable to an unmitigated "heaven of glory." If there is in heaven an end of want, then how can the blessed there go on living?

> If in paradise they do not suffer for want of God, how shall they love Him? And if even there, in the heaven of glory, while they behold God little by little and closer and closer, yet without ever wholly attaining to Him, there does not always remain something more for them to know and desire, if there does not always remain a substratum of doubt, how shall they not fall asleep?[38]

The conception of happiness as a single and static vision, writes Unamuno, is at its base a rationalist idea, one aligned with Aristotle's *bios theoretikos* (life of contemplation). Yet the true human good requires not only vision, but delight. It is possible only if we remain independent in our being from God. It requires, too, a bodily existence of some kind if it is to mean anything. What we long for at bottom, is "a prolongation of this life, and no other," albeit with improvements in its condition. The majority of suicides would not take their lives if they believed that they would otherwise live forever. The self-slayer, he writes, kills himself "because he will not wait for death."

Our thinking about the hereafter is clouded, thinks Unamuno,[39] by the doctrine of hell as a place of eternal punishment. Reflection upon this idea shows that it is unbearable. Attempts to justify it as an article of faith are specious, even ridiculous, when we look at them with seriousness. It is said, for example, that

---

[37] *Ibid.*, p. 256.

[38] *Ibid.*

[39] *Ibid.*, pp. 239 and following.

God is infinite, and so that an offense committed against Him must be requited with an eternity of payment. Could any such rationale hold within the sphere of human ethics? For here surely the gravity of an offense is measured not by the dignity of the offended party, but by the intention of the offender. And what, he asks, becomes of Jesus' "Father forgive them, for they know now what they do"?[40] Indeed do any who offend God fully understand what they do? Eternal punishment, contends Unamuno, is barbarous. Only that a mind that understands punishment as vengeance can begin to entertain it. No one, he adds, can enjoy God in heaven while seeing his brother in hell.

I might digress for a moment to mention, in this regard, my own experience as a philosophy instructor. Years ago, when teaching courses dealing with religious issues, I would occasionally ask students to imagine that the classroom in which we were now located were now the highest heaven, and that the one next door, or across the hallway, were hell. Suppose, I said, that we were able to hear the anguished cries of those in that room while enjoying what was here a paradise. Perhaps some of those next door were acquaintances, even friends or family, in this life. Would we be disturbed by the sounds?

Perhaps, again, they had been our enemies. Would this make the situation any better? The general feeling was that the suffering would be more disturbing if it were the suffering of loved ones. But over time, it seemed to most, it would be disturbing no matter who were the sufferers. Eventually, it seemed, such suffering would become intolerable. Heaven itself might become damnation.

---

[40] *Luke* 23: 34.

Suppose, I said, that the room of the damned were moved further down the hall, so that the screams were less audible, or were moved across town, so that they were not heard, but were only known by some other means. Over time, it seemed, it would make little difference. If the opinion was not unanimous, it was shared to a large extent. And the strongest objections to this scenario, the surest convictions of its evil, came from the most humane and most perceptive students in the class. The more highly developed the student, it seemed, the less he or she was able to entertain the idea of a heaven cognizant of hell.[41]

Of course, it may be objected, heaven need not include this knowledge. Hell, some maintain, is kept from those who are saved. Or perhaps this final division of souls is really a division into wholly different spheres,[42] into different and incommensurate realities, each with its own order. But even if this is the case, I think, a problem remains. For the division still seems to have in it a disturbing finality.

---

[41] This is not to say that such an attitude is unanimous among philosophers. The elect, writes Peter of Lombard in the twelfth century, "shall go forth ... to see the torments of the impious and seeing this they will not be affected by grief but will be satiated with joy at the sight of the unutterable calamity of the impious." This remark, indicative of a good deal of medieval thought, is cited by F. L. Cross in the *Oxford Dictionary of the Christian Church* (Oxford: Oxford University Press, 1963), pp. 1054-55.

[42] Thus C. S. Lewis, for example, says that we might cease to think of heaven and hell as coexisting in "unilinear" time like the histories, say, of England and the United States. Jesus, he observes, speaks of hell less in terms of *duration* than of *finality*. Consignment to the fire is thus treated typically as the end of the story, and not as a new beginning. What is cast, or casts itself, into hell, writes Lewis, is but "remains," and not even a whole person as it has existed in this world. Hell is perhaps not to be thought of as parallel to heaven, but as "the darkness outside," where "being fades away into nonentity." (See *The Problem of Pain*, chapter 8, "Hell".)

Some, perhaps, will find this finality appropriate. Here on earth, they will say, we are given our chance, and after this we must bear the consequences. But such a chance is surely not distributed in any coherent fashion, and the finality in question does not take into account the individual human potential that is often scarcely revealed within this brief lifetime. What would heaven would be without those with whom we have shared the journey? And if we remain with more popular conceptions of damnation, I think, we will see their irrationality.

The Tragic Sense of Life is a book that reveals the pain of its author - his torment at the fact that his own deepest intimations about life and destiny can never find confirmation. The book is produced, he tells us, by a warfare of the heart and the head. That neither side entirely prevails, I think, is a tribute to Unamuno's own integrity. He grasps, in a manner that few have, the reality of the spirit and the complexity of human belief with respect to it. The reader who is steeped in the mainstream of current philosophy may wonder why indeed Unamuno does believe in immortality - may wonder what exactly is his *argument* for it. While such a question is understandable, it misses, I think, his real purpose. Unamuno seeks not to convince, but to *awaken*.

We are backward, he insists, in much of our thought. Traditional religious doctrine, for example, makes it a virtue to accept certain articles of faith no matter what we imagine otherwise. Yet it is not, Unamuno observes, belief in a future life that makes an individual good, but being good that makes him believe in it. Our own love, our own compassion - which is to say, our genuine intelligence - is our safeguard against despair.

Our beliefs arise out of our character, and not the other way around. For this reason there is not always perfect congruence between what a man believes with his head (i. e., with his intellect) and what he knows in his heart. There may likewise exist tension between his own convictions and the letter of his own religious law. A truly elevated human being cannot believe, for example, that anyone is ever separated from his creator for eternity even if he has been raised from birth to accept it. And again, to cite a different but related case, a self-alleged cynic may refute, by his actions, his own professed rejection of values.[43]

St. Emmanuel

Insight of this kind makes Unamuno very different from most in the current mainstream of philosophy. We who now ply the trade stand to learn much from his example. Philosophy, he writes, is a product of the *humanity* of each philosopher.[44] And each philosopher, again, is a man of flesh and bone who addresses himself to other men of flesh and bone like himself. Let him do what he will, he philosophizes not only with his reason, but with his feelings, with his soul and with his body. It is *the man*, insists Unamuno, that philosophizes.

---

[43] Similarly, says Unamuno, if a man tells you that he refrains from wrongdoing only out of fear (say, of punishment hereafter), you can be sure that he would continue in his virtue even if his religious beliefs should change, and would find some other explanation. (p. 262)

[44] *Ibid.*, 28.

How does this make him different? The difference, I believe, is that philosophy, in the main, sees its task as being another version of what is done in the sciences. It is thus an exercise in *detachment*, a technical enterprise, cleansed of emotion and free of crisis. Its aim accordingly is to chisel our ideas into clearer and clearer focus. Its action is like unto that of a blade, whose action, it is supposed, will yield surgical insight into life's deepest problems. In the process philosophy becomes mere performance.

Today's programs in the discipline are principally exercises in abstraction. Little effort is made to explain why it is that comparably talented and educated individuals within the field may have such utterly different ways of understanding life and living it. But there is a reason, and Unamuno sees it. What he sees is that philosophy is not grounded solely in this exercise of logic. Its real source, its life blood, is found in the spiritual condition of that individual who professes it.

The same, thinks Unamuno, is true of literature. If one wishes another angle on his approach to the issue of immortality, and of philosophy as a whole - and for him, as we have seen, they come to much the same thing - one will find no better source than his own story "St. Emmanuel, the Good, Martyr".[45]

Beneath its title is Paul's famous statement, "If with this life only in view we have had hope in Christ, we are of all men the most to be pitied."[46] It is presented as the confidential memoir of a woman named Angela Carballino, who

---

[45] The story is contained in Unamuno's *Abel Sanchez and Other Stories* (Chicago: Henry Regnery Company, 1956).

[46] *I Corinthians* 15: 19.

recalls an extraordinary man of years before, the parish priest in her small village of Valverde de Lucerna. He was, says Angela, "my true father, the father of my spirit," whom she knew far better than her natural father who had died when she was very young. She recalls Don Emmanuel from the time of her childhood, when he was, she recalls, perhaps 37 years of age.

> He was tall, slender, erect; he carried himself the way our Buitre Peak carries its crest, and his eyes had all the blue depth of our lake. As he walked he commanded all eyes, and not only the eyes but the hearts of all; gazing round at us he seemed to look through our flesh as through glass and penetrate our hearts.[47]

He was loved by all, and especially by children. "And the things he said to us!", recalls Angela. Not words, she adds, but *things*. The villagers, she recalls, could scent their sanctity, and they were intoxicated with it.

And how he loved them. His entire life, she remembers, consisted of salvaging wrecked marriages, forcing unruly sons to submit to the wishes of their parents, reconciling parent and child, and above all, she says, consoling the weary in spirit. And he helped everyone to die well.

Angela now remembers various incidents in the life of this Christ-figure who reputedly had left the prospect of a brilliant career in church administration to remain with his village. A young girl, for example, returned dishonored from her time in the city with a child out of wedlock. Don Emmanuel persuaded a boyfriend to marry her and give the child a name. This boyfriend, as it turns out, now has the consolation, in his later years and presently an invalid, of an attentive son to care for him.

---

[47] "St. Emmanuel", pp. 208-09.

On Midsummer's Night, she recalls, the shortest night of the year, it was the custom in the village for old folk to come to the lake to be healed of various complaints of possession and bewitchment. Don Emmanuel, she says, undertook to have the same function as that lake - to be, as it were, a pool of healing. Such was the effect of his presence and his gaze, and above all, she remembers, his miraculous voice, that he effected cures, even though he refused to take credit for miracles. He treated all with kindness, and if he favored anyone, it was the least fortunate, and above all the ones who rebelled.

> The marvel of the man was his voice; a divine voice which brought one close to weeping. Whenever he officiated at Solemn Mass High and intoned a prelude, a tremor ran through the congregation and all within sound of his voice were moved to within the sound of his being. The sound of his chanting, overflowing the church, went on to float over the lake and settle at the foot of the mountain.[48]

And when on Good Friday, she recalls, he intoned Christ's words,[49] "My God, My God, why hast Thou forsaken me?", a shudder went through the crowd, like the lash of a northeast storm on the face of the lake. On one occasion, she writes, his own mother responded, without being able to help herself, "My son!"

Don Emmanuel's effect on people was such that no one dared to tell him a lie. And yet his insistence upon honesty did not come before his mercy. When a judge came to Emmanuel and asked him to obtain a confession from a suspected criminal, he refused, saying that he would not extract a confession from any man that might be the death of him.

---

[48] *Ibid.*, 213-14.

[49] *Matthew* 27: 46.

There was a curious phenomenon that occurred on those occasions when Don Emmanuel gathered together into the church the entire village, young and old, of roughly a thousand persons to recite the Creed: "I believe in God, the Almighty Father, Creator of heaven and earth ..." It was, she remembers, a chorus that had the sound of a single voice, simple and united, forming a kind of mountain, whose peak, Don Emmanuel, was at times lost in the clouds. When they reached the words, "I believe in the resurrection of the flesh and the life everlasting," the voice of Don Emmanuel seemed to be submerged, drowned, she remembers, as if in that lake of voices. In truth, she now realizes, he was silent.

His life, she recalls, was active, and not contemplative. He fled from idleness, which he called the mother of vices, and most of all, she notes, from what he believed was the worst of these, the idleness of the mind. It was, said Don Emmanuel, a substitute for action. There was nothing worse in his mind than remorse over what might have been done. And even then, she notes, she began to sense that this man was himself haunted by some obsession.

Don Emmanuel could not believe that children, if they left the world, were anywhere but in heaven. He believed this no matter what the church itself might say on the subject. A child who was stillborn, or who perished soon after birth, was for him the most terrible of mysteries. It was, he said, as if the infant had killed itself, or had been crucified. He could not believe in hell, yet urged those who came to him to believe in heaven, even if he could not square it with the letter of his own law. Once, she recalls, there came to him an outsider, a man whose son had committed suicide, asking if this son could be buried in consecrated ground despite his sin. Don Emmanuel gave his affirmation, assuring the man that he had no doubt the son must surely have repented of all sin, even in his last moments.

Don Emmanuel was able to restore the spirits of all those who sought him. On one occasion the clown-leader of a visiting troupe lost his wife while in the middle of a performance. Don Emmanuel, who had followed the dying woman to a stable and helped her leave the world in a state of grace, greeted the clown and the others there when the performance was ended. The clown took his hand and told him that he was indeed a saint. Don Emmanuel then took the man's hand in his and replied,

> "It's you who are the saint, good clown. I watched you at your work and understood that you do it not only to provide bread for your children, but also to give joy to the children of others. And I tell you now that your wife, the mother of your children, whom I sent to God while you worked to give joy, is at rest in the Lord, and that you will join her there, and that the angels, whom you will make laugh with happiness in heaven, will reward you with their laughter."[50]

At this time everyone present, she adds, children and elders alike, wept in response - a response that came not only from sorrow, but from a mysterious joy in which all sorrow was drowned.

At sixteen, Angela recalls, she went to him for confession. Unable to enunciate her concerns, she finally poured out her doubts and fears, among them her fear of Don Emmanuel himself. She left the confession consoled, but with a fear, she says, that was turning to pity.

---

[50] "St. Emmanuel", pp. 221-22.

"I was at that time," she recalls, "a very young woman, almost a girl still,"

> and yet, I was beginning to be a woman, in my innermost being I felt the juice and stirrings of maternity, and when I found myself in the confessional at the side of the saintly priest, I sensed a kind of unspoken confession on his part in the soft murmur of his voice. And I remembered how when he had intoned in the church the words of Jesus Christ: "My God, my God, why hast Thou forsaken me?" his own mother had cried out in the congregation: "My son!"; and I could hear the cry that had rent the silence of the temple. And I went to him again for confession - and to comfort him.[51]

There came a time, recalls Angela, when "I began to feel a kind of maternal affection for my spiritual father," a time when she longed "to help him bear the cross of birth."

It was a day of seeming triumph when Angela's unbelieving brother Lazarus took Communion. Yet her sense of foreboding was confirmed later that same day when Lazarus told her in confidence what he could no longer keep a secret. Don Emmanuel, he told her, had asked him to set a good example for the townsfolk - to feign belief, even if he did not feel it, in accepting the sacrament.

How could a priest ask such a thing? It was not deceit, replied Don Emmanuel, for he could dip his fingers in the holy water, and he would end by believing.[52]

> "... And I, gazing into his eyes, asked him: 'And you, celebrating the Mass, have you ended by believing?' He looked away and stared out at the lake, until his eyes filled with tears. And it was in this way that I came to understand his secret."[53]

---

[51] *Ibid.*, 225.

[52] Cf. Pascal, *Pensees*.

[53] "St. Emmanuel", 236.

It was then, recalled Lazarus, that he understood that Don Emmanuel was indeed a saint. He did not believe. Yet his own disbelief he kept secret from the village, solely for the sake of their happiness.

But was it not better to have the truth at any price? Don Emmanuel's answer was that the truth may well be "something so unbearable, so terrible, something so deadly, that simple people could not live with it!" The Church, he explained, let people live. Therein perhaps lay its truth. And his own place in this scheme was to provide them with this consolation, even if it could not be his.

Would Lazarus, himself inclined all his life toward skepticism, and now privy to Don Emmanuel's secret, continue to pray for his deceased mother as he had promised her upon her deathbed? He would, and he would pray for his sister, and now for Don Emmanuel, as well.

Soon afterward Angela and Don Emmanuel met for confession. They wept together, and he told Angela to believe, and to suppress her doubts, if she has them, at any cost. But did he believe? He did.

> "In what, Father, in what? Do you believe in the after life? Do you believe that in dying we do not die in every way, completely? Do you believe that we will see each other again, that we will love each other in a world to come? Do you believe in another life?" [54]

About this he could not lie. Instead he asked her to absolve him. "We quitted the church," recalls Angela, "and as I went out I felt the quickening of maternity within me."

---

[54] *Ibid.*

A curious bond developed between Don Emmanuel and Lazarus, who now accompanied him on all of his tasks with the townsfolk. During which all of the while, notes Angela, "he was sounding deeper in the unfathomable soul of the priest." Don Emmanuel confessed to Lazarus that he was afflicted without end with the temptation to suicide. But he could not allow himself to succumb to it for the sake of those in the village.

Nor could he abide the involvement of the church in political ends. Perhaps there would come, one day, a new society in which wealth were distributed evenly across the whole. What would be the point of it? Would not such an arrangement lead just as surely to tedium and life-weariness? If religion were (in Marx's famous phrase) a mere opiate, let it be such, and it would be something more valuable than all of the social theory in the world.

Don Emmanuel's spirit was weakening, recalls Angela, and his strength was waning. One day, when suffering paralysis, he was carried to the church and preached a final sermon. Before this he called Angela and her brother to his bedside, and told them to continue to pray for all, and to let them dream.

> "When they go to bury me, let it be in a box made from the six planks I cut from the old walnut tree - poor old tree! - in whose shade I played as a child, when I began the dream ... In those days, I did really believe in life everlasting.[55]

He was carried then to the church, and bid all to live in peace and contentment with one another - to live in the anticipation that they would be together again in that other Valverde de Lucerna in the stars overhead.

---

[55] *Ibid.*, p. 252.

Angela and Lazarus were left without Don Emmanuel. Daily Lazarus went to the tomb, and confided to his sister that he could not continue living without his help. For he, like the priest, had seen the truth, and it was death.

It is now years later, Angela explains, and Lazarus, too, has left the world. Her life is different now, for Don Emmanuel taught her how to live. "He taught me by his life," she recalls, "to lose myself in the life of the people of my village." She no longer feels the passing of the years, any more than she feels the passage of the water in the lake. Now, she notes,

> as I write this memoir, this confession of my experience with saintliness, with a saint, I am of the opinion that Don Emmanuel the Good, my Don Emmanuel, and my brother, too, died believing they did not believe, but that without believing in their belief, they actually believed, with resignation and in desolation.[56]

In postscript, Unamuno (who, in his dramatic role of editor, will not tell how he came by this document written by Angela) ventures his opinion that if Don Emmanuel and Lazarus had ever confessed their doubt to the people, they would not have been believed. For the village folk, he explains, would have believed not in their words, but in their deeds. In a village like Valverde de Lucerna, one makes one's confession by one's own conduct. In their own untutored wisdom, these folk saw more deeply into Don Emmanuel than he saw into himself.

"St. Emmanuel" is a masterpiece of fiction, a novel, as Unamuno insists, being the truest and most intimate form of history. In a novel is revealed to us not, with any necessity, the empirical fact of history, but the inward truth of the author's own experience. It is much the same way with a painting, which reveals

---

[56] *Ibid.*, p. 261.

to us not the exact nature of the object, but the painter's apprehension of it - a fact, to be sure, as much as any fact that science reveals.

Reason, Unamuno maintains once again, does not yield us any comfort with respect to our destiny. But the heart is not bound by such limits. Can a case be made upon this condition of internal warfare? Is there a higher reason of some kind that transcends the reason of the intellect?

The answer of this story, I think, lies in the spiritual bond that connects its characters even in the midst of their own professions of doubt. "St. Emmanuel", like Unamuno's whole philosophy, pours out a confession of belief in the midst of darkness. In it is the portrayal of life, of reciprocity, of inward affirmation borne of love. Nowhere is this more poignantly shown than in one passage early in Angel's narrative, remembering Don Emmanuel's silence during the part of the recitation that affirmed belief in the life everlasting. It was, Angela recalls, after she has learned his secret, "as if a caravan crossing the desert lost its leader as they approached the goal of their trek, whereupon his people lifted him on their shoulders to bring his lifeless body into the promised land."[57]

In the embrace of souls lies a truth deeper than reason. Perhaps, Angela tells us, the Don imagines that he does not believe, but this skepticism of the head is shown false by all that he does. And the same is true of Lazarus, whose own deeper faith now courses like a river of new life through his own words. Don Emmanuel, thinks Unamuno, is a living refutation not only of his claim to skepticism, but of skepticism itself. The truth of his spirit is victorious.

---

[57] *Ibid.*, p. 216.

What, Unamuno asks in his greatest work, is our heart's truth, "anti-rational though it be"? It is, he answers, "the immortality of the human soul, the truth of the persistence of our consciousness without any termination whatsoever, the truth of the human finality of the universe."[58] It has, he adds, a kind of "moral proof," formulated as follows: "Act so that in your own judgment and in the judgment of others you may merit eternity, act so that you may become irreplaceable, act so that you may not merit death."

Or perhaps, he adds,

> Act as if you were to die to-morrow, but to die in order to survive and be eternalized. The end of morality is to give personal, human finality to the universe; to discover the finality that belongs to it - if indeed it has any finality - and to discover it by acting.[59]

For those trained in argument, it is not easy to see how this can amount to a "proof" in any sense. Unamuno, of course, does not pretend to have demonstrated the truth of immortality to his reader. Yet sometimes, he believes, we may know something even if we cannot formulate it in compelling manner. Such knowledge is not subject to public confirmation. It arises out of love, out of self-expenditure, out of life-strength that is given to our fellows without expectation.

"The vanity of the passing world and love," he writes, "are the two fundamental and heart-penetrating notes of true poetry."

---

[58] *Tragic Sense of Life*, p. 263.

[59] *Ibid.*

> And they are two notes of which neither can be sounded without causing the other to vibrate. The feeling of the vanity of the passing world kindles love in us, the only thing that triumphs over the vain and transitory, the only thing that fills life again and eternalizes it ... And love, above all when it struggles against destiny, overwhelms us with the feeling of the vanity of this world of appearances and gives us a glimpse of another world, in which destiny is overcome and liberty is law.[60]

This, again, is not a proof. Nor is it intended to be. It is not intended, either, to furnish the reader with any easy confidence in his own immortality. There is far too much confidence, believes Unamuno, with respect to these things, and it exists on each side. The believer, as we have seen, has no rational guarantee. And the sceptic has none, either. For the problem of his own destiny can be dismissed by anything as facile as materialism. His spiritual condition has no intellectual escape. Unamuno's writing is an invitation to the reader to explore himself, and to decide, on the basis of his own inward condition, what he truly believes.

Our real assurance of immortality is found not in reason, but in love - in our own concrete union with others like ourselves. Were there a real pessimism, it would have no witness, but would remain silent. The despair that finds a voice, on the other hand, is a spiritual event, "the cry of misery which brother utters to brother when both are stumbling through a valley of shadows which is peopled with - comrades." (This passage quotes one of the day's periodicals.) In its anguish, says Unamuno, this cry bears witness to eternity.

---

[60] *Ibid.*, p. 39.

H. G. Wells, he notes, has observed that "active and capable men"[61] in religious professions tend to have little concern with personal survival. But this does not mean that such individuals fail to believe, for it is a faith in immortality, a faith "down in their souls like a subterranean river," that nourishes their deeds. Our real salvation, he imagines, lies not in finding intellectual assurance of heaven, but in fighting life's battle without it. The absurd hero Don Quixote, he writes, died and descended into hell,

> and freed all the condemned, as he had freed the galley slaves, and he shut the gates of hell, and tore down the scroll that Dante saw there and replaced it by one on which was written "Long live hope!" and escorted by those whom he had freed, and they laughing at him, he went to heaven. And God laughed paternally at him, and this divine laughter filled his soul with eternal happiness.[62]

Not all of us, of course, will join Unamuno in his anguish. Not all are so structured, and can fathom its depth. But those who can, he believes, will find an answer. In living our lives with courage we will find our strength. In love and in longing we will find the truth. In Don Quixote, thinks Unamuno, one finds such a wisdom. The above quotation, I think, gives this chapter a fitting end note.

Or, if one likes, there is his own:

"And may God deny you peace, but give you glory!"[63]

---

[61] Unamuno quotes here from Wells' *Anticipations*.

[62] *Tragic Sense of Life*, pp. 323-24.

[63] *Ibid.*, p. 330.

Chapter VI

Survival and Soul-Making: The Case of John Hick

> The good that outshines all ill is not a paradise long since lost but a kingdom which is yet to come in its full glory and permanence.
>
> John Hick, *Evil and the God of Love*

No doubt the greatest contribution to the survival issue within mainstream philosophy in recent decades has been made by John Hick. An Englishman born in 1922, Hick has taught religious studies at the University of Birmingham and the Claremont Graduate School in Claremont, California. In this chapter I will examine several aspects of his philosophy, including his account of human destiny as it is developed in his seminal *Death and Eternal Life*. In addition I will discuss his conception of religious belief as presented first in his *Faith and Knowledge* and later in a number of related essays. I will also look at his response to the problem of evil in *Death and Eternal Life* and in his earlier work *Evil and the God of Love*.[1]

---

[1] A brief autobiographical sketch of Hick's own development, from his involvement with evangelical Christian Protestantism to his later embrace of the world's major religious traditions, is contained in "A Spiritual Journey". This essay can be found in his collection *God Has Many Names* (Philadelphia: Westminster Press, 1982).

The Nature of Religious Belief

What does it mean to have, broadly speaking, a "religious" outlook on life? Is such an outlook justified? What is the relationship between religious belief and belief of other kinds? Questions like these occupy much of Hick's writing. In several of his books and essays he undertakes a description of religious belief and a defense of its basic rationality.

There is, writes Hick, "an element of mystery" at the heart of all experience.[2] For we have, it seems, a knowledge that underlies experience itself - a knowledge that precedes its whole content. Consider, for one, our recognition of a world that exists independently of our sense impressions. The existence of this world does not seem to be *derived* from any given fact that the senses disclose. An alternative reading of this experience is possible; we might suppose, after all, that this whole bombardment of sight and sound is just one great hallucination. Certain efforts in philosophy, in fact, involve this kind of exercise.[3] We might, with perfect consistency, entertain the thesis of *solipsism* - the view that the only reality is one's own conscious experience.

---

[2] John Hick, *Faith and Knowledge* (Ithaca, New York: Cornell University Press, 1957), p. 118.

[3] Consider, for example, Descartes' famous "evil genius" hypothesis in Part I of his *Meditations*. It may be, says Descartes, that my experience is really an illusion produced in me by some powerful and malevolent deceiver.

This, of course, would be a wild departure from our usual outlook,[4] yet it does represent a thinkable choice. The belief that our experience represents something real, something outside our immediate awareness, is thus *an interpretation*. This act of reading, of going beyond what is given, thinks Hick, is essential to experience of any kind. For in order to function, to have any notion of objective reality, I cannot be a mere passive recipient of feeling and sensation. I must have some idea of what these things *mean*. (Does the change in my visual field, at this moment, for example, signify merely a change of sense-impression, or does it indicate an object coming my way?)

Interpretation furthermore has levels. Consider, says Hick, my perception of *a rectangular red object* lying on the floor. To this extent I interpret it as a "thing," a "substance" - as something occupying space and time. In addition I may see that this item is a red-covered *book*. I have now a new interpretation, one that includes the previous one and yet goes beyond it. Or consider, again, the various possible reactions to a piece of paper covered with writing. A non-literate individual might interpret it as something man-made, but might not see its purpose. A literate person, but one who does not understand its particular language, might see it furthermore as being a document of some kind. And someone who understands the language will find in it the expression of certain

---

[4] So, for example, our personal relationships, involving "our loves and friendships, our hates and enmities, rivalries and co-operations", would have to be treated not as "transsubjective" meetings with other personalities, but as "dialogues and dramas within oneself." On this way of looking at reality there would be no other persons, but only the appearances of them. Such appearances would have no consciousness of their own, and would not properly be the objects of affection or enmity, nor could their "actions" be judged in any evaluative sense.

ideas. Each, explains Hick, answers the question "What is it?" correctly, but at different levels. And each more adequate level of interpretation presupposes the ones beneath it.

Our reading of experience, then, takes us beyond private sensation. For we take this experience to *represent* something, namely, an external world of space and objects. But the reading goes further. For it is characteristic of human beings to see life not only in these terms, but in terms of "the dimension of personality and responsibility." Our encounter with other human beings gives rise to *moral* awareness. Here we take reality to contain more than just a collection of objects in motion. We find in it value, as well. Thus while I can, Hick says,

> be aware of the bare neutral *existence* of a stone ... I can only be aware of the bare neutral existence of a fellow human being if I have degraded that being in my own eyes from a thou to an it. As a thou he or she evokes in me an awareness, not merely of the existence of a thing, but of the *presence* of a person.[5]

We acknowledge this moral element in various ways, as for example when we find ourselves *obligated* to do something. Consider, says Hick, a traveler on some unfrequented road who comes upon a stranger lying injured and in need of help. At the level of natural significance, it is only an empirical state of affairs, "a particular configuration of stone and earth and flesh." But at the moral level, it is a situation requiring the traveler to give aid.[6]

---

[5] John Hick, *An Interpretation of Religion - Human Responses to the Transcendent* (London: Yale University Press, 1989), p. 145. This work represents Hick's Gifford lectures at the University of Edinburgh in 1986-87. In the passage quoted Hick refers to the 1923 work *I and Thou* by Martin Buber.

[6] *Faith and Knowledge*, p. 111.

In this situation, it seems, a demand, an "imperative," is laid upon him, requiring of him a certain active response. The situation takes on "a preemptory ethical significance" that overrides what inclination he may have otherwise.

Here again, we go beyond the actual data of sensation. This moral element of our experience cannot be deduced from any particular sense impression.[7] If some individual lacks an awareness of value - if he is unmoved, say, by gross instances of abuse or injustice - there is nothing we can *show* him in order to bring him over to our vantage point. If such an individual takes the position of "a moral solipsist ... recognizing no responsibility toward other people, no one can prove to him that he has any such responsibilities." Someone wholly devoid of such awareness can only be viewed, by the rest of us, as being defective in his perception - as suffering from "a defect of his nature analogous to physical blindness."[8]

Thus we take reality, as we have seen, to be more than a theater of private sensation. We take it to involve a world of material events outside our immediate conscious impressions. And we see it furthermore as having a moral dimension. We cannot, thinks Hick, prove these things to be true. Alternative readings of experience are possible. This possibility is inherent in our situation, for there is always my own experience, on the one hand, and the world "in itself"

---

[7] Nor, it might be added, can this element be deduced from any particular inward feeling - say, from the stirring of conscience. For this fact (recalling earlier discussion) is by itself just as ambiguous as sensation. The fact that I have a certain feeling about how I should behave does not tell me whether or not I ought to heed it. Conscience, like sensation, must be interpreted.

[8] *Faith and Knowledge*, p. 113.

on the other. It seems as if there exists an external world; it seems also as if I am involved in a moral encounter with other human beings. But since I can never surmount this limit, can never get outside of myself to "experience the unexperienced," I can never have final confirmation of such basic assumptions.[9]

This second level of interpretation assumes the first. Moral significance presupposes natural significance; it takes for granted the reality of an arena in which oneself is connected with others. Our belief in good and evil assumes that we are taking overt action of some kind in an external world. Relating ourselves to the moral sphere is thus a particular way of relating ourselves to the natural sphere, as well. This paradigm - this logical scheme of "one order of significance superimposed upon and mediated through another" - has further application. As just noted, we commonly take our experience to reveal to us not only a natural order, but a moral one, as well. By the same token, we sometimes take life to have *religious* significance. Herein we find "the highest and ultimate order of significance, mediating neither of the others and yet being mediated through both of them."

Again, as before, we do not derive this element from any particular *feature* of experience. We are not proving anything; rather we are once more interpreting reality *as a whole*. To illustrate, Hick offers the following scenario. Suppose, he says, that I enter a room in a strange building and find myself in what appears to be the meeting of a militant secret society. I see other persons, some of them armed, who take me for one of their fellows. Subtle and violent plans are

---

[9] *An Interpretation of Religion*, p. 134.

discussed for an overthrow of the constitution, and the whole situation is quite alarming, when all of a sudden I notice behind me a gallery with arc lights and running cameras. I see that I have walked by accident onto the set of a film.

Now, of course, my experience has changed: Before me are the same things, but they signify to me something other than what they signified a moment ago. To understand what is involved in religious life, says Hick, let us expand this stage into the world, into the entire universe - this "strange room into which we walk at birth." There is no space left, at this point, for a "gallery," no direction in which we can turn in order to find the real meaning of our situation. We must interpret reality in its entirety, with no further reference available.

A religious believer interprets this whole as a spiritual event. Thus a monotheist, to cite one example, sees the world as mediating the plan and purpose of a divine being. He sees his own situation as requiring of him an according response of trust and obedience. This interpretive leap "carries him into a world which exists through the will of a holy, righteous, and loving Being who is the creator and sustainer of all that is." A perception of this kind is not a reasoned conclusion, nor is it an "an unreasoned hunch." It is instead the believer's apprehension of a divine presence investing all of life. Such a believer, says Hick,

> cannot explain *how* he knows the divine presence to be mediated through his human experience. He just finds himself interpreting his experience in this way. He lives in the presence of God, though he is unable to prove by any dialectical process that God exists.[10]

---

[10] *Faith and Knowledge*, pp. 118-19.

It happens, on occasion, that an individual experiences his entire life in terms of this reality. Thus the Old Testament prophets, to cite one example, "experienced their historical situation as one in which they were living under the sovereign claim of God," and in which it was incumbent on them to act as God's agents.[11]

Consider, then, the fundamental difference that may exist between one individual's experience and that of another. A secular historian, for one, may see in the Biblical drama only the various social and geographic factors giving rise to certain events in a city or empire. But the prophets themselves "saw behind all this the hand of God raising up and casting down and gradually fulfilling a purpose." This interpretation is not *a theory*. It is not something imposed retrospectively upon the facts as a logical device. Rather it is "the way in which the prophet actually experienced and participated in these events at the time."[12] Entering into this framework involves the adoption of fundamental way of seeing and acting towards one's environment. To see the world as being ruled by a divine love, a love all-seeing that sets value upon ourselves, is to see also that a certain kind of life is required of us.

---

[11] For a succinct discussion of the prophets, whose writings constitute a significant portion of the *Tanakh*, or Jewish Bible, see Abraham Heschel's *The Prophets: An Introduction* (New York: Harper and Row, 1962). A more recent account is James M. Ward's *Thus Says the Lord: The Message of the Prophets* (Nashville: Abingdon Press, 1991). For a recent and highly readable translation of the Hebrew scripture, see *Tanakh: The Holy Scriptures* (Philadelphia: The Jewish Publication Society, 1985).

[12] *Faith and Knowledge*, p. 143.

Hick's account of religious belief draws in part from discussion contained in the *Investigations* of Ludwig Wittgenstein. It is possible, observes Wittgenstein, to view a self-same object in different ways, as, for example, when looking at a set of lines and "seeing" it first as one kind of figure and then another - "seeing" it, perhaps, as either concave or convex, or as either a duck or a rabbit.[13] We are familiar likewise with puzzle pictures wherein we "discover" that this scatter of dots or patches is also the picture, say, of a human being standing in a grove of trees. This seeing does not introduce a new object, but involves a new way of seeing what is already present. It will help us, Hick believes, to understand religious belief if we expand this notion of seeing-as into that of *experiencing*-as, into a mode of interpretation involving not just vision, but experience altogether.

Hick applies this notion to the phenomenon of religion worldwide.[14] The starting point of this enterprise is the religious experience of mankind. Such experience, on the face of it, is *transitive* - it impresses itself upon the subject as being not merely experience, but experience of an object of some kind. As such it evokes feelings of awe, dependence, creatureliness, abasement, terror, worship, and joy; a sense of being addressed, claimed, guided, and commanded; an experience of having visions and being illuminated; a special kind of peace and serenity; and a sense of being somehow absorbed into a reality greater than oneself.

---

[13] Ludwig Wittgenstein, *Philosophical Investigations*. Trans. G. E. M. Anscombe (Oxford: Basil Blackwell, 1953). See pp. 193 and following.

[14] See Hick's "Sketch for a Global Theory of Religious Knowledge", contained in the aforenoted *God Has Many Names*.

Again, this is how the world *seems* to those who experience it in religious terms. The fact that certain individuals experience life in this way does not demonstrate, of course, that God exists, or that life has any such higher meaning. Nor, thinks Hick, are we apt to find a demonstration. The world, he believes, is ambiguous in this respect; it offers no confirmation of its own religious meaning, nor confirmation otherwise. The basis of religious belief is not found in any particular argument or empirical fact. To be religious is to experience the world in religious terms. Thus it may happen that two persons live in virtually different worlds, even when their outward perceptions are substantially the same.

But which outlook, it may be asked, is the right one? Life may well seem to us, at times, like a spiritual event. Yet it is theoretically possible that "this entire range of experience is human projection or fantasy."[15] It is possible, as well, that such experience reflects the truth. Which, then, is the right choice?

This question, thinks Hick, turns not upon particular fact, but upon our stance toward experience as a whole. In order to know what stance is appropriate with respect to religious issues, he believes, we would do well to examine our policy toward experience elsewhere. Overall, it is natural, and indeed biologically necessary, for us to trust our most basic inclinations toward reality. We could not live, for example, without some faith in the existence of an external world. (Think of what would happen, for example, to an individual indifferent to the perception that he or she were about to walk into a wall or out of a second-story window.) If we feel that we are in contact with a world of objects and

---

[15] *Ibid.*, p. 79.

events independent of ourselves, it is reasonable for us to act upon this feeling. If we feel that we have a certain moral relation to that world, it is right and natural, again, for us to suppose that this is the case.

This trust, thinks Hick, may extend to religious experience without any compromise of rationality. If one experiences life as a spiritual event, then it is reasonable to act on the basis of this experience, as well.[16] In this regard religious belief has *a structural continuity* with belief of other kinds. We have, in this case as in the ones previous, no theoretical confirmation that we are right. We cannot somehow transcend our own experience and see reality "in itself" over and above what it seems to our conscious apprehension. Perhaps this seeming further dimension of reality is an illusion. But if life presents itself to us as being a spiritual event, thinks Hick, there is no rational advantage in treating it as if it were something else. Nor is there any advantage in remaining undecided.

The key principle of interpretation, once again, is that of meaning. This concept, Hick writes, is "the most general and pervasive characteristic of conscious experience, and it is always relative to a perceiver." All conscious experience is "experiencing-as"; I experience this object, for example, not merely as a set of sensations, but as a *pen*. To experience the thing in this manner - to give it this meaning - is to react to it in one way instead of another (as a thing to write with, rather than to eat with, for example).

---

[16] See again discussion by Richard Swinburne concerning the Principle of Credulity. The relevance of this principle to religious issues in explained in chapter 13, "The Argument from Religious Experience", of Swinburne's *The Existence of God* (Oxford: Oxford University Press, 1979).

Meaning thus involves *action*. To see a thing in a certain way is to have a disposition toward it - to see it not only in terms of how it looks, but in terms of its purpose. Our experience, in this respect, is teleological. Religious experience is no exception; it, too, sees reality in these terms. It is concerned, however, not merely with the end or purpose of particular objects, but with the purpose of life in its entirety. Thus it is also *eschatological*; it is concerned, in other words, with the final end of things - with our own greater development and destiny.

Here, says Hick, lies its real content. Here also is the prospect of its confirmation. Religious belief is concerned with the direction of life as a whole. For this reason it is neither confirmed nor disconfirmed by any particular fact along the way. But its confirmation is possible, for religious belief makes verifiable claims about life's ultimate direction. The fulfillment of this end is the means by which it will (if true, and in a world perhaps far from this one) be confirmed.

But religion, it seems, is not just one thing. In looking at religion across time and place, we are confronted with "the very diverse, and apparently conflicting, beliefs and practices of the various traditions." If these traditions are not all the same, and perhaps not even consistent with each other, then what is the appropriate response? Can all faiths somehow be good or valid regardless? Is one true while all others are false? The most plausible answer, thinks Hick,

> is that the different streams of religious experience represent diverse awarenesses of the same transcendent reality, which is perceived in characteristically different ways by different human mentalities, formed by and forming different cultural histories.[17]

---

[17] *God Has Many Names,* p. 83.

The world's major religious traditions thus represent various ways in which a single and limitless reality is diversely apprehended. In each case, Hick imagines, this reality is "filtered" by the nature and limit of the consciousness that apprehends it. Such filtering, he thinks, may be inevitable. For it may be that "Humankind cannot bear very much reality."[18] A limited creature "is structured to cognise and participate in reality in a particular way"; it is not designed, in its present condition, to absorb the infinite.[19] The world's religions, thinks Hick, may be ways in which God's fathomless nature is apprehended according to the characteristic sensibilities of each culture and the individual within it.[20]

For this reason, he believes, we need to distinguish between the divine in itself and as it is experienced, "between the Real *an sich* and the real as variously experienced-and-thought by different human communities."[21] This thesis is developed at length in a variety of essays[22] devoted to religious experience and

---

[18] *An Interpretation of Religion*, p. 162. Hick quotes the line from T. S. Eliot, *Burnt Norton* (London: Faber and Faber, 1941).

[19] See, in connection with this idea, the discussion of Walter Stace in his "Mysticism and Human Reason", contained in the University of Arizona Bulletin Series, vol. XXVI, May 1955. Relevant portions of this article are reprinted with commentary in the earlier-cited volume *Philosophy Looks to the Future* edited by Richter and Fogg. The element of *paradox* in mystical testimony, writes Stace, may reflect the pouring, as it were, of infinite reality into the finite human "vessel." See also chapter 5, "Mysticism and Logic", in Stace's *Mysticism and Philosophy* (Los Angeles: Jeremy P. Tarcher, Inc., 1960).

[20] *An Interpretation of Religion*, pp. 162-65.

[21] *Ibid.*, p. 236.

[22] See John Hick, *Problems of Religious Pluralism* (New York: St. Martin's Press, 1985).

its interpretation. Borrowing from Kant, he invokes the distinction between *noumenon* and *phenomenon* - between reality on its own, unapprehended by mental structure of any kind, and reality as it appears to human consciousness. We cannot, in our present limited condition, have literal knowledge of God, but we can know God relative to our own particular nature.[23]

What is the relevance of this pluralist view to ourselves, and what impact might it have upon our religious outlook? There is an old controversy, says Hick, about the meaning of *salvation*. In "A Philosophy of Religious Pluralism", he describes various doctrinal strategies within organized Christianity for a resolution. One longstanding position is the *exclusivist* view that salvation is limited to those individuals with a conscious and explicit Christian orientation. Historically this is expressed, for example, in Catholic tradition by the dogma (albeit one effectively negated at the 1966 Second Vatican Council of Churches)[24] *extra ecclesiam nulla salus* (no salvation outside the church). The view has a parallel in Protestantism.[25]

---

[23] It is, says Hick, a restatement of St. Thomas Aquinas' dictum: "Things known are in the knower according to the mode of the knower." (*Summa Theologia*, Part II) See discussion in chapter 14 of *An Interpretation of Religion*.

[24] See Walter M. Abbott, *The Documents of Vatican II* (London: Geoffrey Chapman, 1966).

[25] Cited in Hick's essay "The Christian View of Other Faiths" (*God Has Many Names*) is the Council of Florence (1438-45), which holds that "no one remaining outside the Catholic Church, not just pagans, but also Jews or heretics or schismatics, can become partakers of eternal life; but they will go to the 'everlasting fire which was prepared for the devil and his angels,' unless before the end of life they are joined to the church". In a similar spirit, the evangelical Congress on World Mission at Chicago in 1960 declares, "In the years since the war, more than one billion souls have passed into eternity and more than half of these went to the torment of hell fire without even hearing of Jesus Christ, who He was, or why He died on the cross of Calvary." (p. 30)

It has thus been asserted, at times, that individuals outside the faith - no matter how sincere or virtuous otherwise - are eternally lost. A practicing Buddhist, for example, is apt to be damned if he is unacquainted with Christ or with Christian doctrine. Yet this attitude toward other faiths, Hick notes, is strongly correlated with ignorance of them. As the world becomes smaller, as old caricatures give way to direct contact and responsible scholarship, such an attitude becomes less plausible. And as we become familiar with the phenomena of religious experience across times and cultures, says Hick, we are struck by their profound similarity.[26]

But surely, he contends, this older view is disturbing regardless. For how are we to understand the love and mercy of a creator who condemns (and even, on some accounts, predestines) great portions of the human race to eternal misery? The conception of salvation as "a change in status in the eyes of God from the guilt of participation in Adam's original sin" has thus given way to one involving "the actual transformation of human life from self-centeredness to Reality-centeredness," the latter of which is not bound to a single tradition.[27]

A compromise, he notes, has been proposed in some quarters, a religious *inclusivism* whereby the special saving nature of Christianity is retained while the traditional conception of damnation is avoided. The gist of this view is "that God's forgiveness and acceptance of humanity have been made possible by

---

[26] See, for example, the essay "By Whatever Path ..", contained in this same volume.

[27] "A Philosophy of Religious Pluralism", contained in *Problems of Religious Pluralism*, pp. 31-32.

Christ's death, but that the benefits of this sacrifice are not confined to those who respond to it with an explicit act of faith."[28] Christ's death, on this view, effectively covers all human sin, so that human beings are open to God's mercy even if they are not acquainted with Christ or Calvary.

This, says Hick, appears to be the view advocated by Pope John Paul[29] when he says that "man - every man without any exception whatever - has been redeemed by Christ, and because with man - with each man without any exception whatever - Christ is in a way united, even when man is unaware of it." Such a view thus requires a *widening* of the salvation concept - one that acknowledges "the gradual transformation of human life" wherever it may occur. So understood, salvation may occur within Buddhism or Islam, or in some other, more private context, albeit in each case as the unseen work of Christ.

Surely, believes Hick, this outlook is an improvement over the earlier exclusivism. But what is the real difference, he wonders, between this and the view that salvation occurs outside the realm of Christian faith? There have been many efforts to salvage Christianity's uniqueness while avoiding the exclusivist outlook. Thus Karl Rahner, for example, holds that an outsider who seeks to do God's will is a sort of *honorary* Christian, even if he or she may expressly deny an allegiance. The effort, thinks Hick, is understandable, but once we see the implications, we realize that there is little to separate this modified view from the claim that indeed salvation is possible in many ways.

---

[28] *Ibid.*, pp. 32-33.

[29] *Ibid.*, p. 33. (See John Paul's encyclical *Redemptor Hominis*, 1979.)

> If we accept that salvation / liberation is taking place within all the great religious traditions, why not frankly acknowledge that there is a plurality of saving human responses to the ultimate divine Reality? Pluralism, then, is the view that the transformation of human existence from self-centeredness to Reality-centeredness is taking place in different ways within the contexts of all the great religious traditions. There is not merely one way but a plurality of ways of salvation or liberation.[30]

What is needed, thinks Hick, is a veritable Copernican Revolution in our understanding of human religious experience. Rather than viewing our own tradition (be it Christian, Moslem, Vedic, or whatever) as representing the center of religious truth, we might think of this tradition as being an experiential satellite, as it were, one of many orbiting a single ground of reality. In this way we may regard our own religious experience as having objective worth without supposing that we are somehow arbitrarily favored in this regard.

---

[30] *Ibid.*, p. 34. Hick goes on in this essay to address at length the further issue of pluralism in relation to such traditional and seemingly essential doctrines as that Jesus was God incarnate and that no other such incarnation has existed or will be forthcoming. This pluralistic hypothesis, says Hick, raises a number of questions. What, after all, is this divine Reality to which all of the major world's faiths are supposed to be directed? Can we equate, say, the personal Yahweh of the Hebrews with the impersonal Brahman of orthodox Indian belief? For relevant discussion, see, for example, the essays "On Grading Religions" and "On Conflicting Religious Truth-Claims", contained in *Problems of Religious Pluralism*. See also chapters on the divine *personae* and *impersonae* and the related issue of truth-claims in chapters 15, 16, and 20, respectively, of *An Interpretation of Religion*. A recent collection of essays on Christology and pluralism is contained in Hick's *The Metaphor of God Incarnate* (Louisville: Westminster / John Knox Press, 1993).

Soul-Making and Its Relation to the Problem of Evil

The thesis of pluralism will strike many, I am sure, as being a sound and humane alternative to more conservative options. To many of those who have studied world religion, I believe, the question of which tradition gives us the real spirituality will make about as much sense as asking which gives us the real art or music. While we may harbor a preference for what is closest to home, it would hardly make sense to say that only this artistic expression is good or real. Similarly, perhaps, with religion: If we are honest, thinks Hick, we will see in the world's great religious movements an event of the spirit unfolding in multiple ways according to its various historical settings. A reasonable account, he maintains, will strive to make sense of the religious experience of the whole human race.[31]

Yet there remains another problem. For it seems to be essential to the religious vision that the universe is ultimately a *good* place - that it is shaped by forces of wisdom, power, and unfailing *benevolence*. Or it is believed, at least, that the universe is not malevolent, and not indifferent to our welfare. While this belief in the world's ultimate goodness is not universal,[32] it is surely widespread, and it is central to most religious conceptions, including that of Christianity.

---

[31] It should not be thought, however, that Hick means to say that all religions are equally true or of equal value. See again "On Grading Religions" and other selections in the materials just cited.

[32] It is not prominent, for example, in the conservative tradition of Buddhism, which stresses the need for self-reliance as a means of salvation.

But is this belief realistic? For consider, say many, the pain, the sorrow, the injustice, that exists in the world. Can we really think that we are *cared for* as religious believers tend to imagine?

If God loves us, then why is the world not a kinder place? This problem, to be sure, has exercised many of the greatest minds in history. Perhaps no single issue in all of philosophy is as vexing, nor any as agonizing, as this so-called *problem of evil*. This problem is the greatest obstacle, as well, to belief in a good and merciful creator.

Suppose, says Hume,[33] that someone is told before entering this world that it is the product of great power and benevolence. Would he expect to find the scene now before him? The response of some philosophers, as we have seen, is emphatically negative. If there is cosmic purpose, says Russell, it is the purpose of a fiend.[34] Once a single child has been harmed, says Dostoevsky's Ivan Karamazov, the world stands condemned. He cites the example of a little girl, tortured by her parents, now locked in an outhouse all night in the freezing cold where she cries out to God for protection. "Can you understand," he asks his pious younger brother Alyosha,

---

[33] David Hume, *Dialogues Concerning Natural Religion* (Indianapolis: Hackett Publishing Company, 1980). See Parts X and XI. Thus his character Philo remarks that "if a very limited intelligence whom we shall suppose utterly unacquainted with the universe were assured that it were the production of a very good, wise, and powerful being, however finite, he would, from his conjectures, form *beforehand* a very different notion of it from what we find it to be by experience." (Part XI, pp. 67-68)

[34] See again Russell's "Do We Survive Death?", contained in *Why I Am Not a Christian*.

> why a little creature, who can't even understand what's done to her, should beat her little aching heart with her tiny fist in that vile place, in the dark and the cold, and weep her sanguine meek, unresentful tears to dear, kind God to protect her?[35]

Ivan recalls the example of a general who one day, with minor provocation, takes an eight-year old boy, has him stripped naked in the cold, and then allows him to be chased down and torn apart by a pack of hounds before his mother's eyes. What answer, what cosmic hypothesis, asks Ivan, will explain it! Shall the general, as we sometimes hear, spend eternity in hell? Shall he and the boy and the mother instead rejoice one day together in heaven? There is, thinks Ivan, no answer - no possible explanation of how such things can be permitted in this world. Once done, they cannot be undone, and they cannot be rectified on earth or in heaven.

There exist, as we have seen, various purported defenses of the world's present condition. Few seem compelling. It is said, for example, that God's love is an inscrutable love, one beyond our means to comprehend. This line of argument is offered by Henry Mansel in connection with the religious philosophy of Sir William Hamilton. It is discussed at length by John Stuart Mill in his work *An Examination of Sir William Hamilton's Philosophy*.[36]

Mansel, as Mill explains, follows Hamilton in maintaining "the absolute relativity of all our knowledge." He holds likewise that our efforts to conceive the

---

[35] See again the "Rebellion" section in Dostoevsky's *The Brothers Karamazov*, p. 223.

[36] The relevant portion of Mill's discussion is reprinted in Nelson Pike, ed., *God and Evil* (Englewood Cliffs, New Jersey: Prentice-Hall, 1964).

Absolute or Infinite from our own limited standpoint involves us inevitably in failure. For this reason, he supposes, we cannot infer, from the nature of this world, what infinite qualities its creator may have or lack. We cannot infer, for example, that the pain present in this world rules out the possibility of God's infinite (and thus incomprehensible) goodness.

There is nothing new, writes Mill, in this doctrine. That we cannot understand God, that His ways are not our ways - such propositions have long been used as reasons why "we may assert any absurdities and any moral monstrosities concerning God, and miscall them Goodness and Wisdom." Mansel's strategy, explains Mill, is to maintain that we cannot know such things as wisdom, mercy, justice, and benevolence as they exist in God. For the divine goodness, given its unlimited nature, may not be the goodness that we know in our fellow creatures; it may be some other instead. It is a heresy, holds Mansel, to say that infinite goodness differs "only in degree" from a goodness that is limited. It must differ in kind, as well.

But we must remain true to reason and to language, Mill answers, if we are to have honest inquiry. When we speak of different things, we are obliged to call them by different names. If so, language has no use for such epithets as *just*, *merciful*, and *benevolent*, "save that in which we predicate them of our fellow-creatures; and unless that is what we intend to express by them, we have no business to employ the words." We have no moral or logical entitlement to use these words in any other way. Consider, by way of analogy, our understanding of unlimited space. Among the many, Mill writes,

> who have said that we cannot conceive infinite space, did anyone ever suppose that it is *not* space? that it does not possess all the properties by which space is characterized? Infinite space cannot be cubical or spherical, because these are modes of being bounded; but does anyone imagine that in ranging through it we might arrive at some region which was not extended; of which one part was not outside another, where, though no body intervened, motion was impossible, or where the sum of two sides of a triangle was less than the third side?[37]

A parallel claim, Mill says, can be made with respect to unlimited goodness. If, in ascribing goodness to God, I mean to ascribe to Him some quality other than this one, what can I mean? On what basis do I use the word 'good' to name this mysterious quality? And what reason can I have for venerating it?

To assert in words what we do not think in meaning, Mill argues, is "as suitable a definition as can be given of a moral falsehood." Indeed, if I suppose that God's goodness is not good as I understand it, what reason have I for trusting in His veracity? Our faith itself is grounded in the assumption that God's attributes are the same in kind as those found in His creation. If, writes Mill,

> I am informed that the world is ruled by a being whose attributes are infinite, but what they are we cannot learn, nor what are the principles of his government, except that "the highest human morality which we are capable of conceiving" does not sanction them; convince me of it, and I will bear my fate as I may. But when I am told that I must believe this and at the same time call this being by the names which express and affirm the highest human morality, I say in plain terms that I will not. Whatever power such a being may have over me, there is one thing which he shall not do: he shall not compel me to worship him. I will call no being good who is not what I mean when I apply that epithet to my fellow-creatures; and if such a being can sentence me to hell for not so calling him, to hell I will go.[38]

---

[37] *Ibid.*, p. 42.

[38] *Ibid.*, p. 43.

What can be the difference, after all, between saying that a being is unfathomably good and denying His goodness altogether? To say that His love is so great that it differs in kind from mere *love as we know it* is to say that it is not love, but something else instead. One speaks a language by the rules if one speaks it at all.

Thus there is little prospect, I think, of an answer to the problem of evil along the lines suggested by Mansel. Most other answers, it seems, fare little better. It is said, on occasion, that there must be pain in order for there to exist pleasure. But of course, the amount of pain in the world is very great, and many persons, though no fault of their own, experience little except pain throughout their lives. Nor, I think, can anyone seriously maintain (recalling earlier discussion) that the pain in one individual's life is somehow balanced by the pleasure in that of another. Or to say that good and evil are "relative," and so that creation cannot be objectively evaluated, is hardly better. (Surely, it cannot support belief in divine *benevolence*, which itself presupposes a absolute standard of value.)

Is there, then, any meaningful answer? Hick devotes his book *Evil and the God of Love*[39] to this question. Within the mainstream of Christian tradition, he observes, there exist two principal ways of explaining the condition of the world in which we live. One is the fifth-century response of Augustine, who holds that evil is the consequence of an original "fall" from the paradisal state enjoyed by our first parents. The other is that of Irenaeus, a church father who maintains that the

---

[39] John Hick, *Evil and the God of Love* (San Francisco: Harper and Row, 1977).

world must be understood in terms of the future good at which it aims. The world, on Irenaeus' account, is a moral arena wherein human beings develop qualities of character fitted to their own greater destiny.

In this latter view, thinks Hick, one finds the better and more adequate expression of Christian faith. One finds likewise something essential to religious understanding on the whole. Here, he believes, is the real prospect of making sense of the world in which we live. Instead of thinking of human beings as having been created in finished condition and then falling disastrously away from it, the Irenaen account sees man as "still in the process." This idea counts upon a distinction between the words 'image' and 'likeness' in that passage[40] where God says "Let us make man in our image, after our likeness." Man, thinks Irenaeus, is made in the *image* of God, as a rational and self-conscious creature endowed with freedom of choice and the potential for further development. But he is not yet in the *likeness* of God, which requires something more.

Man as initially created, says Hick, is only as yet "the raw material for a further and more difficult stage of God's creative work." This latter stage is the leading of human beings, through their own free involvement, to a higher quality of existence in the finite likeness of their creator. It thus involves the perfecting of man - the fulfillment of God's purpose for humanity, the "bringing of many sons to glory"[41] and the creating of "fellow heirs with Christ."[42] The fall of man, on this

---

[40] *Genesis* 1: 26.

[41] *Hebrews* 2: 10.

[42] *Romans* 8: 17.

view, is a failure within the second stage of this creative process, one that has "multiplied the perils and complicated the route of the journey in which God is seeking to lead mankind."[43]

Modern anthropology, writes Hick, has made some form of this two-stage conception a virtual necessity. No longer can we think that we have come into being all at once, separate in our development from organic life elsewhere on the planet. But we may see, in this natural process, a creative event whereby we emerge and participate in our own "spiritualization."

The first stage of this creation is simple. It involves the birth of the material universe, and later organic life, and finally personal life in the form of human beings. But with this last event there comes a new kind of reality. For there now exists something with "the possibility of existing in conscious fellowship with God."

This latter stage, Hick explains, is thus essentially different from the first, for it cannot be performed by an outside agency whatever its power. Personal life, by its nature, is "free and self-directing." As such it cannot be perfected from without, but only through its own uncompelled response.

There is a value judgment implicit in this scheme: A creature that has attained to goodness "by meeting and mastering temptations, and thus by rightly making responsible choices in concrete situations," is good "in a richer and more valuable sense" than one created all at once in a condition of guaranteed virtue or

---

[43] *Evil and the God of Love*, p. 255.

innocence.[44] The former kind of goodness has in it "the strength of temptations overcome, a stability based upon an accumulation of right choices, and a positive and responsible character that comes from the investment of costly personal effort." A goodness of this kind, thinks Hick, despite it difficulty, may have in it "a value in the eyes of the Creator which justifies even the long travail of the soul-making process."[45]

The picture being offered herein is thus teleological. Human beings are being perfected as God wills, but this end is not reached by divine fiat or by any fixed mechanical process; rather it owes to "a hazardous adventure" in personal freedom. The process is individual, and not racial; thus human life, on the whole, is probably now "on much the same moral plane" as it was thousands of years ago. Yet during this period countless souls have moved toward fulfillment of the divine purpose.

If God's purpose in making the world is indeed "the bringing of many sons to glory,"[46] Hick explains, this will determine the kind of world that He has created. The error of many antitheistic writers is that they continually assume a conception of the divine purpose quite different from this one. They assume that the purpose of a loving God must be to create "a hedonistic paradise." To the extent that the world departs from this ideal, they imagine, it tells against the claim that its creator is notably good or powerful.

---

[44] *Ibid.*

[45] *Ibid.*, p. 256.

[46] *Hebrews* 2: 10.

Such writers liken God's role to that of a human being providing a dwelling for a pet animal. If the owner is humane, he or she will naturally make the dwelling a pleasant and healthful one. Thus Hume, for example, uses the related example of an architect able to plan a house that will be as *comfortable* for the dweller as possible. Were this house instead a source of "noise, confusion, fatigue, darkness, and the extremes of heat and cold," says Hume, we would not hesitate to blame its planner.[47] The condition of this world, he thinks, is analogous: Its defects show that its architect is less than wholly good and powerful. Surely the convergence of such properties would offer a better result. Nor can we think that a benevolent being, even if limited in power, would have chosen to create a world of such poor quality.

Yet a religious view of life, thinks Hick, does not rest upon this hedonistic assumption. Christian tradition, for example, does not hold that God's purpose in creating the world was to create, all at once, the most agreeable environment possible for the creatures in it. Instead of asking if this world is the most pleasant one imaginable, we might ask instead if it is the kind of world in which *morally conscious beings* may be fashioned, through their own free insights and responses, into rightful heirs of the life for which they are intended. Human beings should be understood not as pets whose lives are to be made as agreeable as possible, but more as children whose first and greatest purpose is "the realizing of the most valuable potentialities of human personality."[48]

---

[47] See again *Dialogues Concerning Natural Religion*, Part XI.

[48] *Evil and the God of Love*, p. 258.

The real question is "How does the best parental love express itself in its influence upon the environment in which children are to grow up?" Surely a parent who loves his children, and who wants them to become the best persons that they may become, does not count their pleasure as being his sole consideration in raising them. He will indeed seek pleasure for his children, will even delight in giving it to them, but he will not seek it "at the expense of their growth in such even greater values as moral integrity, unselfishness, compassion, courage, humour, reverence for the truth, and perhaps above all the capacity for love." To good parents, it is more important to foster quality and strength of character in their children than to fill their lives endlessly with enjoyment.

> If, then, there is any true analogy between God's purpose for his human creatures, and the purpose of loving and wise parents for their children, we have to recognize that the presence of pleasure and the absence of pain cannot be the supreme and overriding end for which the world exists.[49]

The quality of such a world is thus to be judged not by its present incidence of pain and pleasure, but by its fittedness to our own moral development.

This soul-making view tends to see the world as being the God-given environment of human life. But here, Hick says, arises a question. For the claim that the universe has this purpose invites the charge of "anthropocentrism" - of explaining the world in terms of ourselves, rather than as an end in itself.[50] Ought

---

[49] *Ibid.*, p. 295.

[50] Thus Hick cites Irenaeus' claim (*Against Heresies*, v. xxix. 1) that man was not made for creation, but "creation for the sake of man"; and Calvin's statement (*Institutes* i. xvi. 6) that "the universe was established especially for the sake of mankind".

we to think that the whole material universe is intended to serve the purpose of something as fleeting and diminutive as the human race?

The place of man in creation was dwarfed in medieval times, Hick explains, by the belief in angels and archangels above him, creatures unfallen who rejoice "in the immediate presence of God, reflecting His glory in the untarnished mirror of their worship." This scheme has lost its hold on the modern imagination. Yet in its place has come another "minimizer," namely the sheer immensity of the material universe. As our spiritual environment has shrunk, this other horizon has expanded. While the human being was seen as being a minor appendage of the spiritual world, he is now, by some accounts, "an equally insignificant organic excrescence, enjoying a fleeting moment of consciousness on the surface of one of the planets of a minor star." The truth that was symbolized by the angelic hosts "is today impressed upon us by the vastness of the physical universe, countering the egoism of our species by making us feel that this immense prodigality of existence can hardly all exist for the sake of man."[51]

Yet an appreciation of the vastness of our material environment, writes Hick, need not lead us to suppose that we are worthless. For instead of opposing man and nature as rival objects of the divine interest, we might focus upon their solidarity. We are organic to the world. Our actions and our experiences are conditioned by space and time, and apart from this environment we would be nothing, or at least nothing like what we are at present. With this in mind, we may say

---

[51] *Evil and the God of Love*, p. 260.

> that the beauties and sublimities and powers, the microscopic intricacies and macroscopic vastnesses, the wonders and the terrors of the natural world and of the life that pulses through it, are willed and valued by their Maker in a creative act that embraces man together with nature.[52]

By means of matter and living flesh, writes Hick, "God both builds a path and weaves a veil between himself and the creature made in His image." Nature, seen in these terms, has a permanent significance. God has set us within a creaturely environment, and the fulfillment of our nature will take the form of an embodied life within "a new heaven and a new earth." This way of looking at things need not obscure our special nature. Our efforts at theodicy should center likewise upon the soul-making process that seems to be taking place within human life.

Such an account, Hick maintains, must surely be *eschatological* in its direction. It must look not to the past, but to the future. It must explain evil in terms of the divine intention working in our own time toward a fulfillment that lies beyond. Thus it must find the justification of that whole process *in the magnitude of the good to which it leads*.

But this notion of soul-making, it is sometimes thought, is crude in its assumption. Does God, some ask, force us through this gauntlet and then "make it up to us" later? Does He dish out some intended amount of pain so that He may buy it back with gifts afterward?

---

[52] *Ibid.* It is perhaps worth adding, too, that a spiritualistic view of reality need not mean that human beings (or creatures, say, on this planet) are the only beings with a spiritual nature. Countless beings of endless variety may be involved in this process.

This, says Hick, is not what the soul-making view supposes. God does not measure out to us some given amount of pain, nor is pain *per se* even a part of the divine intention. He does not charge us, as it were, for our pleasures, nor pay us back according to our pains. (He does not make us, as Hick puts it, "creditors in a hedonic bank.") Rather what He gives us is *opportunity*: We receive the chance to make our way in this world and to participate, in time, in the greater result at which this process aims.

But if a greater life is the end, it is sometimes asked, why does God not simply create this reality in the first place? If this world aims at our greater development, then why does He not create a universe in which human beings are already elevated and so are residing in a world above their trials? Such a state of affairs must be possible, if it is going to be realized one day. Why then, does God not create it? Rather than use this world as a means to this end, why does He not realize it all at once?

The answer, I think, lies in Hick's earlier claim that a universe in which human beings gain this life by their own efforts has in it a value that it would not have otherwise.[53] Perhaps God could create a world of the kind envisioned, one containing ready-made saints, as it were, immediately enlightened and spared the trial. But a world of that kind, while it might duplicate *in its appearance* the end at which this world aims, would differ from it in one vital respect. Those who inhabit this paradise would not have arrived there by means of their own participation. What they would thus lack is *worthiness* of their present station.

---

[53] See again Hick's discussion on pp. 255 and following.

While they would resemble those who had made the actual journey, they would not be the same creatures. Such a world, in that case, would lack the moral feature that invests this one with its present meaning.

The value of Hick's theodicy, I think, lies in its recognition of the irreducible worth of the individual. Such an account does not explain the existence of suffering in terms of mere abstract principle (that good and evil are subjective, that they are logical complements of each other, or whatever), nor does it try to justify the fate of one person or generation in terms of another. It is the same individual, on this view, who endures the challenge and who participates in the triumph.

May we then believe that God is benevolent? Certainly Hick's view, as expressed in *Evil and the God of Love*, tends in this direction. He does not altogether reject this view, I believe, in his later discussions of cross-cultural religious phenomena. But his answer to the question is now qualified by the model of religious knowledge discussed earlier.

We are familiar elsewhere, explains Hick, with distinctions between appearance and reality, or between realities of different kinds. Kant, again, supposes that the basic character of our experience - our framework, as it were, of space and time - is not an independent fact, but is the way in which consciousness imposes order upon an unqualified reality.[54] Physics, to cite a more

---

[54] See Part I, the Transcendental Aesthetic, in his Transcendental Doctrine of Elements in the first *Critique*. Space and time, he maintains, are "nothing in themselves," but are "merely subjective conditions of all our intuition." (p. 99)

familiar case, has long told us that "the surface of the table, which looks and feels to us as a continuous smooth, hard, brown expanse," is also "a whirling universe of minute discharging quanta of energy in largely empty space."[55]

We must acknowledge, believes Hick, a difference between the divine as it is in itself and as it appears to human experience. The various *personae* and *impersonae* of religious traditions - the gods, goddesses, and formless absolutes that they present as final realities - may represent ways in which the Real is experienced by finite human creatures. Thus traditional terms like 'wise', 'powerful', and 'benevolent', on this model, characterize not this reality on its own, but *as it is apprehended* by us. The Real in itself, on his view, is trans-conceptual; it lies beyond the human categories of moral and religious philosophy. In this respect Hick's mature view goes beyond that of simple affirmation.

But this does not mean that the Real is altogether indescribable or that traditional religious language should be abandoned. Hick does not advocate the view, described earlier, that ultimate reality is unintelligible. Nor does he suggest that we can make no claims appropriate to its nature.[56] For surely, one must think, it is more fitting to say that ultimate reality is wise than to say that it is foolish, more akin to love than to hatred.[57] Our conceptions of good and evil may

---

[55] *An Interpretation of Religion*, p. 242.

[56] See, for example, relevant discussion in chapter 14, "The Pluralistic Hypothesis", in *The Interpretation of Religion*.

[57] All of the major traditions, Hick observes, teach ideals of love and compassion, and not the contrary. The development of sainthood within a tradition is likewise "one valid criterion by which to identify a religious tradition as a salvific human response to the Real." (*An Interpretation of Religion*, p. 307)

not be final, may not characterize the Real as they characterize things in this world, but they move our understanding in the right direction. God, we may think, is more like good than evil, justice higher than injustice. Our moral voice is not an illusion, and we may ask whether or not the universe is a place that is consistent with its demands.

Can we then say that the soul-making view speaks effectively to this question? Some, as we have seen, find it hard to justify this world in terms of what may be in the hereafter. For our present situation, whatever its final direction, holds terrifying possibilities. Think, again, of the things of which Dostoevsky writes. Can benevolence really allow such things? What would possess benevolence to bring forth this state of affairs - to create creatures who are vulnerable and to leave them at the mercy of one another?

But again, we must remember, this view does not count this world as being an end in itself. Such a world, with all its darkness, all its potential tragedy, is yetonly a small part of the story. Here evil may go unpunished. Noble action may be thwarted. Yet it is just such an existence, demanding and precarious, without guarantee, that realizes a spiritual end. By this means we are forged into something better, stronger, more deeply possessed of wisdom, than we might have been otherwise.

Is suffering justified because it makes "better persons" of us? This, one might think, is a rather pat answer. Moreover, it seems to be falsely optimistic. For surely individuals do not always become better for their trials in this world. At times they become worse.

The soul-making view does not assume that such trials *make* us better persons. We may, while here, become worse - we may become, say, more embittered, more egoistic, less principled in our outlook and conduct. But this, again, is consistent with what the view proposes. *A genuine test can be failed.* Our wrong choices - those that tend toward such things, say, as dishonesty, self-pity, and callousness - attest to the severity of the challenge with which we are faced. The adventure, as Hick says, is haphazard.

Nor does this adventure provide, in every case, confirmation of our own moral success. Nothing insures, for the present time, that heroism is victorious, or that it will attach itself to the better cause. We cannot always be sure that we have made the right choice at all. Doubt may accompany even our better choices before and after; uncertainty, it seems, is part and parcel of the struggle. Yet again, it is just in an environment of this kind that the genuine good is called forth. Nor can this end be realized by other means. We are here for the purpose of what even omnipotence cannot achieve, namely the making of ourselves into worthy voyagers upon eternity.

The soul-making view, it is clear, counts heavily upon the notion of free agency. For by this account we actively choose the course - the causes, commitments, and acts of reflection that shape our own spiritual condition. A world in which human beings have this capacity, once again, is a world in which the wrong things may happen. To the extent that human beings are free, the soul-making view supposes, the world admits the possibility of evil. It allows the possibility of wrongdoing, even atrocity, without present justice.

On occasion, however, it is argued that the presence of human freedom need not have this consequence. So, for example, John Mackie,[58] argues that God might have created a world wherein human beings are free but never transgress. Such a world would thus contain the possibility of evil without its reality.

While God, says Mackie, cannot violate logic, He can presumably bring about any state of affairs possible otherwise. Thus He could have created in the beginning, say, a race of automata incapable of moral wrongdoing of any kind. This, it is true, would not be the same thing as creating genuine moral agents. For moral freedom means the capacity for wrongdoing, as well as for doing right. But does this exhaust the creative possibilities?

It is possible, Mackie reasons, that an individual will make a right choice on a given occasion. But if there is no contradiction in a *single* instance of such a choice, how can there be any contradiction in a second, or a third? It seems that there is not. But if so, wonders Mackie, why cannot an individual make a right choice on every occasion? If God, he writes,

> has made men such that in their free choices they sometimes prefer what is good and sometimes what is evil, why could not he have made men such that they always freely choose the good? If there is no logical impossibility in a man's freely choosing the good on one, or on several, occasions, there cannot be a logical impossibility in his freely choosing the good on every occasion.[59]

---

[58] See Mackie's "Evil and Omnipotence", originally printed in *Mind*, April, 1955, and contained in Nelson Pike's *God and Evil*, noted earlier in this chapter.

[59] *God and Evil*, p. 56.

God, thinks Mackie, was not faced with the choice between making "innocent" automata and making beings who might choose wrongly on some occasions. There was open to Him instead the choice of creating beings "who would act freely but always go right." God's failure to choose this possibility thus shows that He is not both all-powerful and wholly good.

Is this correct? It is logically possible, Hick says, that human beings should always choose the good. But it is a further question whether or not they might be *constituted* so as to always choose it. He cites the discussion of Ninian Smart,[60] who maintains that such familiar moral concepts as *courage*, *temptation*, and *generosity*, among others, have no real application to a race of beings who are constructed so as to be wholly good. For such creatures, in that case, would not have to overcome fear, to resist the temptation to be unkind or dishonest, to surmount the inclination toward selfishness, and so on. In which case, wonders Smart, how could they be said to be good as we understand the term?

Mackie's reply, explains Hick, is that "men might have been so constituted as to have been more resistant to temptation than they are,"[61] and so that God could perhaps have created a very different (and much less evil) world without depriving his creatures of their freedom. Thus the question persists, says Hick, "Why did God not realize this possibility in His creation of mankind?" There seems

---

[60] Smart's essay is entitled "Omnipotence, Evil and Supermen", and was printed in the journal *Philosophy* in April, 1962.

[61] *Evil and the God of Love*, p. 307. Yet one must wonder, I think, just how much freedom is left to a creature whose nature is altered in such a fashion. Perhaps we could be made more resistant to temptation than we are at present. But how free can we be if we are made so resistant as to *never* yield to it?

to be no contradiction in the idea that human beings should always choose the good. And if their being of this sort is logically possible, argues Mackie, "then God's making them of this sort is logically possible."[62]

Yet there remains a question, says Hick, whether or not we can imagine God creating beings who are flawless in relation to Himself. For on the Christian view, God created human beings not only so that they might have relationships with one another, but that they should enter also into a relationship with Himself. There is, after all, a religious as well as a moral dimension in the divine purpose. The real question, then, is whether God could have made human beings so that they would freely respond to Himself in a spirit of love, and trust, and faith.

Hick's answer to this question is that God could not create beings of this kind and allow them religious freedom. Consider, he says, the relationship of a patient to a hypnotist. A patient can be made to carry out post-hypnotically a series of actions according to instructions received while in trance. Such actions might be called "free," in the sense that they are not compelled by external forces present at that moment. But under such circumstances, writes Hick, the patient

---

[62] There is, I think, serious doubt that God could *create* beings who would choose rightly on every occasion, even it such choosing is itself logically possible. The fact that something is possible, I believe, does not guarantee the possibility that God can bring it about. For the fact that God has brought it about rules out the possibility of certain features in the thing itself. While the consistently good behavior of morally free creatures seems to be, by itself, a logical possibility, the presence of freedom in this situation entails that it was not insured beforehand by some outside agency. If God builds this eventuality into the universe in advance, He excludes the possibility that it comes about afterward through the free choice of His creatures. Thus there are some things, I think, that have in them no inherent inconsistency, but which God cannot create. (To cite another example, the existence of an uncreated world seems like a logical possibility. Does this mean that God *create* such a world?)

cannot be said to be free *in relation to the person who has hypnotized him*. Similarly, if God somehow builds into a creature the guarantee of a right choice with respect to Himself, such a creature cannot be free in this relationship. It is essential to such personal attitudes as trust, respect, and affection that they arise in a free being "as an uncompelled response to the personal qualities of others."

> If trust, love, admiration, respect, affection, are produced by some kind of psychological manipulation which by-passes the conscious responsible centre of the personality, then they are not real trust and love, etc., but something else of an entirely different nature and quality which does not have at all the same value in the contexts of personal life and personal relationship.[63]

What, again, of the general and the murdered boy? The soul-making view, Hick believes, allows a reply to Dostoevsky's Ivan, who believes that no end can be worth the pain that free agency allows. He discusses this problem in chapter 8 of his *Death and Eternal Life*, a book on which I will focus in the next section.

The atrocity, thinks Ivan, cannot be redeemed. Once it is done, no conceivable turn of events can rectify it or make sense of the world in which it has occurred. The general's damnation will solve nothing. For his suffering, even unto the end of time, cannot remove the pain that he has caused. Nor, Ivan insists, can there be any embrace of mother, son, and general in heaven. The mother cannot, she dare not, forgive the general, even did her son forgive him.

Is it true that nothing can rectify this event? Certainly, I think, an eternity in hell for wrongdoers provides no solution. For the endless pain of the offender does not diminish the present suffering of the victim. Perhaps it will be said that

---

[63] *Evil and the God of Love*, p. 273.

this pain accomplishes a kind of retribution, and so provides the universe with moral balance. But how, again, can an *infinite* amount of suffering do this? As punishment for a misdeed, or for any finite amount of evil, it seems endlessly out of proportion. And how can we think that the universe will be vindicated if it will always contain the suffering of those in hell?[64] Justice, I think, may indeed warrant the general's pain (in some finite measure). But it cannot rectify, by itself, the suffering that he has caused.

What of the other possibility? The mother, says Ivan, cannot forgive the general for what he has done. Yet Ivan, as Hick observes, seems to envision this meeting taking place at a time when the general is essentially the same person that he was at the time of his offense. Ivan, it seems,

> is evidently thinking of this meeting taking place when the general is still the same cruel (or perhaps insane) person who committed the appalling brutality; and he is thinking of forgiveness as a condoning of the general's behavior. But forgiveness does not mean condoning, still less approving, the unspeakably brutal act that was committed.[65]

What we must imagine, says Hick, if we are to come to grips with this question, is not a meeting of mother and general when they are still qualitatively these same people. We must instead try to imagine this meeting at a time, perhaps far distant, when the general has become (by his own making) a morally different creature. We must imagine the meeting at a time when the general has made of himself far more than he is at the time of the offense.

---

[64] See again chapter 5 in this volume.

[65] *Death and Eternal Life*, p. 165.

In this situation it is conceivable, Hick believes, that forgiveness is now possible, and even appropriate. He cites, in this connection, the statement of Pascal, who says that "Time heals griefs and quarrels, for we are no longer the same persons." Neither the offended nor the offender, says Pascal, are "any more themselves," but are like unto nations, once at odds, who meet after two generations.[66]

What kinds of changes in the general are necessary? They are not, I think, simply the changes that come with time to virtually everyone, such as new habits or interests, or differences in appearance and temperament. These are, to some extent, the necessary consequences of experience of any kind, and they are a natural part of an individual's development. The real issue, I think, is whether the candidate has made of himself a better individual than before. Has he addressed his own condition in relation to the offense itself, and has he made the relevant effort, the relevant sacrifice, in this direction? Has he, in short, made

---

[66] Here again, I think, recalling earlier discussion our moral attitudes involve us in a certain conception of personal identity. Pascal's analogy (noted also by both Hume and Parfit) surely has some legitimacy. For each entity, nation and individual, does become something gradually different with the passing of time. But persons, it seems to me, must be fundamentally the same entities over time if this event of forgiveness is to make sense. For what this event involves, I take it, is that the same party who was offended now extends an acceptance to (whom else?) the one who committed the offense. If the one now forgiven is indeed not the same as that one earlier, then what is the point of forgiveness in the first place? But forgiveness does, in many relevant cases, seem appropriate. Thus it appears that our moral attitudes involve us, at times, in a recognition of the profound sameness of persons over time. It also seems true that even serious offenders can become fitting recipients of forgiveness, depending on what they have made of themselves since.

himself *worthy* of forgiveness?[67]

It is conceivable, I think, that over time even the worst actions may be forgiven. The worst suffering, I believe, may be healed, and the worst character improved. With sufficient time there is no limit upon the changes that may contribute to this eventuality. This does not mean that such events will come quickly or easily; indeed individuals like the general, I suspect, are in for whole lifetimes of effort before they will enter into the presence of their victims.

It is conceivable, too, I think, that eternity will provide a good that outweighs whatever evil has arisen on the way to its realization. The present life may furnish us with some intimation of what is be involved in this eventuality. Those who have experienced difficulty, for example, in personal relationships - in feeling anger, say, toward a parent or sibling, or anguish over an unrequited love - know how a future reconciliation may cast this whole experience in a new light. Those who have experienced physical hardship, to cite another case, may likewise see this experience, in time, as having a value that was not at first apparent. They may decide also that it has added something to themselves that they would not wish to be without.

---

[67] Some perhaps will hold that certain offenses, as Ivan suggests, are too heinous to be forgiven. Indeed, if such offenses exist, I must think that the ones that he describes may qualify. But we would do well, I think, to consider the way in which forgiveness for lesser offenses comes about. It may be that some offenses cannot be forgiven at once, or even, perhaps, in the course of a lifetime. But we need to consider, I believe, what is involved in the prospect of an unlimited time period. I suspect that what some persons are saying, when they say that they could never forgive such an action, is that *there will never come a time*, in this world or another, *when they could cease to regard the action of the general as being evil*. But this does not rule out the eventual forgiveness of the general, over some (perhaps immense) course of time and personal change.

There may exist likewise, I think, a vantage point - one remote, perhaps, from the present, yet still imaginable - from which the greatest travail in this world can be looked upon in similar fashion. This misery past will be seen, at that time, not merely as an evil, but as something more. It will be seen as a means to an end, as something now incorporated into a greater reality - one that seen in its entirety can be pronounced good. This reality, we may imagine, will contain understanding. It will contain likewise reconciliation of differences that we may now think impossible. It will contain furthermore a good unending - the kingdom "which is yet to come in its full glory and permanence."[68]

An Adventure into Eternity

The prospect of a future life, then, is integral to Hick's vision of reality. If our lives continue beyond their present limits, where might they lead? It is, writes Hick, a tantalizing mystery, one both vast and daunting. Its lure is irresistible. In the time of the Buddha, there were many views on the scene:

> Is the death of the body the extinction of the person? or does he survive as a continuing consciousness? or as a resurrected person? with a spiritual body? in perpetuity or for a limited period? Will he be born again to live another earthly life? Is there time or timelessness beyond death? Is the individual absorbed back into some great spiritual reality, like a drop returning to the ocean?[69]

---

[68] *Evil and the God of Love*, p. 261.

[69] *Death and Eternal Life*, p. 21.

So it is today. We still do not have sure answers to these questions. One must wonder, indeed, if there is any point in attempting to answer them. But we cannot cease to speculate about death, writes Hick, any more than we can cease to think about life. The issues are equally mysterious, and they are inseparable. We cannot face life without confronting, at some point, the issue of its ultimate direction.

Death and Eternal Life is a massive undertaking, copious in its research and diligent in its argument. It is bolder in its exploration of key issues than any work of its kind before it. In it are addressed such issues as: Do we have reason to believe that there is more to human nature than materiality? May we suppose that all persons are somehow "saved" in the end? What is the relationship between Eastern and Western conceptions of liberation? What may we reasonably expect the next life to be like?

A project along these lines, Hick believes, requires *global theology*, a mission of truth-seeking that does not concern only one portion of the human race or restrict itself likewise to a single religious tradition. Accordingly this project takes into account material from a vast range of sources, east and west, in all its historical variety.

Its method, writes Hick, must be that of spelling out possibilities. We must not suppose that we can have certainty in this domain in the same way that we can have it with respect to issues in this world. We have not proof, and we cannot be sure of all that a future life might involve, even in theory. Our destiny lies ahead, and we cannot know now all that we will know then.

But again, perhaps we can know something. If there is life after death, explains Hick, we may be better able to estimate its proximate rather than its ultimate phases. Thus *Death and Eternal Life* deals, as he puts it, more with *pareschatology* than with *eschatology* - not with the very *last* things (Greek, *eschaton*), but with those things that may hold true on the way.

Our religious sensibility, believes Hick, inclines us to think of the individual human being as a *soul* - to think of it as something possessed of a special value and potentiality. Reflection upon this entity and its development leads us to think of selfhood in terms of "two polar aspects."[70] He calls these the *ego* and the *person*. (Borrowing from classical Indian vocabulary, he uses also the Sanskrit '*atman*' to refer to this second and higher aspect.)

As ego, the self is "an enclosed entity, constituted and protected by its boundaries." As such it is "atomic"; it has itself as its center of value, and seeks to preserve, in its encounters, an "egocentric poise." Thus it lives in that fallen condition of *angst* and estrangement familiar to Continental philosophy,[71] or alternatively in the Buddhist *dukkha*[72] that is the lot of the unenlightened. In such

---

[70] See chapter 2, "What Is Man?", and especially section 5, "From Ego to Atman".

[71] There is, for one, Sartre's dictum (expressed in his play *No Exit*) that "Hell is other people."

[72] This term denotes in Buddhist philosophy the condition that permeates life prior to the event of enlightenment. Although often translated as "suffering," it is perhaps better understood as conveying not pain, but instead the condition of impermanence, and insubstantiality. See Walpola Rahula's earlier cited volume *What the Buddha Taught*, and particularly chapter II, "The First Noble Truth: *Dukkha*".

a condition, this self "is perpetually threatened by the rival egoisms of it neighbors, as well as by the contingencies of the surrounding world."

Yet there is another and higher aspect of the self in tension with this one. This is our personal nature. It is in fact essentially *inter*personal and develops through our involvement with other centers of consciousness like ourselves. As such it is an integral part "of the totality of interpersonal life." This greater potentiality of selfhood "seeks its realization in a society of selves each wholly open to the others in a perfect mutuality" in which egocentricity has been transcended.[73]

An adequate conception of selfhood, writes Hick, must include not only this feature of personality, but it must include a dimension of *depth*, as well. For it is a part of the scheme of religion (and of psychology, as has been noted) that there exists more to oneself than what appears "on the surface." One finds some notion of this depth in much of psychology - for one, in the work of Carl Jung,[74] who maintains that something is needed to explain the existence of certain recurrent images and "archetypes" that exist throughout the world's mythologies. It is also used on occasion to explain what seem to be occasional incidences of telepathy.[75]

---

[73] *Death and Eternal Life*, p. 51.

[74] Hick notes, in this connection, a number of essays in Jung's *Collected Works*. Herbert Read, Michael Fordham, and Gerard Adler, editors (London: Routledge and Kegan Paul). Cited materials date from 1966 to 1970.

[75] See, for example, Whately Carington, *Telepathy* (London: Methuen, 1945). See also section 4 of chapter 6, "Mind and Body", in *Death and Eternal Life*.

The culmination of this book is its fifth and final section, entitled "A Possible Human Destiny". The world's religious traditions, says Hick, differ widely in their ideas about the world and human nature. Yet they point, he thinks, in similar directions. Ideas just noted concerning selfhood and personal development are present virtually everywhere.

There are also, it seems, striking similarities across traditions in accounts of the next world. Consider, for one, the next world as it is understood in the *Tibetan Book of the Dead* and in the literature of western spiritualism. At life's end, according to the Tibetan source, is the prospect of absorption into the clear Light of Reality. This light, thinks Hick, represents the ineffable Void of mainstream Buddhist teaching and the ultimate reality of liberation.[76] But only those of high evolvement (or in Christian terms, who have approached the perfection of "self-naughting") are willing to embrace this event. Most remain, in consequence, within the cycle of rebirth, experiencing for a time the self-manufactured experiences of good and evil issuing from their own constitution.

This idea that the soul creates a *post mortem* world according to its own desires is conspicuously like one found in the material of western spiritualism. One hears, for example, that the next world contains experiences reminiscent of those here, albeit "more beautiful than anything I have seen on earth."[77] The condition of this world seems also to vary with the moral condition of the subject.

---

[76] *Death and Eternal Life*, p. 401.

[77] *Ibid.* The quotation appears on page 10 of Grace Rosher's *Beyond the Horizon* (Greenwood, S. C.: James Clarke, 1961).

"The cold selfish man in Illusion-land," states ostensible communicator Frederic Myers in Geraldine Cummins' *The Road to Immortality*, "may dwell in darkness" for some period of time in the next world, owing to his own egoistic limits.[78]

Some element of wish-fulfillment seems to be present in each case. But furthermore there exists, across the two traditions, a common theme of spiritual evolution, and of an increasingly higher existence with one's own continuing progress. The theme is present in some form, as Hick shows, not only in these two examples, but in the broader mainstreams of the world's great religious traditions.

In what further direction do these converging paths seem to lead? If salvation, he argues, involves the thorough transformation of human character, then this process must continue in some fashion beyond present limits. For it is an observable fact that many leave this world having made little progress toward the goal, and that few reach it within this lifetime.

Do traditional ideas about heaven and hell speak to this issue? The idea of a single earthly career followed by an eternity in one place or the other, thinks Hick, is inadequate. The doctrine of hell, for one, is morally intolerable,[79] and traditional ideas of heaven offer little prospect of the growth that seems to be involved in the soul-making process.

---

[78] *Ibid.*, p. 405. See Geraldine Cummins, *The Road to Immortality* (London: The Aquarian Press, 1955). Hick quotes from page 48 of Cummins' book.

[79] For Hick's discussion of this point see especially section # 2 of chapter 10, "Later Christian Thought".

For this reason, the concept of multiple lives is much more plausible. This need not mean that an individual recycles time and again in this world,[80] as some popular notions would have it. But the idea of a continued growth invites the idea, in some form, of a series of lives each bounded by birth and death. For the prospect of death, Hick maintains, is integral to such things as risk, danger, self-sacrifice, and others, which invest life with moral significance. But with the lessons of each life, he imagines, may come progress to higher levels. Thus it may be that human beings continue their careers by means of a plurality of lives in a plurality of worlds, and not simply by continued returns to this one, but in an ongoing ascension.[81]

The world's major religious traditions speak characteristically not only of progress, but also of liberation - of a final transcending of our present bounds altogether. This liberation is commonly imagined to be a kind of *unitive* state wherein oneself is somehow merged with ultimate reality. In the Vedic tradition, again, there is the idea of *atman* being absorbed into Brahman;[82] in Buddhism, the

---

[80] Indeed the thought of countless returns to this world may be as daunting as that of eternal punishment. "Man," writes Nicolai Berdyaev, "is haunted by three nightmares: the religious nightmare of the eternal punishment of hell; the occultist and theosophical nightmare of evolution and reincarnation in an infinitude of worlds; and the nightmare of mysticism, which is the annihilation of human personality in God." See Berdyaev's *Freedom and the Spirit* (New York: Charles Scribner's Sons, 1935), p. 325.

[81] See section 5 of chapter 20, "A Possible Pareschatology". For a criticism of more popular ideas of reincarnation and the notion of past lives, see chapter 19, "Reincarnation - Discriminations and Conclusions".

[82] This theme, as noted in a previous chapter, is reiterated in several of the *Upanishads*.

promise of *nirvana*, and with it release from the ties of craving that presently bind.[83] In the Christian tradition, says Hick, there is something comparable to this. It is expressed in the mystical tradition of the unitive life, "in which a human will becomes one with the divine will." It is expressed also in the broad ideal "of "self-giving love and in the modern rediscovery of personality as essentially interpersonal."[84] This element is given voice by Paul, who says, "it is no longer I who live, but Christ who lives in me."[85] Hick cites the related discussion of Evelyn Underhill, who speaks of "a final swallowing up of that wilful I-hood, that surface individuality which we ordinarily recognize as ourselves."[86] Thus in Christian mysticism there is something analogous to the widespread eastern conviction that "our approach to Ultimate Reality involves the transcending of ego-hood."[87]

Need this mean that in liberation we cease to exist as individuals? Modern insights into the nature of personality, says Hick, may provide a clue as to what is actually involved in this transcendence. Throughout much of Western history the human being has been looked upon as something wholly individual, as a

---

[83] The nature of this release (or literally "blowing out", that is, of selfish desire) is portrayed differently in the two principal schools of Buddhism, the Theravada, or "Doctrine of the Elders", and the Mahayana, or "Great Raft" of salvation. See Hick, chapter 21, "Moksha, Nirvana and the Unitive State".

[84] *Death and Eternal Life*, p. 442.

[85] *Galatians* 2: 20.

[86] Slightly amended in *Death and Eternal Life*, pp. 445-46. The original passage can be found on page 425 of Underhill's *Mysticism* (New York: New American Library, 1974).

[87] *Death and Eternal Life*, p. 446.

distinct substance independent of its fellows. Yet in recent times,[88] there has come an emphasis upon "the essentially interpersonal nature of personality."[89] Reflection upon who we are and how we develop suggests to us that our involvement with others is integral to our own existence, that there must ultimately be *two* persons if there is to be even one. This development has import for the question of another life. "Could it be," asks Hick, "that as the separate ego-selves attain to their several human perfections the boundaries between them become more transparent and human existence becomes more corporate than individual?"

The distinction between self as ego and self as person suggests that as an individual becomes more and more developed he or she becomes less and less an ego. The developed personality, it seems, is essentially outward-looking. Ego is a limit upon this development. A perfected individual might thus be imagined to be a personality without egoity, "a living consciousness which is transparent to the other consciousnesses in relation to which it lives in a full community of love."[90]

Herein, says Hick, we have

---

[88] Hick cites here the example, noted earlier, of Martin Buber, whose *I and Thou* expresses the idea that human nature cannot be understood solely in terms of "I-It" relationships of the kind that one has toward theoretical activity, but must include as well attention to the "I-Thou" that involves the encounter of one person over against another. See again Martin Buber, *I and Thou*. Trans. Ronald Gregor Smith (New York: Charles Scribner's Sons, 1958.)

[89] *Death and Eternal Life*, p. 459.

[90] *Ibid.*, p. 460.

> the picture of a plurality of personal centres without separate peripheries. They will have ceased to be mutually exclusive and open to one another in a richly complex shared consciousness. The barrier between their common unconscious life and their individual consciousnesses will have disappeared, so that they experience an intimacy of personal community which we can at present barely imagine.[91]

This blurring of individuality, says Hick, may be hard to grasp, yet it is not altogether foreign to present thought. The traditional idea of God as being a *unity* and still *three persons*, for example, may suggest an instance of this mutuality. As such it may offer some glimpse of "a community so intimate and harmonious as to constitute a single corporate person."

At this point, we verge upon our conceptual limits. Yet these questions cannot be ignored. Is this development best understood as taking place within time, and as within an embodied state? Time is the dimension within which change occurs; thus it seems to be a requirement for our continuing development. This development seems to involve likewise an interaction between distinct persons within a common environment. As such it seems to require the conditions of embodiment and temporal progress. But when the process is complete, it may be otherwise. Perhaps it will be that in progressively higher worlds,

> The interpersonality of mutual love becomes the universal principle of life, whilst self-protective egoity withers away, so that the individual's series of lives culminates in a last life beyond which there is no further embodiment but instead entry into the common Vision of God, or nirvana, or the eternal consciousness of the atman in its relation to Ultimate Reality.[92]

---

[91] *Ibid.*

[92] *Ibid.*, p. 464.

Hick's discussion, I believe, is indispensable reading for anyone who is interested in the issue of human destiny. Its topic, as he himself admits, is speculative, but this topic cannot be avoided by anyone who has an inkling of his own spirituality and entertains concern with his own direction.

Part of my discussion in the next chapter will bear the influence of Hick's thought. In this final chapter I will recall some previous discussion, noting, for one, the literature of psychical research and the so-called near-death experience. I will delve a bit further into such literature, and into discussions it has inspired, noting a few of its recurrent themes and their relation to my own previous discussion. Finally I will note a few intimations of a greater life, as I see them, contained within our present experience.

Chapter VII

The Prospect of Another Life

Nothing can possibly convey to you the brilliance of the color, always the color, that seems to abound in such full measure in the neighborhood of the rivers. Perhaps it is that the streams themselves reflect back so much colorful light from the flowers that this effect of seeming preponderance of color is produced.

Anthony Borgia, *Here and Hereafter*

The acts of your days on days make a certain-shaped thing of you. Then in the rhythm of life the influences too big for control strike a sharp blow or stroke or influence or vibration of some kind, that overcomes your plan or sense of direction. And this same stroke arranges your relationships quite automatically. Suddenly you fit into the place where the thing you shaped will go with mathematical nicety. It is though a lot of scattered things were dancing about; and *clap!* They were all in a pattern. You call it fate, or luck, or destiny, but all the time it is just the preparation of your days on days, your own deliberate handiwork.

Stewart Edward White and Harwood White, *Across the Unknown*

In the ninth round, three times inside a minute, King's right hooked its twisted arch to the jaw; and three times Sandel's body, heavy as it was, was levelled to the mat. Each time he took the nine seconds allowed him and rose to his feet, shaken and jarred, but still strong. He had lost much of his speed, and he wasted less effort. He was fighting grimly ...

Jack London, "A Piece of Steak"

"Science itself," writes Huston Smith, "never did cage us." But from its reports, he continues, we built ourselves a cage and entered it. Hearing from science only statements about the physical world, we inferred - wrongly - that the physical world is all that exists.[1]

It is one thing, as Smith suggests, to say that science deals only with material things, and another to say that these are the only things real. In preceding chapters I have defended what might be called, on the whole, an otherworldly account of reality. I have suggested that human beings are more than material creatures, and consciousness likewise more than a by-product of the material events with which it is associated. I have maintained that no particular fact of science demands of us a reductionist alternative.

Nor do reductionist accounts seem especially convincing in the moral sphere. Our encounter with good and evil, I have maintained, encourages an account of reality that extends outside the bounds of material nature. I have argued further that our present response to moral demand involves us implicitly in a belief in our own survival.

I have maintained, as well, that certain elements of the paranormal hold the prospect of a continuation of our adventure beyond its present boundaries. I have suggested that the material of psychical research, for example, provides occasional evidence to this effect.

---

[1] See Smith's Foreword to William Johnston's edition of *The Cloud of Unknowing*.

Belief in such things as mediumship and otherworldly visions is open, once again, to familiar objections. Such beliefs, to be sure, are in fashion - paranormal claims abound these days in party talk, occult bookstores, and mass level entertainment media. But rarely, I think, are these claims sincere, much less are they trustworthy. Their dubiousness has led many to think that supernaturalism itself is illicit, that its literature is not merely suspect, but inherently worthless. Alleged evidence of the afterlife, notes renowned astronomer Carl Sagan, is never impressive. Purported exercises in "channeling" (a voguish form of oral mediumship), for example, fail always to provide us with anything testable in the way of assertion. Belief in survival, he concludes, is irrational. The integrity of a scientist requires allegiance to hard fact, and not to any such "comforting fantasy."[2]

Fact indeed is better than fraud or fantasy. And the bulk of today's "psychics" and "channelers," I am certain, can be dismissed on one ground or another. But it is by no means clear, as we have seen, that one can "write off" all of the paranormal in this fashion. While Sagan's criticism of certain targets is apt, his own selection emphasizes the doubtful and even the ludicrous.[3] In this chapter, and recalling some of the previous discussion, I wish to devote a bit more

---

[2] Carl Sagan, *The Demon-Haunted World* (New York: Ballantine Books, 1996). See especially pp. 203-09.

[3] Sagan cites in this same section the example of J. Z. Knight, who channels "Ramtha", a soul who lived 35,000 years ago and who now speaks fluent English, says Sagan, with what sounds like the accent of an Indian Raj. Why, asks Sagan, does Ramtha never oblige us with a few details of life and society in that era? ("I know," he adds parenthetically, "he speaks English with an Indian accent, but where 35,000 years ago did they do that?")

attention to alleged glimpses of the other side, relying both upon the classical literature of psychical research and upon more recent and related material.

What does such literature purport to tell us about the next world? Has it any plausibility? Might it, in some instances, represent a reasonable cashing out of discussion elsewhere in this volume? I have suggested (particularly in chapter 4) that there may exist genuine cases of contact with the other side. In this chapter I will deal, in part, with the element of the paranormal once again. I will examine some of its recurrent themes and the broad conception of the next world that emerges from its literature. I will argue that such material is indeed worth examination and that we stand to gain something from the effort. In conclusion I will discuss certain intimations of a greater life as they are contained, by my reckoning, in ordinary life experience.

A Classic Study

In recent years much excitement has arisen over the so-called near-death experience - the experience of those who have "crossed over" and returned, or have seen the next world as they departed this one. One finds the experience present, in some form, throughout the ages.[4] Cases may bear a conspicuous similarity, even across vast differences in culture and personal temperament.

---

[4] A splendid account is contained in Carol Zaleski's *Otherworld Journeys* (New York: Oxford University Press, 1987).

Today, more than twenty years after its first printing, Ray Moody, Jr.'s *Life After Life* remains perhaps the best introduction to this phenomenon. A medical doctor with a Ph. D. in philosophy, Moody's interest in survival developed out of his encounters with ill or dying patients and his investigation (prompted largely by his students) of the issue in his classes.

There are, Moody writes, two basic and fundamentally different conceptions of death present in the human race from time immemorial. The first[5] of these holds that death is "sleep" or "forgetting" - that it is, in other words, annihilation. The second maintains that it is instead "the passage of the soul or mind into another dimension of reality."[6] Those who have had the near-death experience have no doubt as to which of these is the case, for they are certain that it is the latter. The experience, as will be noted shortly, has effected conversions of outlook in even the staunchest skeptics.

Certain characteristics of this experience, Moody observes, repeat themselves across a wide range of circumstance. "What has amazed me," he writes, "since the beginning of my interest are the great similarities of the reports, despite the fact that they come from people of highly varied religious, social, and educational backgrounds."[7]

---

[5] See Ray Moody, *Life After Life* (New York: Ballantine Books, 1988). See discussion in chapter 1, "The Phenomenon of Death". One finds this former view expressed, says Moody, in Homer's *Iliad*, where death is called "death's sister." The association of sleep and death continues today in various ways, as for example when a pet is "put to sleep."

[6] *Ibid.*, p. 13.

[7] *Ibid.*, p. 15.

To illustrate, he offers a composite description that by now has become classic.

> *A man is dying and, as he reaches the point of greatest physical distress, he hears himself pronounced dead by his doctor. He begins to hear an uncomfortable noise, a loud ringing or buzzing, and at the same time feels himself moving very rapidly through a long dark tunnel. After this, he suddenly finds himself outside his own physical body, but still in the immediate physical environment, and he sees his own body from a distance, as though he is a spectator. He watches the resuscitation attempt from this unusual vantage point and is in a state of emotional upheaval.*[8]

After awhile, this individual collects himself and becomes more used to this odd condition.

> *He notices that he still has a "body," but one of a very different nature and with very different powers from the physical body he has left behind. Soon other things begin to happen. Others come to meet and to help him. He glimpses the spirits of relatives and friends who have already died, and a loving, warm spirit of a kind he has never encountered before - a being of light - appears before him. This being asks him a question, non verbally, to make him evaluate his life and helps him along by showing him a panoramic, instantaneous playback of the major events of his life.*[9]

At some point, the subject finds himself approaching a line or barrier representing the transition from this world to the next. He learns that he cannot cross this line, but must return to finish his time here. He resists, owing to the fact that he is overwhelmed by the joy and peace that he has found in this new environment. Nonetheless, and to his disappointment, he reunites with his body and continues with life in this world.

---

[8] *Ibid.*, pp. 21-22.

[9] *Ibid.*, p. 22.

Later, Moody continues, he tries to tell others of his experience, but finds that he has trouble doing so. For "he can find no human words adequate to describe these unearthly episodes." He also finds that others tend to scoff at what he tells them, and so he stops making the effort. Yet the experience affects him no less profoundly for this difficulty.

While the experience of near-death subjects varies in its details, the features noted above occur often enough, in some mixture, to warrant the preceding description. Such accounts, notes Moody, bear also a dramatic resemblance to those contained in diverse sources of classical literature. Among such sources, he observes, are Plato, the New Testament, the mystic Emmanuel Swedenborg, and the Tibetan *Book of the Dead*.

Consider, Moody says, the dialogues of Plato. While Plato was an example *par excellence* of Greek rationality, he was, in addition,

> a great visionary who suggested that ultimately truth can only come to one in an almost mystical experience of enlightenment and insight. He accepted that there were planes and dimensions of reality other than the sensible, physical world and believed that the physical realm could be understood only by reference to these other, "higher" planes of reality.[10]

Plato, as we have seen, located reality outside the world that is disclosed by the senses. This world stands to reality, on his view, much like shadows on the wall of a cave[11] to the objects on which they depend. The journey of the philosopher is like unto a climb out of this dungeon to the world above.

---

[10] *Ibid.*, p. 116.

[11] *Republic*, Book VII, 514 a and following.

Thus Plato was interested chiefly in the spiritual and incorporeal aspect of the human being. The material body, he believed, was merely a vehicle for the soul's present use. Life, on this view, is a journey homeward. Along the way we are jarred into the recollection of eternal truth by our contacts with these flawed examples - fragmented and derivative instances of such things as truth, goodness, wisdom, and beauty - that we find around us. A good part of Plato's writing deals with the soul and its fate after its departure from this world of appearances. Death is escape from a fleeting world of shadow; it is return home to the greater life that awaits. It is likewise a full awakening to what has been forgotten upon our entrance into this world here below.

Thus Plato contends, as Moody says, that "the soul that has been separated from the body upon death can think and reason even more clearly than before," and can see things now in their true nature far more readily than when imprisoned in the flesh.[12] Compare this, says Moody, with the testimony of the apostle Paul, originally himself an adversary of the Jesus movement, who experienced a conversion while traveling the road to the town of Damascus.[13] The brilliance of this vision, its life-shattering impact, is reminiscent, observes Moody, of what occurs in near-death experiences. There is also Paul's statement in his first letter to the church at Corinth, in which he claims that there are

---

[12] *Ibid.*, pp. 116-17. Moody cites the examples of Plato's *Gorgias*, *Phaedo*, and *Republic*. Concerning the notion of a judgment or (in NDE parlance) "review" at life's end, see, for example, Plato, *Gorgias*. Trans. Donald J. Zeyl (Indianapolis: Hackett Publishing Company, 1987). See especially 523 a and following.

[13] See *Acts* 26: 13 - 26.

"celestial bodies" as well as "bodies terrestrial."[14] He speaks, in a related context, of "things which eye saw not, and ear heard not, and which entered not into the heart of man, Whatsoever things God prepared for them that love Him."[15] While the apostle thus offers no exact or literal description, his words are alive with promise.[16]

Paul's account, says Moody, resembles those of certain subjects who find themselves to be embodied, in some fashion, even while released from the flesh. These subjects commonly report that this other body is different from the ordinary one and is not subject to its limitations. Paul says that while the material body is weak and ugly, the spiritual body will be strong and beautiful. The statement is reminiscent, Moody believes, of near-death experiences in which the spiritual body seems whole and complete even when the material body has been broken. Such reports suggest likewise that the spiritual body seems to have no defined age and to be unlimited by the aging process.[17]

---

[14] *I Corinthians* 15: 35 - 52. There are, writes Paul, "celestial bodies, and bodies terrestrial: but the glory of the celestial is one, and the glory of the terrestrial is another ... So also is the resurrection of the dead. It is sown in corruption, it is raised in incorruption: It is sown in dishonor, it is raised in glory: It is raised in weakness; it is raised in power: It is sown a natural body, it is raised a spiritual body. There is a natural body, and there is a spiritual body ..."

[15] *I Corinthians* 2: 9. (Cf. *Isaiah* 64: 4 and 65: 17.)

[16] Worth noting also is Paul's autobiographical statement in the second epistle to the church at Corinth, that "I know a man in Christ, fourteen years ago ... caught up even to the third heaven ... how that he was caught up into Paradise, and heard unspeakable words, which it is not lawful for a man to utter ... (*II Corinthians* 12: 2-4). American Standard Version.

[17] *Life After Life*, p. 115.

The Tibetan Book of the Dead, cited in the previous chapter, is a remarkable work compiled from the teachings of various sages over centuries in prehistoric Tibet and passed on initially by word of mouth. It was apparently written down for the first time in the eighth century A. D., but was long kept hidden from the outside. The individuals who compiled this information, explains Moody, viewed death as a skill - as something that could be done "artfully" if one possessed requisite knowledge. The book was read as a guide to a dying person in his final moments. Herein it was thought to serve two functions.

> The first was to help the dying person keep in mind the nature of each new wondrous phenomenon as he experienced it. The second was to help those still living think positive thoughts and not hold the dying one back with their love and emotional concern, so that he could enter into the afterdeath planes in a proper frame of mind, released from all bodily concerns.[18]

The book contains a lengthy description of stages through which an individual passes after death. On leaving the body, the subject is said to enter into a void, in which he may hear various noises like those of thunder and the whistling of the wind, after which he finds himself outside the mortal body.

> He notices that he is still in a body - called the "shining" body - which does not appear to consist of material substance. Thus, he can go through rocks, walls, and even mountains without encountering any resistance. Travel is almost instantaneous ... His thought and perception are less limited; his mind becomes very lucid and his senses seem more keen and more perfect and closer in nature to the divine. If he has been in physical life blind or deaf or crippled, he is surprised to find that in his "shining" body all his senses, as well as all the powers of his physical body, have been restored and intensified.[19]

---

[18] *Life After Life,* p. 120.

[19] *Ibid.,* pp. 121-22.

This individual may encounter other beings with similar bodies, and may also encounter a brilliant light. The book counsels one approaching this light to have only love and compassion for others. It describes also the great peace and contentment of dying, as well as the "mirror" that contains his or her life story with perfect accuracy. While this ancient work, says Moody, contains descriptions of stages through which his own subjects (having returned) cannot yet have passed, its similarity with contemporary accounts is "nothing short of fantastic."

A further parallel is the work of Emmanuel Swedenborg, a Scandinavian who wrote his accounts in the eighteenth century. Swedenborg, says Moody, first gained prominence as a scientist and later underwent a religious crisis. Soon he began to tell of encounters with the other side. Contained in his accounts are the themes of passing over, meetings with other beings, life-review, a quasi-bodily mode of existence, and others.[20]

What does one make of these similarities? They do not seem to be accounted for by prior *influence* of these older sources upon contemporary subjects. But this, says Moody, is hardly an adequate explanation. True, many subjects were familiar with parts of the Bible, and some were acquainted with Plato. But none in this particular group were acquainted with Swedenborg or with the Tibetan material. Some recurrent details of their experiences, in fact, do not appear in the Bible or in Plato, yet they agree remarkably with these other, more esoteric sources.

---

[20] *Ibid.*, 122-26.

Have we, then, proof of survival? The near-death experience does constitute a proof, of sorts, for those who have it. For these individuals are typically convinced beyond doubt of its reality and of the greater life that it reveals. But this does not decide the theoretical question of how such experiences ought to be understood. For this encounter is, after all, a private *experience*. As such is open to interpretation. It is, to be sure, psychologically interesting. But whether or not it is veridical (which is to say, truth-telling) is another matter.

Can we write it off, on the other hand, as mere hallucination? Some imagine that this is the case. Granted, they say, experience is vivid. It may even transform lives. But this only means that the experience is forceful. Perhaps it can still be explained in natural terms - in terms of certain deep tendencies of the human psyche and the biological events in which this structure is based. Thus a mere change in pressure within the inner ear, observes Sir Cyril Burt, may produce the sensation of rising or floating.[21] The near-death experience, like religious vision on the whole, thinks Sagan, is peculiarly reminiscent of our own natural birth.[22]

---

[21] Burt makes this observation in his 1968 work *Psychology and Psychical Research*. His claim is discussed by Paul and Linda Badham in their book *Immortality or Extinction?* (London: Macmillan Press, Ltd., 1982). See chapter 5, "The Evidence from Near-Death Experiences". See also Moody's discussion in chapter 5 of *Life After Life*.

[22] Carl Sagan, *Broca's Brain* (New York: Random House, 1979). See chapter 25, "The Amniotic Universe". The mystical core of religion, thinks Sagan, "is neither literally true nor perniciously wrong-minded. It is rather a courageous if flawed attempt to make contact with the earliest and most profound experience of our lives." (p. 309)

Materialist philosophers are right, I believe, in saying that near-death experiences are open to more than one interpretation. The majority of such experiences can, in theory, be accounted for in terms of material events with no obvious contradiction. It is true that some people have the feeling that they have left their bodies and perhaps have journeyed also to other worlds. But evidence, we must remember, is an empirical notion; it is concerned, in other words, with what can be seen and examined in a shared public arena. The reality of such experiences, as experiences, is for all practical purposes an established fact. But as such it belongs to the realm of psychology, and not metaphysics. Any further reading of such experiences takes us by definition outside the bounds of science. Thus I agree that such experiences do not by themselves provide us with *evidence* of world beyond this one.

But this does not mean, I think, that a materialist interpretation of the near-death experience is the only one possible, or that it is warranted over the other and trans-worldly alternative. There are two levels of inquiry, says William James, concerning religious experience. The first is empirical, and has to do simply with its psychological features. (This much is for science.) The second is philosophical, and concerns our interpretation. Metaphysical claims are not outwardly testable - we have no scientific gauge of the reliability of a vision. But this, thinks James, does not rule out its *evaluation*. The measure of its worth, he maintains, lies simply in its content. Does its message accord with our own good sense and moral instinct? What is its impact on the subject?[23]

If we cannot publicly confirm the experience, neither can we dismiss it on the basis of its concomitant material conditions. We cannot judge, for example, that some purported revelation is illusory because the subject is generally frail, or suffers high fever at the time of its onset. We know, of course, that fever can produce illusion with respect to material events. But we have no way of gauging its reliability, James insists, with respect to things beyond. (In this other realm, "103 or 104 Fahrenheit might be a much more favorable temperature for truths to germinate and sprout in" than the normal one.) Nor can we assume that illness or trauma is any less likely an occasion for being visited. The presence of God may attend these moments as much as any other. We must then judge the experience on another ground, namely, what it *gives* to the one who has it.

How impressive, then, is the face-value content of the near-death experience? What is its impact? On the whole, it seems, its message abounds in love and assurance. To this extent, it is in keeping with what one might expect from a higher source. As to its aftereffect, no less is true. If increased optimism, compassion, and inclination to self-assessment are any criteria, the experience surely passes James' test. It not only alters the life-outlook of subjects, but seems to bestow upon them *a moral intelligence*. In this respect it deserves, it seems, a better explanation than that of illusion or material accident.

---

[23] See William James' discussion of religious experience and its interpretation in his classic *The Varieties of Religious Experience* (New York: Macmillan Publishing Company, 1961). See especially Lecture I, "Religion and Neurology", for discussion of the materialist bias. (The *Varieties* is comprised essentially of James' Gifford Lectures at Edinburgh at the turn of the century.)

"I appreciate things more," reports a subject interviewed by near-death researcher Kenneth Ring. "Life is precious. And it is a gift of God."[24] "I have no fear of letting people know how I feel about them now," states another. "I remember telling my brother two or three years ago [after the experience] how much I loved him ... now, I have a real sense of beauty." "I value people more," reads one more of these. "I don't think I value worldly goods that much."

Kindness, mercy, a wholesome interest in the condition of others; a genuine sense of the greater reality of which we are a part - the experience tends to bring with it a dramatic elevation of outlook and personal conduct. Typically, its effect is lasting. It may occasion total departure from a lifestyle that was heretofore selfish and without kindness or imagination. Rarely, if ever, does trauma or drug use bring about such change. Thus there is reason, I think, to suppose that the near-death experience is essentially different from the experiences with which sceptics often compare it. If the experience brings transformation by an experience, if love and wisdom are its product, we have some reason to suppose that the experience is genuine.

I have said that an unusual experience does not by itself provide empirical evidence of survival. Yet at times, it seems, it may contain something so extraordinary that it does indeed take us outside the bounds of conventional

---

[24] Kenneth Ring, Ph. D., *Life at Death* (New York: Quill Press, 1982). See chapter 8, "Aftereffects I: Personality and Value Changes". The cited quotations appear on pp. 141 and following. Ring lists a number of these examples, which are fully representative of Moody's findings. He reiterates this theme of drastic and permanent life-change in his subsequent work *Heading Toward Omega* (New York: Quill Press, 1985). See chapter 5, "Value Changes Induced by NDE's".

understanding. For some of these experiences, as I have noted in prior discussion,[25] seem to convey *empirical knowledge* that defies ordinary explanation. (I will cite further examples in a moment.) Thus again, I think, it is hard to dismiss them always as hallucination.

Nor do they seem like hallucinations of any familiar kind to those who have them. Near-death subjects themselves, it is worth noting, are never impressed with efforts to explain their experiences in such terms. Those with firsthand knowledge of psychoactive drugs, for example, say that the experiences are profoundly distinct. Nor do they think that the near-death encounter is explainable as the result of trauma or a related "defense mechanism."[26]

---

[25] See again discussion of Myers' work.

[26] A detailed account of alternative lines of interpretation is contained in Karlis Osis and Erlendur Haraldsson, *At the Hour of Death* (New York: Avon Books, 1977). As the authors observe, certain physiological factors, such as those of fever, brain-starvation, malfunction of the nervous system, and the presence of pain-killing drugs, are often suggested as possible explanations of near-death visions. Yet research does not turn up the expected correlations between these conditions and reported experience that one might expect. Nor does there appear to be the correlation involving belief-states (a subject's expectation, say, of death or recovery) that psychological explanations would predict. While the presence of a certain drug is correlated with a given kind of hallucination, there seems, again, to exist a profound difference between hallucinations of the "normal" kind and the near-death experience. For example, the visions of other persons linked with a specific medical condition were normally of persons still living, while those of NDE subjects were invariably of persons who were deceased. See once more the related and very detailed discussion see Paul and Linda Badham in *Immortality or Extinction?*

Recurrent Themes and Alleged Glimpses

I have suggested in this chapter and elsewhere that life may contain an element of the paranormal, that belief in another order of reality does not of itself compromise our intellectual integrity. There exists, too, as I have noted, a broad family of literature concerned with this order. One, as noted earlier, is produced by oral mediumship. Another owes to so-called "automatic writing," in which purported otherworld communicators transmit information by the hand of the go-between. In this section I will delve a bit further into this material. I will look also at some of the discussion that it has engendered in the past century. I will cite relevant themes in this literature and relate them briefly to discussion in previous chapters.

What might the next world be like? Our thinking draws of necessity upon present experience. Any notion of another life, observes psychical researcher James Hyslop, must involve sensation. Consider, for one, the New Testament book of *Revelation*, with its promise of *streets of gold*.[27] Even if we read this account as being symbolic, says Hyslop, its meaningfulness depends in some measure on its intended material analogy.[28]

---

[27] See, for example, *Revelation* 21: 21, "And the twelve gates were twelve pearls; each one of the several gates was of one pearl: and the street of the city was pure gold, as it were transparent glass." (American Standard Version)

[28] James Hyslop, *Contact With the Other World* (New York: The Century Company, 1919), p. 353.

This idea of a material heaven extends across a very wide range of literature, including that of scripture, psychical research, and the near-death experience. The next world, by all accounts, seems to be structurally akin to this one; whatever its particular features, it is still a world of space and time, of actions and encounters, a world in which we may continue to express ourselves in ways much like those at present.

Accounts along these lines sometimes meet with derision, owing, perhaps, to the fact that they are not ethereal enough for some tastes. But surely it stands to reason the next life has something in common with this one. For if this present life is what spiritual sources, on the whole, make it out to be, it serves a certain educational purpose. It is in some sense *preparatory* to the next. If so, it must bear that life some analogy. Indeed it is hard to imagine what life would be in the absence of space or time, or whether our existence without them makes sense.

This does not mean that the two worlds are altogether alike. The broad consensus of such sources is that the next world is a brighter and kinder place than this one. Thus Moody's subjects, for example, are always talking about *light*, about *warmth* and *acceptance*, and the difficulty that one has conveying, in ordinary language, the unearthly beauty on the other side. Their testimony is joined in veritable chorus by those in various sources of mysticism and psychical research.

Many otherworld reports, as I have noted, come through the pen. "My life here has been a charmed one," reports one of these, allegedly a spirit who died as a small child now speaking from the other side. This source describes "enrapturing scenes of beauty being constantly presented to view, like the ever varying landscapes delineated on the canvas by a skilful artist." These places "are vocal with celestial harmony, and the air is redolent with the perfume of flowers."[29]

There are flowers, agrees the account penned by Anthony Borgia, of unearthly fragrance. An astonishing feature of this other world, it continues, is "the sound of music that enveloped them, making such soft harmonies as corresponded exactly and perfectly with the gorgeous colors of the flowers themselves."

Further, it is reported, there exists a profound connection between sound and color.

> In the spirit world all music is color, and all color is music. The one is never existent without the other. That is why the flowers give forth such pleasant tones when they are approached ... The water that sparkles and flashes colors is also creating musical sounds of purity and beauty.[30]

---

[29] James Hyslop, *Contact with the Other World* (New York: The Century Company, 1919), pp. 367-68.

[30] Anthony Borgia, *Life in the World Unseen* (Midway, Utah: M. A. P. Publishing, 1993), p. 70. This account claims to be the report of Robert Hugh Benson, a writer and clergyman who left this world in 1914 and who communicates through the hand of Anthony Borgia. The remark about color and sound having a correspondence is a strange one, yet it is curiously reminiscent of some of the things that mystics in this world have said on occasion. Cf. Underhill, who quotes St. Martin as reporting that "I saw flowers that sounded, and saw notes that shone." Such persons, she says, have moments of experience "in which the senses are fused into a single and ineffable act of perception, and color and sound are known as aspects of one thing." (*Mysticism*, p. 7) Did we realize, she adds, the extent to which our common view of things is dependent on the peculiarity of our own structure, we might be less contemptuous of those who offer such flights of expression.

"I felt *filled* with light," reads another, as delivered through the hand of Helen Greaves, "that is the only way I can express it."[31] This literature has common ground with the reports of many near-death subjects, who tend to say things quite similar. A "day" on that side, writes Rebecca Springer in recalling her own glimpse of the next world,

> was full of glorious radiance, a rosette golden light, which was everywhere. There is no language known to mortals that can describe this marvelous glory. It flooded the sky; it was caught up and reflected in the waters; it filled all heaven with joy and all hearts with song.[32]

Another theme, just as prominent, is that of *reunion*. No one, near-death researcher Elizabeth Kubler-Ross is convinced, dies alone. In general, "the people who are waiting for us on the other side are the ones who loved us the most."[33] Typically this meeting involves reunion with a departed spouse, parent, or sibling.

This theme of rejoining loved ones is very old in purported accounts of life on the other side. "Our home life in heaven complete," exclaims Rebecca Springer, in recounting her lessons learned from an otherworld visit, "no partings forever!"[34] "I recognized my grandmother," reads a more recent source,

---

[31] Helen Greaves, *Testimony of Light* (Essex, England: Neville Spearman Publishers, 1969). This account purports to communicate from the other side the experiences of Frances Banks, a former Catholic Sister who left this world in 1965.

[32] Rebecca Rutter Springer, *My Dream of Heaven* (Midway, Utah: M. A. P. Publishing, 1995), p. 61. Springer's story was originally published in the nineteenth century.

[33] Elizabeth Kubler-Ross, *On Life After Death* (Berkeley, CA: Celestial Arts, 1991), p. 15.

[34] *My Dream of Heaven*, p. 129.

> and a girl I had known when I was in school, and many other relatives and friends ... They all seemed pleased. It was a very happy occasion, and I felt that they had come to protect or to guide me. It was almost as if I were coming home, and they were there to greet or welcome me.[35]

Such accounts, many of which have been collected by the Society for Psychical Research, have inspired a good deal of reflection on the part of those who have examined them. It does not seem likely, writes philosopher and Society member Minot Savage, "that the going out into that other world is into a strange and lonely country."[36] When we came into this world, he explains, we were expected and were welcomed with love and care. He adds,

> I do not believe that the next step ahead in the universe is into something poorer than was the occasion of our coming here. So I believe that we shall find ourselves among friends, in a place that shall seem very much like home ...[37]

There is a tendency in some quarters, again, to dismiss alleged near-death visions as being illegitimate. Perhaps, it is said, these reports owe to some kind of delusion. Or perhaps they are simply manufactured. Their commonality with this other literature may owe to deliberate copying by those who have read other stories. Or again, it has been suggested, certain accounts already in print or in the public mind may find their way by clairvoyant or telepathic means into the mind of the automatist, whose speech or writing then gives the material new

---

[35] See again Moody's *Life After Life*, which contains many such descriptions as well as discussion of their evidential value.

[36] Minot Savage, *Life Beyond Death* (New York: The Knickerbocker Press, 1899), p. 273.

[37] *Ibid.*

expression.[38]

Of course, an explanation along the lines of extra-sensory ability is already disturbing enough to the materialist view. For materialism has a hard time accommodating channels of communication of the kind that these explanations require. But while telepathy may seem like a less fantastic hypothesis than disembodied survival, it is not obvious that such an explanation has an advantage over that of full-fledged otherworldly vision. Certain near-death subjects, as noted earlier, seem to acquire knowledge by their experience that strongly suggests communication from the other side. One such case, representative of many, is found in a precursor of Moody's book, a short and posthumously published work entitled *Death-Bed Visions*[39] by medical doctor and psychical research pioneer Sir William Barrett.

Barrett relates the experience of his wife, a distinguished surgeon, in the room with a Mrs. B., who was in labor and suffering heart failure. Although the child was saved, Mrs. B. passed over. About an hour before this, the woman had a vision of her deceased father, who seemed to beckon her to the next world. "It is difficult," writes Lady Barrett, "to describe the sense of reality conveyed by her intense absorption in the vision."[40] At this time, she was replaced at the bedside

---

[38] This idea was suggested to me by John Hick in a private conversation some years ago.

[39] Sir William Barrett, *Death-Bed Visions - The Psychical Experiences of the Dying* (Northamptonshire: Aquarian Press, 1986). The book was first published in 1926. See related discussion in Barrett's earlier-cited *On the Threshold of the Unseen*.

[40] *Ibid.*, p. 11.

by hospital Matron Miriam Castle, who describes a further event in the woman's final moments. "I was present shortly before the death of Mrs. B.," relates Castle,

> together with her husband and her mother. Her husband was leaning over her and speaking to her, when pushing him aside she said 'Oh, don't hide it; it's so beautiful.' Then turning away from him towards me ... Mrs. B. said, 'Oh, why there's Vida,' referring to a sister of whose death three weeks previously she had not been told. Afterwards the mother, who was present at the time, told me, as I have said, that Vida was the name of a dead sister of Mrs. B.'s, of whose illness and death she was quite ignorant, as they had carefully kept this news from Mrs. B. owing to her serious illness.[41]

Barrett obtained a separate and corroborating statement from Mrs. B.'s mother Mary C. Clark, who was present at the time. In it Clark notes the puzzlement on the face of her dying daughter, who, again, had not been informed of her sister's passing. Barrett goes on to consider various explanations of the occurrence, and shows that it is difficult indeed to explain it by means of misperception of any kind. He discusses other such cases in the same chapter.

Kubler-Ross recalls a similar case (one of a good number in her long acquaintance) of a twelve-year old girl who crossed over and returned. She had been reluctant to share the experience with her mother, since she did not want to tell her that she had found a place more beautiful than the home in which they lived. Finally needing to share the experience with someone, she confided to her father that she had been in a place of great beauty. One of the things, she said, that made it special was being there with her brother, who regarded her with great love and tenderness. But she could not understand how such an experience was

---

[41] *Ibid.*, pp. 12-13.

possible when she did not have a brother. On hearing this the father wept, confessing to her that she had in fact had a brother who had died some three months before she was born. The existence of this deceased sibling had been kept altogether from her knowledge.

Purported communications from the other side, as Hyslop has noted, tend to represent the next world as "a finer form of matter." Yet the idea, he adds, is hard for some to entertain. For how, they ask, can there be material objects that resist detection? It is one thing to say that a thing is elusive, but these heavenly objects, it seems, resist detection altogether.

Certain descriptions of the next-world environment have at times provoked ridicule even within sympathetic ranks. One of these involves a purported communication to Oliver Lodge (a noted physicist and Society member) from his son Raymond. In a sitting with the renowned medium Gladys Osborne Leonard, "Raymond" announces that "there are laboratories over here, and they manufacture all sorts of things in them. Not like you do, out of solid matter, but out of essences, and ethers, and gases."[42] He claims that these manufacturers are able to produce, among other things, cigars and mixed drinks. He claims furthermore to live in a house made of brick.

Is belief in another world then irrational? Whatever the merits of any particular revelation, there is nothing inherently absurd or implausible, thinks Hyslop, in the idea of a hidden material world. Physical science, he observes, "has

---

[42] Sir Oliver Lodge, *Raymond* (New York: George H. Doran Company, 1916), p. 197.

resolved the atoms which have been supposed to be the basis of matter as known by the senses into ions and electrons which are supposed to be ethereal in their nature."[43] A distinction between sensible and supersensible exists, he explains, within science itself, as witness the examples of the air, certain gases, and X-rays, among others. Perhaps we would even do better, he adds, to abandon the classical division of reality, in a kind of all-or-nothing fashion, into mind and matter, and think of it more in terms of levels or gradations.

"Scientists,"observes Savage in a similar vein, "are perfectly familiar with states of matter that they are not cognizant to any of our senses."[44] Vision, we know, occurs only when vibrations impinge upon the eye at a given number per second , and ceases when those vibrations pass beyond that range. It may be, he writes, that there exist independent worlds, "some possibly existing in different parts of space, but others perhaps pervading each other unseen and unknown in the same space." For all we know, there may be spiritual entities with us in this world, "pervading the atmosphere all around us, real, thrilling and throbbing with life, a life more intense than any we know anything about or can dream of, and our present senses take no cognisance of them whatsoever."[45]

There is, again, a long tradition of belief in a realm that is material in its composition, yet undetectable by ordinary sensation. This view finds expression

---

[43] James Hyslop, *Life After Death - Problems of the Future Life and Its Nature* (New York: E. P. Dutton and Co., 1918), p. 255.

[44] *Life Beyond Death*, p. 279.

[45] *Ibid.*, p. 278. For related discussion see Lodge's *Phantom Walls* (New York: G. P. Putnam's Sons, 1930).

across a wide range of both occult and mainstream religious traditions.[46] It accords also with much of the literature of psychical research. "The astral world," writes theosophist writer Annie Besant, "is a definite region of the universe, surrounding and interpenetrating the physical, but imperceptible to our ordinary observation because it is composed of a different order of matter."[47] "We have an astral fac-simile of the material body," claims purported communicator George Pelham, noted earlier, in a seance with Mrs. Piper.[48] Nor is this idea of refined matter altogether foreign to mainstream religion. More than one writer has noticed, for example, the similarity between this astral body and that body of which Paul speaks in *I Corinthians*.[49]

This idea of entities embodied yet invisible, Savage admits, will seem fanciful to some. But perhaps, he says, it helps to make sense of certain unusual

---

[46] Whatever pain or enjoyment a soul tastes in Hades, argues Church Father Tertullian, "in its prison or lodging, in the fire or in Abraham's bosom, it gives proof thereby of its own corporeality." The passage appears in Tertullian's *de Anima*, chapter 7. It is reprinted in Antony Flew, ed., *Body, Mind, and Death* (Toronto: Macmillan, 1969), p. 92. Tertullian notes also the experience of a certain female seer, who speaks of seeing a soul "soft and transparent and of an etherial color, and in form resembling that of a human being in every respect.". (*de Anima*, chapter 9, also contained in the passage just noted)

[47] Annie Besant, *Man and his Bodies* (Adyar, India: Theosophical Publishing House, 1967), p. 34. This book had its first printing in 1896. The theosophical movement developed late in the nineteenth century out of interest in both spiritualism and classical Indian religion. For a recent account of this "esoteric physiology" and its theoretical scheme, see again Benjamin Walker's *Beyond the Body - The Human Double and the Astral Planes*.

[48] *Human Personality*, vol. II, p. 614.

[49] See chapter 6, "The Possibility of a Future Life", in Hyslop's *Life After Death*. (Hyslop also cites this parallel in chapter 21, "Mode of Life After Death", in *Contact with the Other World*.)

features of human experience. Consider, for one, those "warnings," sudden and elusive, that sane individuals occasionally seem to receive.[50] These experiences, Savage explains, may be the interference of some near ally who happens, by some circumstance, to have the opportunity.

One finds in the near-death literature some reiteration of the idea, prevalent in both religious and scientific traditions,[51] that there is far more *to oneself* than the ordinary consciousness. Many subjects report an expansion of faculties during their out-of-body episodes. They may also feel, as noted earlier, that in their freed state they were not limited by their outward age. Over the years, says Moody, he has asked some of his child subjects how "old" they were during the experience - whether or not, that is, their liberated body is one of a child or one of an adult.[52] "A surprising number of them," he writes, "say that they are adults during the episode, although they can't say how they know this." This, he believes, may accord well with religious ideas. For if one thinks of this experience in terms of the spirit leaving the flesh, "it could mean that the spirit itself is an ageless entity that finds itself housed in an ever-changing body."[53]

---

[50] Savage cites, as one example, the experience of a friend who suddenly heard and obeyed a voice and leaped from one side of her car to the other, just before a collision demolished the side on which she had been sitting.

[51] See again related discussion in chapter 4 of this volume.

[52] Ray Moody, Jr., *The Light Beyond* (New York: Bantam Books, 1989), p. 74.

[53] *Ibid.*, pp. 74-75. Moody admits that this is not the only explanation, however, since it may be that children are made "so comfortable" by those beings they encounter that they naturally feel like their peers.

The next world, as we have seen, is described in curiously similar ways across this wide and cross-related body of psychical and spiritualist literature. What, now, of its moral properties? Again, it seems, there exist broad currents of agreement. Much of the literature also bears in an interesting way, I think, on discussion in previous chapters.

The consensus of most near-death and related literature is that there exists no single and perfect division of the human race with respect to the next life. There are not two eternal groups, each with its own fixed destiny, as some traditional religious doctrines maintain. Overall there is little notion of hell, in the popular sense of the word; rather the next world, it seems, is a plurality, a series of places each corresponding to the condition and ongoing development of its inhabitants.

What strange ideas we have while on earth, says the departed brother of Rebecca Springer when she encounters him on the other side. We imagine that death of the body brings about in us some absolute change, for better or worse. But in fact, he claims, we bring to the new life the same tastes, the same desires, the same knowledge, that we have acquired in this one. If we were not sufficiently good before our passing, we are not made instantly wise or elevated in the moment of transition. What, he asks, would be the point of acquiring worthy knowledge over the course of a long and active life, only to undergo a complete change the very second we are done with it? We are building for eternity, he maintains, all during our earthly life. The purer our thoughts, the nobler our ambitions, the further we progress, and the higher our station on the other side.[54]

A kindred outlook is expressed by Savage, who says, "I think we have distorted all our ideas of the other life by our theological speculations, and by supposing that death is a line, the moment we have crossed which, our destiny is fixed, and we are either devils or angels forever."[55] More likely, he maintains, we carry in ourselves heavens and hells. It is these inward fires of our own making, if anything, that will disturb our peace in the next world. We take with us, for better or worse, what we have wrought in this life. From our own actions, and what they make of us, there is no escape. If we wish happiness on that side, suggests Savage, we might start now by cultivating in ourselves what is good and positive.

Many collections of near-death experiences have been published in the years since Moody's book first appeared. One of the more recent, stressing also this idea of otherworld levels, is Mally Cox-Chapman's *The Case for Heaven.* We might bear in mind, notes Cox-Chapman, that Jesus' statement[56] that in his Father's house there are "many mansions." The Greek *'monai'*, notes Cox-Chapman, might well refer not only to mansions, but to abiding-places, to places of rest along the way. The third century philosopher Origen, she adds, uses the

---

[54] *My Dream of Heaven*, p. 23.

[55] *The Life Beyond Death*, p. 272.

[56] *John* 14: 2.

term to describe resting places of the soul on its journey to God.[57] Thinking in such terms, we might well imagine that "any number of realities revealed in near-death experiences are indeed mansions in Heaven."[58]

How does this claim, taken at face value, relate to previous discussion? It accord well, I think, with the view[59] that the universe is a moral order, that it is ultimately *a place of justice*. The absence of hell from its scheme may seem like a defect to some, who imagine that this prospect affords rightful punishment to those who have done terrible things in this world. But if justice is our concern, we would do well, I think, to reconsider.

Those who favor the idea of hell need to ask themselves, it seems to me, whether or not they truly believe (as most of them claim) in the unfailing goodness of their creator. They must ask themselves likewise what is the relationship between this creator and His (or Her) subjects. The same historical tradition that embraces the notion of hell also maintains characteristically that God is love.[60] How are these claims to be reconciled?

Let us imagine that some individual has lived, on the whole, a bad life. Let us suppose that he now faces the prospect of damnation. If we believe also

---

[57] *The Case for Heaven*, p. 23.

[58] *Ibid.*

[59] See again discussion in chapter 3 in this volume.

[60] See, for example, *I John* 4: 8. This idea is stressed also in the fourth gospel, considered by many to be the scriptural cornerstone of the Christian faith. For relevant discussion, see also William Barclay, *The Mind of Jesus* (San Francisco: HarperCollins, 1976). Especially worth note in this regard is chapter 11, "What Jesus Said About God".

that God is love - that God indeed has loved this individual with a love immeasurable all the days of his life - then we must ask one question. What now happens to this relationship? If this one dying is not (by whatever criterion) in the right spiritual condition, this love is withdrawn. In its place comes wrath unending.[61] Yet how, I ask, has this event of death (through whatever fluctuation of the moment - a passing virus, a sputtering plane engine, a chance storm or flood, perhaps) so transformed the situation?

The event itself (ordinarily no choice of the one dying) does not seem to alter, in any decisive way, the nature of this mortal creature. Why then this sudden and absolute change? We are far more in keeping with the dictates of both reason and conscience, I believe, if we think along alternative lines.

But such an individual, it may be said, has already had chances. Perhaps he *deserves* punishment. Should everyone, after all, float off into some cosmic bath of joy and sunlight when done here? Yet perhaps this perfect reward is not the only alternative to fire and brimstone. By no means does the literature I have cited, in preceding paragraphs, promise unconditional happiness to all. Some near-death experiences, it might be noted, are painful.[62] In this way they may serve as a warning to those who have them.

---

[61] Some no doubt will quarrel with my description, saying that God's love for this individual is eternal, and that it is not replaced with anything else. But from the point of view of the one damned, I think, it is scarcely important.

[62] See, for example, Maurice Rawlings, *Beyond Death's Door* (Nashville: Thomas Nelson, 1978). Rawlings' treatment of the material is criticized, however, by Paul Badham, who believes that Rawlings incorporates material that can better be classed as nightmare or delirium. See again chapter 5 of the Badhams' *Immortality or Extinction?*

There are dark realms, insists the Borgia source. For there are some whose lives here have been "spiritually hideous." This fact has nothing to do, he adds, with the image such individuals have maintained in this life. Some of these now in darkness may have had lives that were outwardly successful and even sanctified. But in the next life there is no such tension between fact and appearance. Content is decisive. God does not need to punish such individuals, explains this account, for here they punish themselves.[63]

There is a difference between this conception of punishment and the more traditional one. For punishment as understood here is finite. It is likewise *proportionate to the degree of the offense*. Thus I believe that this alternative conception is more reasonable.

In order to see this point, we might consider for a moment what justice means in this world. First and foremost, I must think, it involves some notion of moral *balance*. It has to do with reciprocity. For this reason it does not prescribe the same reward or punishment in every case. In the case of punishment, for example, it prescribes (ideally, at least) the penalty weighted *o the degree of the offense*. This degree is determined, moreover, not merely by the outward form of the offense (be it murder, theft, rape, or any other), but *by the degree of its viciousness*. For this reason, I believe, accounts of the kind just noted express a

---

[63] *Life in the World Unseen*, pp. 83 and following. Cf. Swedenborg, cited earlier, who says that "no part of the punishment is done by the Lord - it is done by the evil itself. For an evil thing and its punishment are so closely joined that they cannot be separated." See section # 550 of Emmanuel Swedenborg, *Heaven and Hell*. Trans. George F. Dole (West Chester, Pennsylvania: Swedenborg Foundation, 1979). This book was first published in Latin in 1758.

sounder conception of justice than those that operate, in effect, all-or-nothing. They recognize that good and evil are matters of degree, that no individual likewise is wholly and consistently one or the other, and that no amount of action within a finite lifetime merits infinite punishment.[64] They remind us also that our present efforts to understand and dispense justice are at best approximations. We cannot know the moral condition of other human beings, nor even our own, with any finality in this world. Nor, again, does our present moral status in the eyes of others determine our destiny. For it is what is inside us, our real substance, that matters. But on the other side, if we may judge by some of these accounts, it is different. For there justice is not merely approximated. Instead truth prevails in its entirety. It is not obscured or circumvented.

This notion of our continuous development and according fate finds an interesting parallel in the mainstream of classical India. That seeker who falls short of liberation in this life, says the lord Krishna to the warrior Arjuna in the epic *Bhagavad Gita*, wins nonetheless "the heavenly worlds of the doers of right," and dwells there for "endless years" before returning to finish the task.[65]

---

[64] It is said, on occasion, that desert is really not the issue. For no one, it is claimed, deserves salvation. Cited in this connection are certain key passages, such as Paul's remark (*Romans* 3: 23) that "all have sinned, and fall short of the glory of God," and so that God acts on the side of leniency in sparing anyone. For this reason some conservative types insist that justice is the last thing that anyone should desire from their creator. But if this is the case, then the divine justice is strangely and hideously different from any that we know.

[65] See *The Bhagavad Gita*. Trans. Franklin Edgerton (Cambridge: Harvard University Press, 1972). Edgerton appends a collection of very worthwhile essays to this translation. See also chapter 5 of Swami Prabhavananda's *The Spiritual Heritage of India* (Hollywood: Vedanta Press, 1980).

No effort, it appears, is ever wasted. In this same tradition, as noted earlier, one finds a highly refined spiritual exercise called *yoga*, literally a *yoking* or *union* of oneself with Ultimate Reality. This practice, explains Huston Smith, has lines of specialization, each fitted to respective types of personal constitution. One of these is *karma yoga*, the path of *work*, as distinguished from those paths that emphasize respectively *knowledge*, *meditation*, or *devotion* as their principal means. "If I chop down a tree that blocks my view," Smith explains,

> each stroke of the axe unsettles the tree; but it leaves its mark on me as well, driving deeper into my being my determination to have my way in the world. Everything I do for my private wellbeing adds another layer to my ego, and in thickening it insulates me more from God. Conversely, every act done without thought for myself diminishes my self-centeredness until finally no barrier remains to separate me from the Divine.[66]

What is suggested by this passage, as is suggested by much of the literature of psychical research, is a conception of salvation quite different from those more common in the Western mainstream. Our destiny, according to this line of thought, is not decided once and for all by any particular fact about our present condition, be it membership in a given religious organization, an article of belief, or allegiance to a certain religious figure. Instead, it seems, we are what we make of ourselves, for better or worse and in varying degree, all day long and throughout our lives. Each day, and in all of our actions, we are making ourselves something different from what we were before. Our fate will be determined principally by just this activity.

---

[66] Huston Smith, *The World's Religions* (San Francisco: HarperCollins, 1991), p. 38.

There persist, of course, many questions about the next world. One of these involves the experience of those on the other side in relation to ourselves. Can they see us now? And if so, are they distressed by the problems that we presently face? Those who have departed this world would suffer great anxiety, it seems, if they were aware of these difficulties. Are they thus denied this knowledge?

The discussion of Minot Savage, I believe, is once again worth attention. Does it seem likely, he asks, that we are taken from our families, at life's end, and kept from all sight of them? More likely, he believes, the bond that has united us in life remains present across the worlds. But this, adds Savage, need not mean that those on the other side must bear our burdens as we bear them, or that they must share in the pain that exists on this side. For things may be assessed in another fashion on that side, and the perception there may be very different from our own. He offers herein a splendid insight.

Consider, says Savage, how it is in this world. We may at times see our loved ones in situations that seems to them quite dire while we do not share their alarm.

> A mother, as she sits in her home with her little child playing at her feet, sometimes has an experience like this. The child breaks her doll or plaything of one kind or another; and this is a heart-breaking sorrow to the little one; but it does not break the heart of the mother at all. She picks the child up in her lap, clasps her to her heart, soothes and comforts her. She knows that it is but a passing sorrow, and is not going to cloud the child's life forever.[67]

---

[67] Savage, *Life Beyond Death*, pp. 281-2.

"So it seems to me," he continues,

> that those who have found out to a certainty what the grand issue of life means, cannot be troubled because we shed a few tears over a loss in Wall Street or because we have a pain which may last us for a week. They know what is before us, they know it is to be victory in time ...[68]

Speculation about the next world is not confined to those who have left the religious mainstream. In *Faith and Reason*, noted Christian philosopher Richard Swinburne[69] offers a way of thinking about the next world as an extension of present belief in an all-wise creator. To understand heaven, thinks Swinburne, one ought to think first about what makes for a meaningful life here on earth. For that world, he imagines, is continuous in its values with this one.

What, he asks, are the most worthwhile tasks that an individual might pursue in this world? They are those of "developing our understanding of the world and beautifying it, developing our friendship with others, and helping others toward a deeply happy life."[70] So, then, will such activities characterize heaven, in better and surer forms than we have found them here. Heaven will be the residence of those who have started in this world to do its tasks "for a short time with limited tools and understanding, with many obstacles to success, and desires for other things."[71] In short, it will be a place of action, purpose, and creativity in

---

[68] *Ibid.*, p. 282.

[69] Richard Swinburne, *Faith and Reason* (Oxford: Oxford University Press, 1981).

[70] *Ibid.*, p. 131.

[71] *Ibid.*, pp. 135-36.

their highest forms, wherein God's unlimited nature allows us growth toward perfection. The next life is thus continuous in its nature with this one.

Another worthwhile discussion from this more conservative quarter is that of Richard Purtill, who discusses the future life and its possible characteristics in his earlier-cited book *Thinking About Religion*.[72] Popular ideas about reincarnation, thinks Purtill, offer little in the way of a satisfactory resolution of the question of human destiny.[73] Traditional thinking about heaven and hell, he adds, is little better. Consider the case of an individual who has committed some brutal series of crimes against innocent people and yet repents in his final moments. Such an individual, on the mainstream view, is thought to be "saved." But does he now deserve, does he share, the same fate as an individual whose whole earthly life has been exemplary?

The traditional view of the Catholic Church, he notes, is that such an individual must first endure fires of *purgatory* to be fit for heaven. Purgatory, in its popular conception, says Purtill, is thus a kind of torture chamber with suffering, and not education, as its sole end. But if a man, he writes,

> relived that evil, seeing it as his victims felt it, the man could fully realize and fully reject the evil. The only adequate purgatory might be to suffer what you made others suffer - not just an equivalent pain, but *that* pain, seeing yourself as the tormenter you were to them.[74]

---

[72] See especially chapter 10, "Life After Death: What Would It be Like?"

[73] See again the introduction contained in this volume.

[74] *Thinking About Religion*, p. 148.

In this case, says Purtill, you might truly understand your evil and reject it. As for those inward sins of rage, or hatred, or envy, which harm no other person, purgation might consist of "seeing these as God sees them, in their full squalor and meanness and nastiness." Seeing them so, one might likewise be able to fully repent of them.

In concluding this section, I note again the discussion of Elizabeth Kubler-Ross, which summarizes many recurrent themes of paranormal experience. It expresses also, I think, what is contained in the germ of religious awareness. One of these is the idea that death is actually but a *transition* from one mode of life to another. Death of the body, writes Kubler-Ross, is identical with "what happens when the butterfly emerges from its cocoon." It is no more than "moving from one house into a more beautiful one" when the old one has served its purpose.[75]

One hears also, she says, of a *return to wholeness* that has been lost in some cases by accidents of the flesh. People who were blind, writes Kubler-Ross,

> can see again. People who couldn't hear or speak can hear and speak again. Those of my patients suffering from multiple sclerosis, being able to move only in a wheelchair and having trouble uttering a sentence, tell me full of joy after they return from a near-death experience: "Doctor Ross, I could dance again."[76]

The near-death experience, it appears, is shaped in some degree by the cultural environment in which it occurs. "I have never," writes Kubler-Ross, "encountered a Protestant child who saw the Virgin Mary in his last minutes, yet

---

[75] Elizabeth Kubler-Ross, *On Life After Death* (Berkeley, Cal.: Celestial Arts, 1991), p. 10.

[76] *Ibid.*, p. 13.

she was perceived by many Catholic children." You are thus received, she says, by those who mean the most to you. In this respect the experience varies with circumstance. Yet certain characteristics are present across these lines. Before stepping out of the body, she notes, "in exchange for those forms which you will keep for eternity, you pass through a phase which is totally imprinted with items of the physical world." The particular features of this phase will vary with the expectation of the subject.

In her own case, she goes on to say, "I was allowed to cross a pass in the Alps covered with wild flowers. Everyone is met by the heaven he or she imagined."

> After you have passed this tunnel, bridge or mountain pass, you are at its end embraced by light. It is extremely bright, and the more you approach this light the more you are embraced by the greatest, indescribable, unconditional love you could ever imagine. There are no words for it.[77]

No words: This theme of *ineffability* figures always in the classic literature of mysticism.[78] It is likewise present in virtually every piece of literature concerning the near-death experience. Ordinary ways of describing sound and beauty, and indeed even space and time, do not capture it.[79]

---

[77] *Ibid.*, p. 16.

[78] See, for example, James' discussion in Lecture 16 of his *Varieties*, which lists this characteristic as one of the defining features of mystical encounter.

[79] Cf. a Moody subject who reports that "our world - the one we're living in now - *is* three-dimensional, but the next one definitely isn't. And that's why it's so hard to tell you this. I have to describe it to you in words that are three-dimensional. That's as close as I can get to it, but it's not really adequate. I can't really give you a complete picture." (*Life After Life*, p. 26)

In much the same vein, there is expressed herein a *lack of limitation* of the kind that ordinarily binds us. The events of this higher are governed not by material law, but by the truths of the spirit. Thus if for example a young American dies in Asia and thinks of his mother in Washington, "he will bridge the thousands of miles through the power of thought in a split second and will be with her."[80] Time and again it is stressed also that this world is a place of *education*, a place, writes Kubler-Ross, "that you had to go through in order to pass certain tests and learn special lessons." What occurs here - what we learn or fail to learn - makes a difference. But once having finished this school, one is allowed to go home - "to go home - to graduate!"[81]

Intimations of a Future Life Contained within Daily Experience

All of this talk of visions and other worlds, I think, is immensely interesting. Yet it is also elusive. Even if we are receptive, in some measure, to claims of this kind, there remains an element of uncertainty. Have we, when all is said and done, any real confirmation of the next world? For all of the rumors, all of the marvelous stories and alleged peerings, it seems, we lack a final demonstration.

---

[80] *On Life After Death*, p. 14.

[81] *Ibid.*, p. 17.

This point was noted by William James in his essay "Final Impressions of a Psychical Researcher".[82] "I confess," writes James,

> that at times I have been tempted to believe that the Creator has eternally intended this department of nature to remain *baffling*, to prompt our curiosities and hopes and suspicions all in equal measure, so that, although ghosts and clairvoyances, and raps and messages from spirits, are always seeming to exist and can never be fully explained away, they also can never be susceptible of full corroboration.[83]

James' discussion is cited by Colin Wilson, who refers to this problem of uncertainty as "James' Law". Some such principle, thinks Wilson, will occur sooner or later to practically everyone who investigates the paranormal. The evidence, he notes, is plentiful, but "it *always* leaves room for doubt."[84]

Yet this, I think, may stand to reason, if we consider what is typically involved in a religious view of life in the first place. In our present condition, maintains John Hick, we remain "at an epistemic distance" from our creator.[85] We are confined, in other words, to a situation in which we have neither perfect confirmation nor perfect disconfirmation of our greater destiny. Suspended, for

---

[82] Contained in John J. McDermott, ed., *The Writings of William James* (Chicago: The University of Chicago Press, 1977), pp. 787-99. The essay was originally published under the title of "Confessions of a Psychical Researcher" in the *American Magazine* of October, 1909.

[83] *Ibid.*, p. 788.

[84] *Afterlife*, p. 159.

[85] See again Hick's earlier cited book *Philosophy of Religion* (Englewood Cliffs, New Jersey: Prentice-Hall, 1990). Relevant discussion is found in several places, including chapter 4, "The Problem of Evil", and Chapter 6, "Evidentialism, Foundationalism, and Religious Belief".

now, between these two possibilities, we are thus free, in an important sense,[86] and able to pursue our destiny as the soul-making process requires.

This does not mean, either, that the material of psychical research is without value. Nor does James himself advocate skepticism with respect to the survival prospect. We have not full confirmation, he thinks, but there is evidence for those who look for it.

Here again, I think, it is as it should be. There is not proof of the next life, it seems, in the same way that there is proof in science or mathematics. This does not rule out, of course, that certain individuals (for reasons perhaps best known to Providence) may be vouchsafed an answer, as we have seen, on rare occasion. But the answer to the survival question is not available to us as other answers may be. And yet again, there may exist levels of affirmation according to the seriousness of the inquirer. Those who refuse the adventure, of course, will shut themselves off from any of its possible discoveries. (They will not, for example, have the experience of contact with a genuine medium, as may take place on rare occasion.) Those who are serious in their inquiry are sometimes rewarded, it appears, in a manner that befits their own devotion. Those individuals, by the same token, who know nothing of serious investigation, those who can instead rest content with unthinking acceptance of their religious training, or who are satisfied with mindless tabloid declarations ("proof" of heaven being a periodic weekly favorite), will have the affirmation that is fitted to their mentality.

---

[86] See related discussion in the preceding chapter of this volume.

Justice, reunion, joy, understanding, emancipation from life's present ills and limitations - these are among the recurrent and unmistakable themes of the literature that deals with the prospect of life hereafter. In these words we find, I believe, the echo of our own deepest instincts. We find in them likewise, I think, some sense of our spiritual direction.

I believe also that the content of daily life may hold its clue. Thus in conclusion I will turn from this rather exotic business of higher planes and transworld dictation to consider the issue in a plainer light. For we find intimations, I think, not only in things far afield, but also in our present life encounters. Contained in this fabric, I believe, are inklings of a greater reality.

As noted earlier, our moral experience is instructive. Consider, for one, the example of *courage*. It is a familiar thing, one that we find (or find portrayed) before us much of the time. We admire this quality. We find it celebrated in world literature. Take, for one, Herodotus' famed account of the battle at Thermoplyae in the war between the Greek allies and the massive army of the Persians. The Greek Spartan forces, having held a strategic post time and again, now find themselves betrayed by an informer and confronted by overwhelming invasion. Under crushing attack, they keep their post. They are at last forced to a hilltop where they fight to the end. "In that spot," writes Herodotus, "the Greeks defended themselves with daggers - those who had any of them left - yes, and with their hands and with their teeth," even as they were buried by the assault.[87]

---

[87] Herodotus, *The History* (Chicago: University of Chicago Press, 1993). Trans. David Grene. See section 7.210 and following.

Granted, the event itself is remote. Its details are open to debate and historical revision. We do not know, for example, if the Spartans chose the optimal strategy in remaining at their post after it had been betrayed. Yet we commonly say that episodes like this one are nonetheless "inspiring" - that such courage is "commendable," that it offers some lesson as to what a man should be, both on the battlefield and off it. Such an apprehension is not peculiar - it extends across a wide range of personal types and cultures. Ordinarily we do not suppose that it commits us any particular view of the cosmos. But in embracing this view we acknowledge, I believe, a reality that transcends the natural world. We express the conviction that value is real; we express likewise our apprehension that we ourselves are embarked upon a venture that exceeds anything passing material concern. We realize that we are summoned - called upon to pursue our own convictions to their end.[88] Herein we confront our own spirituality.

---

[88] No less worth attention, in this regard, are the things we say about behavior that is despicable. Consider the attitude that we have toward individuals, say, who engineer (often for monstrous gain) the sale of crack cocaine to young buyers in the inner cities. We may say of such persons that they are "trash" or "scum" and that they deserve perhaps the severest form of retribution available.

The reaction of some readers to this point will be that words like 'scum' are but slang outbursts - that they may express personal feeling, but have no part in the real diagnosis of human behavior. I say in reply that such persons are not being true, in this case, to their own feelings. What would be their response to someone who kidnaped their daughter, made her dependent upon a drug and turned her out on the street for profit? They might say that they would despise the dealer, perhaps even would kill him. But further, I think, they would claim that they are *justified* in this attitude, which involves more. The reader who rests content with a subjectivist account of values might ask himself why he does not embrace the lifestyle of the pimp or the dealer. The bare fact that he chooses otherwise expresses a judgment (implicit, perhaps, but present nonetheless) of value of a more serious kind, it seems to me, than such an account can provide.

Consider, to take a different but related example, the case of sporting activity. Think of how we admire the "heart," the "gameness," of an athlete who confronts physical challenge in the arena of baseball, or gymnastics, or distance running. Those who have watched contests in the prize ring (or better yet, have engaged in them) will recognize that moment when an exhausted fighter must, in the parlance of the game, "suck it up" - must surmount his own agony.

What is contained in this event? Is the individual before us merely a piece of machinery, a chance assemblage of flesh and circuitry causally programmed for this outcome? Is what we see at bottom the empty dance of particles in motion?

It is theoretically possible, I think, that this is the case. It may be that this spectacle that rouses our souls is not what we imagine. Perhaps instead it is part of an unconscious and inexorable flow of events from all of time - the crest of a single wave on which is carried the birth of stars and the primal stirring of life in the sea.[89] But we do not experience the event in this fashion. We see it as a *drama*, as a contest of flesh and mettle whose outcome, as yet, *may be one thing or another* - as something not fully decided until the last effort is spent.

In this triumph of will we perceive the triumph of spirit. We thus find it fitting to describe it as valiant, as heroic, as something *chosen* rather than necessitated. Materialism, it seems, has little room for such ideas. Again, I do

---

[89] It is possible, I say, but not obvious. In order to see the oddness of this view, consider in mind's eye what the world might have been like on some given day ten million years ago. If the thesis of determinism is correct, and all events are but inevitable consequences of events preceding, then this envisioned moment contains and necessitates all the details of the world as it is at this very instant. Given this one distant past moment as it was, nothing else could be the case now.

not deny that the materialist account is one option. Perhaps, and for all that I have said to the contrary, it is true. But if we wish to give it our allegiance, it seems to me, we must dispense with descriptions of the kind just noted. For on this account, such descriptions reflect only our *naivete* with regard to the real cause. By its reckoning the fighter who "overcame odds," and who fought his way back from the brink of defeat (or who lost, yet managed to lose with honor) is but one more accident; the perseverance of a childhood polio victim to become a world-class distance runner, another swell on that same ocean; the nightly effort of an abandoned young mother to obtain the skills necessary to provide her child with a fighting chance in the world, a further chance configuration.

Thus we are faced, it seems to me, with a choice. Do we believe that such things as courage and valor (whether in the ring, on the battlefield, or in the classroom) are accidents, or do we believe that they are something more? Is value an illusion or that it is real? We must choose one way or another.

Our common sense respect for value has ties, I believe, with classical philosophy. Consider, once more, our judgments as to what is good, or fine, or virtuous. Plato, as noted earlier, holds that such judgments involve a kind of *recollection*. Thus when I encounter some particular instance of beauty, for example, it not only pleases me, but occasions in me the awareness of *truth*. It is a reflection of the archetypal source from which it comes.[90]

---

[90] This Greek conception of value has not only endured, but has found its way into mainstream Christian thought, as well. Thus our encounter with beauty, writes J. B. Phillips, "is a pointer to something, and it certainly points to something beyond the present limitations of time and space." J. B. Phillips, *Your God is Too Small* (New York: Macmillan, 1961), p. 70.

Those who teach Plato in the college, I notice, make this notion of form and remembrance a standard part of the lesson, but they make little effort to relate it to ordinary life-concerns. Instead they fill whole terms with questions of a very abstract kind, asking, for example, whether there may exist a Form or Type of *the horse*, and if so, of a certain *kind* of horse, and what more we must accept if we go in this direction.[91] Such issues, technically possible yet existentially vacant, do little by themselves, I think, to explain the real value in Plato. For this value lies not merely in his ability to entertain, but to *uplift* - to raise our vision above the passing scene that claims our attention. Plato, if read with the whole intelligence, enables us to understand, for example, the meaning of *beauty*, whether of object or (more importantly, thinks Plato) of the soul. He enables us to see likewise the folly of current lame notions that such a thing exists "in the eye of the beholder." Real value, Plato tells us, lies in the worth of what is beheld.

For some, I grant, this world may be enough. In a popular film of some years back, a young woman disavows herself of any belief in another world, for what can be greater, she wonders, than Mozart, than Bach, than the love that she

---

[91] To be sure, a good deal of this activity owes to Plato himself, who subjects this notion of form and archetype, at times, to rigorous and sometimes hair-splitting examination. Thus in his *Parmenides*, for example, the Eleatic sage asks a young Socrates if there is a single essence of "hair or mud or dirt," or other such unglamourous objects. Does one eternal Form, he asks, *cover* a set of its instances as a sail might be spread out over a group of men? Does it thus have area-parts as the sail does? If a "largeness" accounts for many large objects, asks Parmenides, is not "a second form of largeness," over and above the first, needed to characterize this whole set of entities together? (See *Parmenides* 130c and following.) But today's near-exclusive devotion to such issues, I think, ignores the greater vision that inspires these dialogues, whose drama runs deeper than mere dialectical exchange.

finds here in this one? Such an attitude is possible, I realize, but so is another. In beholding the creation of a Michelangelo or a Mozart we commonly imagine that we behold something that is valuable; we imagine that we have before us not merely something that is enjoyable, but something that has objective worth. We suppose that it exceeds other efforts of similar kind.

If reality is material, how can one shape, one sequence of rhythm, be greater than another? It is eternity, I believe, that bestows upon any human accomplishment its greatness. A poem, a statue, a work of prose literature, has value to the extent that it apprehends what is timeless.

Truth lies beyond. This world is not its residence. Our best examples of beauty here are tinged. Our best loves are denied, for the moment, their full expression. Within us, by contrast, is the apprehension of a good real and unsurpassable, one barely intimated even in life's greatest moments.

From daily encounter is born a sensibility. A kinship develops among those who have shared a task, a journey, an adventure. Thus two lovers speak not only of their physical intimacy, but of their *union*. In so doing they acknowledge a reality that defines all of human encounter.

There are some, perhaps, who will deny this reality, but they find, in time, that they cannot exist without it. Thus the mind-set of a hardened criminal, for example, one day melts with the admission of his own self-deceit. He literally cannot live with himself. His old life is not merely difficult, or uncomfortable. It is a lie. For this reason it is untenable. He can no longer exist in moral isolation from his fellows. While relatively few of us are hardened criminals, life carries each of us forward, I believe, in a similar direction. Each of us learns, in some fashion, that he or she is not entirely separate from others. We find, in certain moments, a connectedness that runs to the very ground of our being.

This apprehension may not be vividly present in each individual's experience. I do not suppose that it is constantly present in the hearts of very many. But it is present nonetheless. And it is not, it seems to me, a mere accident of nature. Instead it is a harbinger of reality. Consider what happens when we disregard this instinct - the case, say, in which we commit some slight, or fail to give others their due. What does this involve? On the reductionist view, it means merely that we have transgressed, say, some rule of propriety or civil statute. Such a rule, on this view, has no inherent worth, and any allegiance to it is the result of some accident of biology arising out of chemical reaction.

The moral voice insists that something more is awry. It tells us that we have done something truly and grievously wrong. This experience presents itself to us not merely as *feeling*, but as the *indication*, in some way, of the real order of things. Whether or not this reading is correct, it is, I think, the one that we implicitly accept if we treat this voice with respect.

And whatever our theoretical leanings, we tend to regard moral feeling as being worth our attention. We regard it, fact, as being an essential part of ourselves. For while we may not always find this feature of our experience to be pleasant (consider, say, the insistent message of a troubled conscience), we would not be rid of it, I believe, if we were given the chance. This bond, this undercurrent of personal contact, points us once more in a spiritual direction.

We speak at times also of the irreducible *worth* of human beings. We do this often enough, I think, that it may be said to constitute a basic part of our ordinary experience. How does this element bear upon our picture of the universe? Here again, I think, common sense leads upward. This apprehension is given unsurpassable expression by John Haynes Holmes in his sermon "Ten Reasons for Believing in Immortality".[92]

In human beings, thinks Holmes, is living revelation. Within us, he maintains, there exists a curious discord, a lack of coordination, as he puts it, "not only between our personalities and our physical bodies, but also between our personalities and the physical world." Our souls have promises and potentialities that should not and cannot be subject to "the chance vicissitudes of earthly fortune." Or what shall we say, when we see some life "of great achievement, of character and beauty and noble dedication to man-kind ... cut off sharply before its time by an automobile accident, a disease germ, a bit of poisoned food?"

> What shall we think when we see a Shelley drowned in this thirtieth year by a heedless sea, a Phillips Brooks stricken in the prime of his manhood by a diphtheric sore-throat, a Captain Scott frozen in mid-career by an accident of weather? Is it possible that these lives of ours are dependent upon a fall of snow, a grain of dust, a passing breeze upon the sea? Is it possible that our personalities, with all their potencies of spirit, can be destroyed, as our bodies can be broken, by all the material forces of the world? Are we to believe that eternal powers can be annihilated by transient accidents?[93]

---

[92] This sermon is contained in Paul Edwards and Arthur Pap, eds., *A Modern Introduction to Philosophy* (New York: The Free Press, 1973).

[93] *Ibid.*, p. 256.

Says Holmes, "I cannot think so!" He cites the example of Professor G. H. Palmer, who, having lost his wife, now asks, "who can contemplate the fact of it and not call the world irrational if, out of deference to a few particles of disordered matter, it excludes so fair a spirit?"

It is "beauty" and "noble dedication," says Holmes, that confront us, and that leave this world at the behest of transient forces. In the oration of Brooks and the last resolute courage of Scott, we find a quality of the spirit. This quality, of course, is not confined to famous examples. It surrounds us. In meditating upon it, we find insight. We perceive ourselves as spiritual beings embarked upon a voyage, one alive with the challenge of growth and exploration. We recognize, among our fellows, those who have trod the way before us, and when we encounter wisdom and compassion amidst the struggle, we understand, as perhaps not before, life's meaning.

It is this recognition, I believe, that inspires Kant. It pours from Unamuno with every sentence. There is revelation, says the Spaniard, in the act of embrace. In the mutual sheltering of mother and child, of man and wife, we find depths of reality. Indeed we find it even in the antagonism of struggle.[94]

How does apprehension of this kind bear upon philosophy? We must be wary, once again, of counting personal experience as logical demonstration. This

---

[94] There is, he writes, "much more humanity in war than in peace." War, he maintains, "is a school of fraternity and the bond of love"; human love, he contends, "knows no purer embrace ... than that between victor and vanquished on the battlefield." (*Tragic Sense of Life*, pp. 279-80) One need not, I think, be as enamored of warfare as is Unamuno in order to see the lesson he offers. In our most intimate encounters with human beings are contained insights into the nature of human life and destiny.

seeming "irrationality" of our death, I think, does not rule out its theoretical possibility. For it may be that we happen to live in a universe that caters to no such values and harbors no sympathy with the impulses that arise within it. That material forces should exercise final authority over a "radiant" spirit is (if true) unfortunate, but it is not *per se* contrary to reason.

Should we then withhold affirmation? Some, I imagine, will take this position. Such feelings as those Holmes expresses, they may say, are lovely, but philosophy must not be guided by sentiment. Better, then, to set them aside - only in this way can we be objective. But neutrality, recalling earlier discussion,[95] does not seem to hold any advantage with respect to our other faculties. We are not neutral, for example, regarding the testimony of our eyes, or our moral experience. Let us suppose, for the sake of argument, that we share Holmes' apprehension of eternity. How should it bear upon our wider outlook?

We are within our rights, I believe, to take such apprehension as being legitimate. On what grounds need we disqualify it? Granted, it is not in keeping with theoretical economy: It involves us in a richer and wider view of reality than we might have otherwise. Materialism, it may be argued, is "cheaper," since it acknowledges only those truths gathered by the senses. But the cheaper view, I think, is not obviously better. For why must we think that *sensation* is our only contact with reality? Why not suppose that other aspects of our experience connect us with it, as well?

---

[95] See again, for example, Hick's discussion of religious belief and its basis.

Immortality, thinks Holmes, is befitting of our own magnificence. He says this, I believe, because in character he finds something awesome. In reflecting upon it we are not merely pleased, nor impressed, but humbled. We experience the soul as immortal. Nothing else will suffice to express our admiration. We must understand others (and ourselves) in these terms if we are true to our own experience. If nobility of character is a mortal event, there is something utterly wrong with what it inspires within us. We experience others within a religious framework, and it is neither honest nor rationally advantageous for us to state the case otherwise.

Further account of this phenomenon is hard to come by, though I am reminded of a possible analogy. Suppose that someone marvels at the sight of the sun one afternoon breaking through the clouds and is moved, at that moment, to affirm the reality of a supreme being. Does such an individual have grounds for this affirmation? There are, in fact, some who might say this - who might *infer* from this spectacle, say, the existence of a divine artist. I think, however, that the experience is best understood not as argument but as revelation. One who beholds this marvel does not infer from it God's existence, but experiences it as being God-given. The sun speaks, as it were, of a source worthy of all praises. It strikes within us a chord that lies deeper than that of the intellect. It reminds us of the truth already present in our hearts, and leads us on with the assurance that joy and truth are one at last.

So it is, I believe, with personal splendor. Here again we give utterance in the spirit. Just as this vision of light may move us, in the outward delight of sensation, to affirm the majesty of creation, so might our insight into personal worth move us, in hope and in humility, to affirm that persons are immortal. That transient accidents of physics might really "exclude so fair a spirit" is not impossible, but it is incongruous with our own deepest instinct. In last analysis, the thesis of mortality is strangely comical, and I am moved, in this context, to say that it is unlikely, as well. Belief in survival is an integral part of experiencing the real and potential worth of humanity. In last analysis it is perhaps not a belief, in the ordinary sense, at all, but a mode of religious perception.

There is no greater issue, no more momentous prospect than that of survival. A single soul, says Unamuno once again, "is worth all the world" - a single eternity worth more than all the fleeting moments lived by all the beings who shall ever inherit the earth. If we are but "mud in motion," reflects the medium Geraldine Cummins, we lose all prospect of true optimism and higher dignity. She cites the words of Macneile Dixon, who says,

> No theological or metaphysical twitterings can rebut the demonstrable hollowness of life, its inherent futility. The passing show may have its interest, but how slight and ephemeral, how painful an interest. We are offered, it seems, a sip from the cup of life, which is then for ever withdrawn ... Proclaim to men that 'Death is the only immortal', and religion receives its mortal wound. Announce to them that all human history is a mere scramble for wealth or power, all loves and loyalties time's broken pottery - it is ruin and every man knows it. Men will not be easily consoled for so much courage, so much endurance, so much faith, so much affection, so much sweetness cast into the void.[96]

---

[96] This quotation appears in page 152 of Cummins' autobiographical work *Unseen Adventures* (London: Rider and Company, 1951). Though Cummins does not cite exact pages, the quote comes from Professor Dixon's Gifford Lectures.

Some may find Dixon's assessment of this world to be pessimistic. But one need not, I think, have an unduly low estimate of the present life to appreciate the importance of the next. In eternity is contained the only real prospect of this world's rectification.

If indeed we are destined for more than this life, where might the road lead? Again the old questions arise. On one hand, as noted earlier, is the view that we continue endlessly[97] as the selfsame beings that we are at present. On the other we are said to one day transcend this present mode altogether. By one reckoning, we are forever distinct and finite individuals. By the other, not. Ought we to think of our fate as being a continuation, in perpetuity, of ourselves, or as being instead an absorption of self into some higher reality?

Here, it seems, is a dilemma. For surely there is something odd in the idea that we simply continue on the path without end. Where can a path lead if we must tread it forever? And what can we accomplish if a goal remains before us always. Yet if we transcend those conditions (our personal nature, our existence in space and time, and so on) that make for our present mode of life, then it is hard to see what is left of us.[98]

---

[97] This, again, is Kant's view of moral progress. See also Unamuno's discussion.

[98] It is perhaps worth adding that the earlier problem of *proportion* (that is, the fittedness of effort to reward), cited in connection with the doctrine of endless punishment, arises once more with this idea of liberation. For the end promised, it seems is without limit, while the progress toward the goal (even if extended over multiple lifetimes) is presumably finite. Yet the problem in this case, I believe, is less troubling. For an endlessly giving divine nature makes more sense, I think, than an endlessly vengeful one.

The world's major religious traditions seem to point, on balance, toward the latter alternative. They affirm not only survival, but an end at which the journey aims. Typically this end, or *eschaton*, is thought to involve union, in some sense, with an ultimate reality and so also a transcendence of our present limits. Thus Christians, for example, speak at times of a diminution of selfhood with their growth in Christ, and of a vision in which individuality is absorbed into the source that gave it birth.

Something analogous seems to hold in the Indian tradition. The *Upanishads*,[99] again, liken the soul's journey to that of a single river, at first separate "in name and form" from others and later joining them in a common sea. The true self, we sometimes hear, is without limit. "You can have what you want," explains Huston Smith in summarizing the message of Vedic Indian tradition.[100]

What we really want, he explains, beyond all of the false and trifling ends that occupy our time, is being (*sat*), consciousness (*chit*), and joy (*ananda*). We want these things not just for a time, or in their usual admixture. We want them whole and unadulterated. This, says Smith, is Hinduism's promise - an end from which there is no return, and one that explodes all present limitation into infinity. There is liberation, and the repayment on our effort is infinite.

---

[99] *Mundaka Upanishad* III. 2. 8. The word '*Upanishad*' comes from a conjunction of Sanskrit words meaning "to sit down near" (that is, near a teacher). These materials are discussed in detail by Swami Nikhilananda in his four-volume work *The Upanishads* (New York: Ramakrishna-Vivekananda Center, 1952).

[100] See *The World's Religions*, pp. 13 and following.

This promise, it seems, is affirmed elsewhere. The Tibetan *Book of the Dead,*[101] as we have seen, speaks of absorption into the *Clear Light*. And in Geraldine Cummins' earlier-cited manuscript, purported otherworld communicator F. W. H. Myers speaks of an ultimate "merging" with the God of all creation.[102]

The themes of union and self-transcendence are noted often by Evelyn Underhill in her classic work *Mysticism*. All mystic thinkers, she writes, declare the mutual attraction between the "spark" of the soul, the "free divine germ" within, and the source from which it has come. She speaks, in this connection, of the annihilation of self when "utterly merged" in the divine ocean, and again of "the doing away of separateness" in a Dark Night of mystic purgation.[103]

Can one speak coherently of both mystical union and a retention of individual sameness? There is a limit, I think, on what we apprehend of the remote future. We cannot know, in concrete terms, what liberation may be like. Yet the exercise, I believe, is worthwhile for what it may yield to our understanding here and now.

---

[101] W. Y. Evans-Wentz, ed., *The Tibetan Book of the Dead or the After-Death Experiences on the Bardo Plane, according to Lama Kazi Dawa-Samdup's English Rendering* (London: Oxford University Press, 1957). See also discussion by John Hick, citing this edition, in chapter 20 of *Death and Eternal Life*.

[102] See again *The Road to Immortality*.

[103] See, for example, chapter 9, "The Dark Night of the Soul". It is worth noting, however, that Underhill herself does not take this to mean that selfhood is abolished. This insistence upon self-annihilation, she believes, is exaggerated in some cases. The tendency of Indian mysticism "to regard the Unitive Life wholly in its passive aspect," results, she maintains, from a distortion of truth. (p. 434) Yet description is difficult, for in our encounter with the Absolute, we are "caught up to a plane of vision beyond the categories of the human mind." (p. 423)

A moment's reflection upon this issue discloses one fact - namely the tremendous change that may occur within us if indeed our life continues on the other side. In reflecting on the next life we are apt to envision human beings as retaining indefinitely their current demeanor and appearance. We picture those on the other side as they looked at the end of this life, or perhaps at the peak of their earthly activity. But surely there is no warrant for this. Our state of appearance even here is fleeting. Perhaps it is only the gradual nature of this change that keeps us from fully seeing it. Yet it occurs, sometimes dramatically, even within short periods.

If our appearance changes, think of what happens to our consciousness. Consider, says Hick, what has taken place within us in the last few decades. We are very different creatures now than we were then. If this transition has been gradual, it has been no less profound. "When I read the diary which I wrote when I was fifteen years old," Hick writes, "I know that it is my diary, and with its aid I remember some of the events recorded in it; but nevertheless I look back upon that fifteen-year old as someone ... whom I do not *feel* to be myself."[104] What, he asks, will it be like to read this diary in *fifty million* years' time?

With experience comes development. Nowhere is this more apparent than in one's own case. As I reflect upon events within myself over the last few decades, I find vital change. As I project this event forward (even within the span of this life), I see further developments awaiting. Carrying it into the limitless future, I see that I may be, in time, incomparably more than I am at present.

---

[104] *Death and Eternal Life*, p. 410.

I see also that while I entertain this prospect, I can scarcely comprehend it. My present thought does little justice, I am sure, to what the future has in store. My real end, my real nature, may be scarcely intimated at this time. Even those things that I now count as being basic to my identity (say, being male and Caucasian) do not impress me, as I reflect upon them, as being eternal. Others (such as my present concern with the morning sports page) seem laughable. At some distant point, I must think, I will be a thoroughly different creature from the one than I am at present. Thus while there may exist something within me that is eternal, the "me" of the remote future will bear this one little resemblance.

I think, however, that we must be careful as to what we infer from this fact. In looking back, says Hick, we find our past selves to be virtually different people from ourselves now. Thus again, I may look at something that I have written in childhood and feel distant from the composer of that material. For I am qualitatively different from that individual; my habits, interests, and trains of thought are quite unlike his own. But does this mean that he and I are distinct individuals?

Granted, if my only acquaintance with that earlier person is my perception now of that writing, I may feel myself to be as different from him as from some other altogether. If I must rely on the writing for my only acquaintance, then I view this individual from the outside, as it were, and learn about him in much the way I might learn about an altogether different individual. But when I *remember* the experience, my view is quite different. When I recall, say, riding through the Black Hills of Montana in 1955, seeing Custer's last battle site and wondering what the fight must have looked like, I feel that I am wholly identical with that four-year old observer, even if I am now very different in character.[105] It does not seem to me that time and change diminish this relationship in the least.

The real connection between past and present selves, I concede, is indeed quite mysterious. But whatever difficulties may attend that issue, we need not be wholly agnostic, I think, with respect to our destination. For there are moments in life, moments of moral and intellectual advancement, that reveal its broad direction. And whatever may be said about liberation, some notion of our basic and enduring individuality, I believe, is essential to it. For if liberation is the end of our singular and personal existence - if individuality, in other words, is an illusion - how are we to make sense of the activity of the finite and struggling entity who now progresses toward the goal? We cannot, I think, unless we acknowledge the identity of this progressing individual with the one that is liberated. Or if liberation is the end of an existing individuality, it seems to be tantamount to annihilation.

Perhaps it will be said, on the other hand, that annihilation is the goal. This appears to be the case with at least one line of Buddhist thought.[106] But this view, I think, is implausible. If annihilation is the goal, then non-existence must be thought by the seeker to be preferable to existence - and preferable, then, not just to the average run of life as it is commonly experienced, but even to life in the

---

[105] See again related discussion in chapter 2, particularly regarding Swinburne and the Principle of Credulity as it relates to memory.

[106] This view of the *Theravada* school is discussed and criticized by Hick in section # 3 of chapter 21 in his *Death and Eternal Life*.

higher stages of its evolution nearing the end of the line. Such a claim is surely contrary to appearances and to the very spirit of Buddhist practice.

Nor, I think, does it make sense to say that our present individuality is an illusion, or that the idea is contrary in some way to a genuine religious spirit. If the individual is indeed a mere phenomenon, it is hard to see why any self-interested concern should arise as to its welfare now - why choices should be made by anyone regarding anything - whether it be, say, his present occupation or lifestyle, or some higher attainment down the road?

Nor need anyone be concerned, it seems, with the welfare of anyone else. One cannot benefit oneself, nor benefit others, if there is no *one* who stands to be benefitted. (Indeed on this assumption even a self-annihilationist philosophy cannot be pursued with any reason.) It is *as individuals* that we construct our philosophies and pursue our destinies at all. Whatever we think about our final destiny, it is as singular entities, discrete and persisting, that we are obliged to treat one another along the way.

Once again, I believe, plain experience offers a clue. We may gain some insight into our destiny if we think, for a moment, about what is involved in our union with others in this world. This element, as we have seen, is central to Hick's discussion. It figures also in James Martineau's *A Study of Religion*. Consider, says Martineau, what is involved in our most intimate encounters in this world. He recalls a young woman who has lost her husband, and who now pours out her grief to their friend (the famed theologian Friedrich Schliermacher) seeking assurance. In the midst of sorrow, she writes,

> there are yet blessed moments when I vividly feel what a love ours was, and that surely this love is eternal, and it is impossible that God can destroy it; for God himself is love. I bear this life while nature will; for I have still work to do for the children, his and mine: but Oh God! with what longing, what foreshadowings of unutterable blessedness, do I gaze across into that world where he lives! What joy for me to die! Schlier, shall I not find him again? Oh my God! I implore you, Schlier, by all that is dear to God and sacred, give me, if you can, the certain assurance of finding and knowing him again.[107]

Schliermacher bids her to think of his death as "a melting away into the great All" and to abandon thoughts of "the personal life" to which we cling in vain. And what then? "Is her problem solved?" asks Martineau. "Does she open her arms and cling no more to 'personal life'?"[108] Rather she might reason as follows.

> When I loved and knew God in my Ehrenfried, there were two objects of my love; for one of them was by my side, and prayed with me to the other in the unseen. Now that he has left me alone, and "is living eternally in God," are they still two lives, or only one? And when I love my husband eternally in God, am I to have two objects of affection, or only one? If two, then have I still the same dear soul to cleave to that has upheld me here: and the love which passes to him, will he not reciprocate? and if there is this interchange, what is it but the inmost essence of the personal life? Love, - knowledge, - where persons are not; can there be a greater contradiction? If I am to have but one object of affection, the human being merged in the Divine, then how is it that I shall not vanish too, but still remain capable of apprehending and loving what is higher than myself?[109]

This train of thought, believes Martineau, would be perfectly natural. It would also indicate a pupil who is wiser than her teacher. The idea of the soul's

---

[107] James Martineau, *A Study of Religion* (Oxford: The Clarendon Press, 1900), vol. II, p. 337. Two volumes.

[108] *Ibid.*

[109] *Ibid.*, p. 339.

"merging" into a greater whole, he says, gives rise to certain confusions. Our thought on the subject sometimes leaves behind, as a result, the very thing most real of all. The notion that progress leads us toward an end of selfhood, he contends, contains fallacies both moral and mathematical in kind.

This "pantheistic disparagement" of personal life, explains Martineau, supposes that self-surrender means self-negation - that "when we have completely attained, our separation dies away, and God is all in all," and so we cease to be individuals. But surely, this reasoning is fallacious. Doubtless, he writes,

> there is here a *'self'* which is sacrificed: but by whom? By another *'self'* that lives and loves the more intensely, when that foe is slain. The will which disciplines itself into harmony with God's does not cease to be a will when its goal is reached and the concord is entire. Is it not a *voluntary* relation, perfected between spirit and spirit, and consciously present in the affections of both?[110]

This whole process of self-abandonment, of dropping false concerns, thinks Martineau, is itself *personal* activity - "the putting forth, from my own centre, of thought, of effort, of love: and in the consummation which is said to extinguish them actually have their highest realization." To think otherwise, he explains, "is to confound *harmony between two* with *absorption in one*." We think also that a limitless reality must somehow absorb everything into itself - that "the infinite, instead of admitting any finite side by side with it, must embrace and merge it." Such thinking "confounds the *infinite with the total*, and erroneously assumes that the infinite is denied if we speak of anything besides."[111]

---

[110] *Ibid*, p. 340.

[111] *Ibid.*, p. 341.

That something is infinite, says Martineau, does not make it the only thing real. Thus while omniscience, to cite an example, comprehends all things, its reality does not preclude that of intelligence apart from itself. By analogy, "the range and depth of a great human mind does not exist at the expense of lesser intelligences around; and Newton who weighed the planets could live under the same roof with the house-keeper that prepared his porridge." Neither, then, does the limitlessness of divine wisdom annihilate reason within ourselves.[112]

Martineau's discussion helps us to see, I think, what is wrong with efforts to evaporate the self, in the name of sophistication, into some faceless Absolute. Insight into our real nature is gained by attention to what is contained in our own present growth and maturation. We ordinarily think that these things involve us in a greater intimacy with our fellows. As such they may offer us some portent of our real direction.

Thus I close this discussion on a note at once plain and telling. Wisdom distributes itself widely, I believe, across the range of human experience. To this end I have drawn at times, and especially in the present chapter, on sources quite far removed from the mainstream. Philosophers, I think, would do well to extend the breadth of their vision, at times, outside that of current fashion. They must do this, I am convinced, if they are to come to real grips with the problems that concern them.

---

[112] *Ibid.*, pp. 341-42. Indeed, he adds, if it is metaphysically impossible for a finite subject to coexist with an infinite, it is not an impossibility that begins in death; it must have place on this side as much as on the other. And yet here we are, it seems, "holding the very relation supposed to contradict itself."

With this in mind I end with the peculiarly apt remarks of Stewart Edward White,[113] inspired by his relationship with his late wife.

> You know the cozy, intimate feeling of companionship you get sometimes when you are in the same room; perhaps each reading a book; not speaking; not even looking at one another. It is tenuous, an evanescent thing - one that we too often fail to savor and appreciate. Sometimes, in fact, it takes an evening or two of empty solitude to make us realize how substantial and important it really is.
>
> Then, on the other hand, you know how you draw closer by means of things you do together. And still more through talk and such mental interchanges. And most of all, perhaps, in the various physical relationships of love and marriage.
>
> Now when you stop to think of it, all these latter material contacts, right through the whole of life, are at root and in essence aimed at really just one thing: that rare inner feeling of companionship suggested feebly in the sitting-by-the-fire idea. That is what we *really* are groping for in all friendly and loving human relations, hampered by the fact that we are different people more or less muffled from each other by the barriers of encasement in the body.[114]

Herein, it seems, is contained an inkling of what is involved in the soul-making process. If we cannot see just where the path leads, perhaps we can know something, at least, of the way in which it opens before us. Our present experience with others may give us a foretaste of what is ultimately involved in the adventure of self-transcendence.

---

[113] This quote is taken from Stewart Edward White and Harwood White, *Across the Unknown* (New York: E. P. Dutton and Co., 1943). White was a novelist in the early part of the century whose works include *The Call of the North* (New York: Grosset and Dunlap, 1903) and other tales of frontier adventure. In later years, he produced several books issuing from his wife Betty's seemingly direct contact with the next world. Among his later works, *The Unobstructed Universe* (New York: E. P. Dutton, 1940), perhaps his most famous, purports to offer a firsthand account of that world provided by Betty from the other side.

[114] *Ibid.*, pp. 334-35.

What is effected in this process is perhaps not our extinction, nor our absorption, but our gradual breaking free of those barriers that keep us presently from the existence for which we are intended. Thus the outcome, to cite a familiar paradox, is that in losing our lives we may find them, and that in giving of ourselves we may become gainers in the highest sense. For persons who experience life in such terms, it is an adventure of the greatest kind, and it is one indeed that has only begun.

Bibliography

Abbott, Walter, *The Documents of Vatican II* (London: Geoffrey Chapman, 1966).

A. J. Ayer, *Language, Truth and Logic* (New York: Dover Publications, 1952).

Badham, Paul, *Christian Beliefs About Life After Death* (London: Macmillan, 1976).

Badham, Paul and Linda Badham, *Immortality or Extinction?* (London: Macmillan Press, Ltd., 1982).

Baillie, John, *The Interpretation of Religion* (New York: Abingdon Press, 1928).

Barclay, William, *The Mind of Jesus* (San Francisco: HarperCollins, 1976).

Barrett, William, *Death of the Soul - From Descartes to the Computer* (New York: Anchor Books, 1987).

_____, *Irrational Man* (New York: Anchor Books, 1990).

Barrett, Sir William F., *Death-Bed Visions - The Psychical Experiences of the Dying* (Northamptonshire: Aquarian Press, 1986).

_____, *On the Threshold of the Unseen* (New York: E. P. Dutton and Company, 1918).

Berdyaev, Nicolas, *Freedom and the Spirit* (New York: Charles Scribner's Sons, 1935).

Besant, Annie, *Man and his Bodies* (Adyar: Theosophical Publishing House, 1967).

Borgia, Anthony, *Life in the World Unseen* (Midway, Utah: M. A. P. Publishing, 1993).

Brenner, Charles, *An Elementary Textbook of Psychoanalysis* (New York: Anchor Books, 1974).

Brown, Stuart C., ed., *Reason and Religion* (Ithaca, New York: Cornell University Press, 1977).

Buber, Martin, *I and Thou* (New York: Charles Scribner's Sons, 1958). Trans. Ronald Gregor Smith.

Burtt, Edwin, *The Metaphysical Foundations of Modern Science* (New York: Doubleday, 1932).

Butterfield, Herbert, *The Origins of Modern Science* (New York: The Free Press, 1957).

Carington, Whately, *Telepathy* (London: Methuen, 1945).

Catlin, George, *North American Indians* (New York: Penguin Books, 1989). Editor Peter Matthiessen.

Cervantes, Miguel de, *Don Quixote* (New York: Modern Library, 1998). Trans. Samuel Putnam.

Choron, Jacques, *Death and Western Thought* (London: Collier Books, 1963).

Cobb, John, Jr., and David Ray Griffin, *Process Theology* (Philadelphia: Westminster Press, 1976).

Comte, August, *Introduction to Positive Philosophy* (Indianapolis: Hackett Publishing Company, 1988). Trans. Frederick Ferre.

Crossan, John Dominic, *Who Is Jesus?* (New York: HarperCollins Publishers, 1996).

Cummins, Geraldine, *The Road to Immortality* (London: Aquarian Press, 1955).

_____, *Unseen Adventures* (London: Rider and Co., 1951).

Davis, William C., *Three Roads to the Alamo* (New York: HarperCollins, 1998).

Dasgupta, Surendranath, *A History of Indian Philosophy* (London: Cambridge University Press, 1922). Five volumes.

Dostoevsky, Fyodor, *The Brothers Karamazov* (New York: W. W. Norton and Company, 1976). Trans. Constance Garnett.

Douglas, Alfred, *Extra Sensory Powers - A Century of Psychical Research* (Woodstock, New York: Overlook Press, 1977).

Eastman, Charles, *The Soul of the Indian* (Lincoln, Nebraska: The University of Nebraska Press, 1980).

Edgerton, Franklin, trans., *The Bhagavad-Gita* (Cambridge: Harvard University Press, 1972).

Edwards, Paul, general editor, *The Encyclopedia of Philosophy* (New York: Macmillan, 1967).

Edwards, Paul and Arthur Pap, eds., *A Modern Introduction to Philosophy* (New York: Macmillan, 1973).

Eliot, T. S., *Burnt Norton* (London: Faber and Faber, 1941).

Evans-Wentz, W. Y., ed., *The Tibetan Book of the Dead or the After-Death Experiences on the Bardo Plane, according to Lama Kazi Dawa-Samdup's English Rendering* (London: Oxford University Press, 1957).

Feinberg, Joel, ed., *Reason and Responsibility* (Belmont, California: Wadsworth Publishing Company, 1978).

Flew, Antony, *Body, Mind and Death* (Toronto: Macmillan, 1969).

_____, *God, Freedom and Immortality* (Buffalo: Prometheus, 1984).

Fosdick, Harry Emerson, *Adventurous Religion* (New York: Harper and Brothers Publishers, 1926).

Frankl, Viktor, Man's Search for Meaning (New York: Washington Square Press, 1984).

Gauld, Alan, *Mediumship and Survival* (London: Paladin Books, 1983).

Graham, George, *Philosophy of Mind* (Oxford: Blackwell Publishers, Ltd, 1993).

Greaves, Helen, *Testimony of Light* (Essex: Neville Spearman Publishers, 1969).

Gunaratna, V. F., *Rebirth Explained* (Kandy: Buddhist Publication Society, 1971).

Gurney, Edmund, Frederic Myers, and Frank Podmore, *Phantasms of the Living* (London: Kegan Paul, Trench, Trubner, and Co., Ltd., 1918).

Guttenplan, Samuel, ed., *A Companion to the Philosophy of Mind* (Oxford: Blackwell Publishers, 1996).

Hamilton, Edith and Huntington Cairns, eds., *Plato - Collected Dialogues* (Princeton, New Jersey: Princeton University Press, 1961). Various translators.

Happold, F. H., *Mysticism - A Study and an Anthology* (London: Penguin Books, 1988).

Harrison, G. B., ed., *A Book of English Poetry* (London: Penguin Books, 1950).

Hartshorne, Charles, *The Logic of Perfection* (La Salle, Illinois: Open Court Press, 1962).

Herodotus, *The History* (Chicago: University of Chicago Press, 1987). Trans. David Grene.

Hick, John, *Death and Eternal Life* (Louisville, Kentucky: Westminster / John Knox Press, 1994).

_____, *Evil and the God of Love* (San Francisco: Harper and Row, 1977).

_____, *Faith and Knowledge*

_____, *God Has Many Names* (Philadelphia: Westminster Press, 1982).

_____, An Interpretation of Religion - Human Responses to the Transcendent (London: Yale University Press, 1989).

_____, *The Metaphor of God Incarnate* (Louisville, Kentucky: Westminster / John Knox Press, 1993).

_____, *Philosophy of Religion* (Englewood Cliffs, New Jersey: Prentice-Hall, 1990).

_____, *Problems of Religious Pluralism* (New York: St. Martin's Press, 1985).

_____, ed., *Classical and Contemporary Readings in the Philosophy of Religion* (Englewood Cliffs, New Jersey: Prentice-Hall, 1964).

_____, ed., *The Existence of God* (New York: Macmillan, 1964).

The Holy Bible Containing the Old and New Testaments (New York: Thomas Nelson and Sons, 1901). American Standard Version.

Hume, David, *Dialogues Concerning Natural Religion* (Indianapolis: Hackett Publishing Company, 1980).

_____, *A Treatise of Human Nature* (Oxford: Clarendon Press, 1951). L. A. Selby-Bigge, editor.

Huxley, Aldous, ed., *The Perennial Philosophy* (New York: Harper and Row, 1970).

Hyslop, James, *Contact with the Other World* (New York: The Century Company, 1919).

_____, *Life After Death - Problems of the Future Life and Its Nature* (New York: E. P. Dutton and Company, 1918).

Inglis, Brian, *Natural and Supernatural: A History of the Paranormal* (Dorset: Prism Press, 1992).

James, William, *Memories and Studies* (New York: Longmans, Green, and Company, 1911).

_____, *The Varieties of Religious Experience* (New York: Macmillan, 1961).

_____, *The Will to Believe and other essays in popular philosophy* and *Human Immortality* (New York: Dover Publications, 1956).

Janet, Paul, *Theory of Morals* (New York: Charles Scribner's Sons, 1905).

Johnson, Paul, *The Quest for God: A Personal Pilgrimage* (New York: HarperPerennial, 1996).

Johnson, Raynor, *The Imprisoned Splendour* (New York: Harper and Brothers, 1953).

Johnston, William, ed., *The Cloud of Unknowing* (New York: Image Books, 1996).

Kant, Immanuel, *Lectures on Ethics* (New York: Harper and Row, 1963). Trans. Louis Infield.

_____, *Lectures on Philosophical Theology* (Ithaca, New York: Cornell University Press, 1978). Trans.

_____, *Critique of Practical Reason* (Amherst, New York: Prometheus Books, 1996). Trans. T. K. Abbott.

_____, *Critique of Pure Reason* (Indianapolis: Hackett Publishing Company, Inc., 1996). Trans. Werner S. Pluhar.

Kubler-Ross, Elizabeth, *On Life After Death* (Berkeley: Celestial Arts, 1991).

Kaufmann, Walter, *The Faith of a Heretic* (Garden City, New York: Doubleday and Company, Inc., 1961).

Labor, Earle, Robert C. Leitz III, and Milo Shepard, eds., *Jack London - Short Stories* (New York: Collier Books, 1991).

Lamont, Corliss, *The Illusion of Immortality* (New York: Frederick Ungar Publishing Company, Inc., 1965).

_____, *The Philosophy of Humanism* (New York: Philosophical Library, 1957).

La Mettrie, Julien Offray, *Man a Machine* (La Salle, Illinois: Open Court Press, 1993). Trans. Gertrude Bussey.

Lewis, C. S., *The Abolition of Man* (New York: Touchstone Books, 1996).

_____, *Mere Christianity* (New York: Touchstone Books, 1980).

_____, *The Problem of Pain* (New York: Simon and Schuster, 1996).

_____, *Surprised by Joy - the Shape of My Early Life* (San Diego: Harcourt, Brace and Company, 1955).

_____, *The Weight of Glory and Other Addresses* (New York: Collier Books, 1980).

Lewis, Hywel, *The Elusive Self* (Philadelphia: Westminster Press, 1982).

Lodge, Sir Oliver, *Raymond* (New York: George H. Doran Company, 1916).

Lorimer, David, *Survival? - Body, Mind and Death in the Light of Psychic Research* (London: Routledge and Kegan Paul, 1984).

Lucretius, *On the Nature of the Universe* (London: Penguin Books, 1994). Trans. R. E. Latham.

Maas, Peter, *Underboss: Sammy "The Bull" Gravano's Story of Life in the Mafia* (New York: HarperCollins, 1997).

Mach, Ernst, *The Analysis of the Sensations* (London: Open Court Publishing Company, 1914).

Martin, Malachi, *Hostage to the Devil: The Possession and Exorcism of Five Living Americans* (New York: Harper and Row, 1987).

Martineau, James, *A Study of Religion* (Oxford: Clarendon Press, 1900).

Matovina, Timothy, *The Alamo Remembered* (Austin: University of Texas Press, 1995).

McDannell, Colleen and Bernard Lang, *Heaven - A History* (New Haven, Connecticut: Yale University Press, 1988).

McDermott, John J., ed., *The Writings of William James* (Chicago: The University of Chicago Press, 1977).

Mill, John Stuart, *Utilitarianism* (London: Longmans, Green and Company, 1910).

Moody, Raymond, *Life After Life* (New York: Ballantine Books, 1988).

_____, *The Light Beyond* (New York: Bantam Books, 1989).

Myers, Frederic, *Essays - Classical* (London: Macmillan. 1888).

_____, *Human Personality and Its Survival of Bodily Death* (Salem, New Hampshire: Ayer Company, Publishers, Inc., 1992). Two volumes.

_____, *Science and a Future Life* (London: Macmillan and Company, 1893).

Newman, John H., *A Grammar of Assent* (New York: David McKay Company, 1947).

Nicholson, Kelly, *Body and Soul: The Transcendence of Materialism* (Boulder, Colorado: HarperCollins Publishers, 1997).

Nielsen, Kai, *Ethics Without God* (London: Prometheus Books, 1973).

Nikhilananda, Swami, trans., *The Upanishads* (New York: Ramakrishna-Vivekananda Center, 1952).

Nofi, Albert A., *The Alamo and the Texas War for Independence* (Conshohocken, Pennsylvania: 1992).

Osis, Karlis and Erlendur Haraldsson, *At the Hour of Death* (New York: Avon Books, 1977).

Parfit, Derek, *Reasons and Persons* (New York: Oxford University Press, 1984).

Pascal, Blaise, *Pensees* and the *Provincial Letters* (New York: Modern Library, 1941). Trans. W. F. Trotter and Thomas M'Crie.

Penfield, Wilder, *The Mystery of the Mind - A Critical Study of Consciousness and the Human Brain* (Princeton, New Jersey: Princeton University Press, 1975).

Perry, John, ed., *Personal Identity* (Berkeley: University of California Press, 1975).

Phillips, D. Z., *Death and Immortality* (London: Macmillan, 1970).

Pike, Nelson, ed., *God and Evil* (Englewood Cliffs, New Jersey: Prentice-Hall, 1964).

Plato, *Gorgias* (Indianapolis: Hackett Publishing Company, 1987). Trans. Donald J. Zeyl.

_____, *The Republic* (San Francisco: HarperCollins, 1968). Trans. Allan Bloom.

Popper, Karl and John C. Eccles, *The Self and Its Brain* (New York: Springer International, 1977).

Prabhavananda, Swami, trans., *Shankara's Crest-Jewel of Discrimination* (Hollywood: Vedanta Press, 1978).

_____, *The Spiritual Heritage of India* (Hollywood: Vedanta Press, 1980).

_____, trans., *The Upanishads* (Hollywood: Vedanta Press, 1947).

Purtill, Richard, *Thinking About Religion* Englewood Cliffs, New Jersey: Prentice-Hall, 1978).

Rachels, James, *The Elements of Moral Philosophy* (New York: McGraw-Hill, 1993).

Rahula, Walpola, *What the Buddha Taught* (New York: Grove Weidenfeld, 1974).

Rampa, T. Lobsang, *You - Forever* (London: Corgi Books, 1965).

Rashdall, Hastings, *The Theory of Good and Evil* (London: Oxford University Press, 1907). Two volumes.

Rawlings, Maurice, *Beyond Death's Door* (Nashville: Thomas Nelson, 1978).

Read, Herbert, Michael Fordham, and Gerard Adler, eds., *Jung's Collected Works* (London: Routledge and Kegan Paul, 1970).

Reichenbach, Bruce, *Is Man the Phoenix?* (Grand Rapids, Michigan: Eerdmans, 1978).

Radhakrishnan, Sarvepalli, *Indian Philosophy* (London: George Allen and Unwin Ltd, 1923). Two volumes.

Richter, Peyton and Walter Fogg, eds., *Philosophy Looks to the Future* (Prospect Heights, Illinois: Waveland Press, 1978).

Ring, Kenneth, *Heading Toward Omega* (New York: Quill Press, 1985).

_____, *Life at Death* (New York: Quill Press, 1982).

Ring, Merrill, *Beginning with the Pre-Socratics* (Mt. View, California: Mayfield Publishing Company, 1987).

Rosher, Grace, *Beyond the Horizon* (Greenwood, South Carolina: James Clarke, 1961).

Russell, Bertrand, *Religion and Science* (London: Oxford University Press, 1961).

_____, *Why I Am Not a Christian* (New York: Simon and Schuster, 1957).

Sagan, Carl, *Broca's Brain* (New York: Random House, 1979).

_____, *The Demon-Haunted World* (New York: Ballantine Books, 1996).

Santayana, George, *Reason in Religion* (New York: Dover Publications, 1952).

Savage, Minot, *Life Beyond Death* (New York: The Knickerbocker Press, 1899).

Sherrington, Sir Charles, *The Integrative Action of the Nervous System* (Cambridge: Cambridge University Press, 1947).

Sherry, Patrick, *Spirit, Saints and Immortality* (Albany, New York: State University of New York Press, 1984).

Singer, Peter, *Practical Ethics* (Cambridge: Cambridge University Press, 1993).

Smith, Huston, *Forgotten Truth* (San Francisco: HarperCollins, 1992).

_____, *The World's Religions* (San Francisco: HarperCollins, 1991).

Smith, Suzy, ed., *Frederic Myers' Human Personality and Its Survival of Bodily Death* (New Hyde Park, New York: University Books, Inc., 1961).

Snell, Bruno, *The Discovery of the Mind* (Cambridge, Massachusetts: Harvard University Press, 1953). Trans. T. G. Rosenmeyer.

Springer, Rebecca Rutter, *My Dream of Heaven* (Midway, Utah: M. A. P. Publishing, 1995).

W. T, Stace, *Mysticism and Philosophy* (Los Angeles: Jeremy P. Tarcher, Inc., 1960).

Streeter, B. H., A. Clutton Brock, et al., *Immortality: An Essay in Discovery Co-ordinating Scientific, Psychical and Biblical Research* (New York: Macmillan, 1917).

Stroud, Barry, *Hume* (London: Routledge and Kegan Paul, 1977).

Swedenborg, Emmanuel, *Heaven and Hell* (West Chester, Pennsylvania: The Swedenborg Foundation, 1979). Trans. George F. Dole.

Swinburne, Richard, *The Evolution of the Soul* (Oxford: Clarendon Press, 1987).

_____, *The Existence of God* (Oxford: Oxford University Press, 1979).

_____, *Faith and Reason* (Oxford: Oxford University Press, 1981).

St. Teresa of Avila, *Interior Castle* (New York: Doubleday, 1989). Trans. E. Allison Peers.

Tierney, Brian, Donald Kagan, and L. Pearce Williams, eds., *Great Issues in Western Philosophy* (New York: McGraw-Hill, 1992).

Tillich, Paul, *The Courage to Be* (New Haven, Connecticut: Yale University Press, 1980).

Tolstoy, Leo, *The Death of Ivan Ilych* (New York: Signet Book, 1960). Trans. Aylmer Maude.

Tyrrell, G. N. M., *The Personality of Man* (Middlesex: Penguin Books, 1960).

Unamuno, Miguel de, *Abel Sanchez and Other Stories* (Chicago: Henry Regnery Company, 1956).

_____, *The Tragic Sense of Life* (New York: Dover Publications, 1954). Trans. J. E. Crawford Flitch.

_____, *The Tragic Sense of Life in Men and Nations* (Princeton, New Jersey: Princeton University Press, 1972). Trans. Anthony Kerrigan.

Underhill, Evelyn, *Mysticism* (New York: New American Library, 1974).

Van Biema, David, "Does God Exist?", *Time* (New York: Time, Inc., March 24, 1997). Vol. 149, no. 12.

Van Over, Raymond and Laura Oteri, eds., *William McDougall: Explorer of the Mind* (New York: Garrett, 1967.

Vesey, Godfrey, *Personal Identity: A Philosophical Analysis* (Ithaca, New York: Cornell University Press, 1977).

Walker, Benjamin, *Beyond the Body - the Human Double and the Astral Planes* (London: Routledge and Kegan Paul, Ltd., 1984).

White, Stewart Edward and Harwood White, *Across the Unknown* (New York: E. P. Dutton and Company, 1943).

Whitehead, Alfred North, *Process and Reality* (New York: Macmillan, 1929).

Wilson, Colin, *Afterlife* (Garden City, New York: Doubleday and Company, 1987).

Wilson, Margaret, *Descartes* (London: Routledge and Kegan Paul, 1993).

Wittgenstein, Ludwig, *Philosophical Investigations* (Oxford: Basil Blackwell, 1953). Trans. G. E. M. Anscombe.

***The Works of William Shakespeare Complete* (Roslyn, New York: Walter J. Black, Inc., 1937).**

Wright, Robert, *The Moral Animal: Why We Are the Way We Are* (New York: Vintage Books, 1994).

Zaleski, Carol, *Otherworld Journeys* (New York: Oxford University Press, 1987).

Index

Principal Names

A

B

C

D

E

F

G

H

I

J

K

L

M

N

O

P

R

S

Key Subjects

A

B

C

D

E

G

H

J

K

L

M

N

O

P

Q

R

S

T

U

V

W

About the author:

Kelly Nicholson is the author of *Light on the Horizon* and *Body and Soul: The Transcendence of Materialism*. He has taught philosophy in mainland China and the Slovak Republic, as well as in Utah and the Pacific Northwest. In 1998 he was a Visiting Fellow at the University of Wales.

Kelly received his Ph. D. in philosophy from the Claremont Graduate School in 1989. He is a longtime sports fan who delights in baseball action and memorabilia. At present he resides in the state of Utah.

To order additional copies of this book, or other books written by the author, you may contact Homeward Bound Publishing, Inc. Place your order via phone, fax, mail, or e-mail.

Toll Free: 1-888-433-1130

Fax: 1-801-816-1170

e-mail: homewardpb@aol.com

www.need2read.com

The cost of this book per copy is $34.95, plus $6.50 for shipping and handling. We accept most credit cards. You may also send check or money order to:

Homeward Bound Publishing, Inc.
Post Office Box 1468
499 East Parowan Way
Draper, Utah 84020